The Multifaith Movement: Global Risks and Cosmopolitan Solutions

Anna Halafoff

The Multifaith Movement: Global Risks and Cosmopolitan Solutions

Anna Halafoff
Faculty of Arts and Education
Deakin University
Burwood, VIC, Australia

ISBN 978-94-007-5209-2 ISBN 978-94-007-5210-8 (eBook)
DOI 10.1007/978-94-007-5210-8
Springer Dordrecht Heidelberg New York London

Printed on acid-free paper

Springer is part of Springer Science+Business Media (www.springer.com)

for Cosmo

Foreword

This book examines the rise of multifaith initiatives to counter global risks of terrorism and climate change at the turn of the twenty first century. Recent increases in religious diversity in most societies has led to the rise of multifaith engagement to promote healthy interreligious relations and has brought diverse religious groups together in partnerships designed to address major issues confronting humanity. As James A. Beckford notes, most contemporary sociological studies focus on negative or controversial aspects of religion—up until now there has been little sociological research on the positive peacebuilding and social capital enhancing aspects of religion—nor has there been such an in-depth qualitative study of the multifaith movement.

Multifaith relations in the twenty-first century have moved from marginal activities engaged in by a boutique minority of liberal Christians and a few 'others' to genuinely interreligious activities collaboratively conducted by people from a wide variety of religious origins and from diverse orientations within religious groups. Embodied understanding about how different religions work for those that practice them is essential to intergroup respect and harmony. Mere textbook learning will not do. As religious voices return to the public sphere, those who develop and apply social policy need to not just be aware of religious difference but to have the ability to respect and work with different beliefs and practices. Presuppositions that a 'secular voice' will provide an objective or inclusive way to deal with diversity are no longer tenable. The notion that all religions are essentially the same quickly comes unstuck. In this context Anna Halafoff contributes new knowledge by examining multifaith engagement through the lens of social movement and cosmopolitan theory.

This book is important not only for sociologists of religion, as it provides a missing sociological narrative about how the multifaith movement is a product of contemporary sociological developments, but it is also critical reading for multifaith practitioners and policy makers.

Halafoff provides a helpful history of the multifaith movement including a review of the movement's principle aims. This book also assists the reader to appreciate the impact that social, cultural and environmental issues have had on multifaith activities. Many people mistakenly think that multifaith initiatives are a post 9/11 phenomenon, however they need to better understand the multifaith movement in order to appreciate the different ways it has worked and how the focus of this movement has changed over time.

The *netpeace* framework Halafoff develops stresses the need for communication and collaboration across multiple sectors, including religion and state, in response to common crises. It also provides a critical framework useful in comparing the ways different societies 'manage' religious diversity, and how societies differ in the ways social issues are defined and multifaith responses are constructed.

Finally, while frequently dismissed as a 'soft option', Halafoff explains how multifaith engagement is an important and effective part of countering violent extremism strategies, stressing the need for governments to partner with religious communities to better understand grievances and address them according to cosmopolitan principles—the key here is communicative action embodied in real relationships.

Successful negotiation of life in an increasingly globalised world requires that all citizens, agencies and governments realise just how interconnected we are. With this comes the implication that it is more necessary than ever to learn to live peacefully and respectfully with one another. Societies and the religions that operate within them must learn the value of respecting the rights of all others, even those who differ on matters of faith and ethics. This book will help to make this need a reality.

UNESCO Chair in Interreligious and Intercultural Relations – Asia Pacific, Monash University

Gary D. Bouma

Acknowledgements

This book could not have been completed without the assistance of the multifaith leaders who participated in this study, my academic colleagues, and my family.

A total of 56 multifaith leaders from Australia, the United Kingdom and the United States of America were interviewed for this project. I would like to thank each one of them for their time and interest in my research. I was particularly moved by their kindness, wisdom, generosity and commitment to the multifaith movement. These qualities enabled them to welcome me into their homes and offices, and to share their valuable insights with me, in the hope that this research may be able to provide a greater understanding of the global multifaith movement.

I am also very grateful to Professor Gary D. Bouma and Dr. Jo Lindsay for their guidance, wisdom, tireless enthusiasm, and good humour. Professor Rae Frances, all of the staff at the Monash University's School of Political and Social Inquiry, and Deakin University's Centre for Citizenship and Globalisation, also expressed a strong interest in my research and provided words of encouragement. Thank you in particular to Associate Professor Pete Lentini, Professor Greg Barton, Bill Kelly, Rachel Woodlock, Ela Ogru, Sue Stevenson, Professor Fethi Mansouri and Cayla Edwards.

Finally, I must thank my wonderful son Cosmo and his wise mother Irina. I could not have undertaken this project, or completed this book, without the patience, understanding and support of everyone mentioned above.

Contents

Abbreviations

AFIC	Australian Federation of Islamic Councils
AIF	Affinity Intercultural Foundation
AIMA	Australian Institute of Multicultural Affairs
AIS	Australian Intercultural Society
AMF	Australian Multicultural Foundation
APRO	Australian Partnership of Religious Organisations
C-100	Council of 100 Leaders
CCES	Council for Christian Education in Schools
CRALD	Culturally, Religiously and Linguistically Diverse
CSIS	Centre for Strategic and International Studies
DEECD	Department of Education and Early Childhood Development
DET	Department of Education and Training
FIRIS	Fairness in Religion in Schools
FECCA	Federation of Ethnic Communities' Councils of Australia
GCG	Globalization for the Common Good
GRE	General Religious Education
GREE	General Religions and Ethics Education
IARF	International Association for Religious Freedom
ICCN	Interfaith Climate Change Network
ICNY	Interfaith Center of New York
ICV	Islamic Council of Victoria
IFNUK	Inter Faith Network for the UK
IFYC	Interfaith Youth Core
IGO	Inter-Governmental Organisation
IIC	International Interfaith Centre
IIPC	Interreligious and International Peace Council
LKPY	Loving Kindness, Peaceful Youth
MAS Freedom	Muslim American Society Freedom
MMYN	Multifaith Multicultural Youth Network
NACRE	North American Coalition on Religion and Ecology
NCC	National Council of Churches

NGO	Non-Governmental Organisation
NMAC	National Multicultural Advisory Council
NRMs	New Religious Movements
NRPE	National Religious Partnership for the Environment
OMA	Office of Multicultural Affairs
PEA	Presbyterian Elders Association
PWR	Parliament of the World's Religions
REENA	Religions and Ethics Education Network Australia
RfP	Religions for Peace
RfPA	Religions for Peace Australia
RI	Religious Instruction
SRE	Special Religious Education
SRI	Special Religious Instruction
TCIU	Tanenbaum Centre for Interreligious Understanding
TFF	Three Faiths Forum
ToU	Temple of Understanding
Tripartite Forum	Tripartite Forum on Interfaith Cooperation for Peace
UN	United Nations
URI	United Religions Initiative
Vatican II	Second Vatican Council
VMC	Victorian Multicultural Commission
WCC	World Council of Churches
WCF	World Congress of Faiths
WCRP	World Conference of Religions for Peace
WFDD	World Faiths Development Dialogue
WFF	World Fellowship of Faiths
WMC	World Missionary Conference
WPR	World's Parliament of Religions
WRE	World Religions Education
WWF	World Wildlife Fund
WWI	First World War
WWII	Second World War

Chapter 1
The Multifaith Movement, Global Risks and Cosmopolitan Solutions

Although our current era has been characterised as one of fear, risk and uncertainty it has paradoxically also been described as one of great hope and global interdependence. Reactions to the tragic events of September 11, 2001 provide evidence of this dichotomy as a politics of fear has since permeated so-called Western societies, accompanied by a growing interest in collaborative cosmopolitan solutions to counter global risks, such as terrorism and, more recently, climate change (Bauman 2006; Beck 2006). The rise of the multifaith[1] movement at the turn of the twenty-first century is exemplary of these cosmopolitan strategies—aimed at addressing risks and advancing common security—both locally and globally.

Following the September 11 terrorist attacks on the World Trade Center in New York, Muslim Australians experienced an increase in discrimination and attacks against them and their places of worship. A culture of fear, perpetuated by discourses of exclusion that emanated from the former Prime Minister John Howard's Government, also contributed to rising Islamophobia, migrantophobia and critiques of multiculturalism in Australia. However, religious communities

[1] There is very little explanation available regarding the terminology used to describe relations among different religions, and among religious groups. Patrice Brodeur and Eboo Patel (2006: 2) observe that there has been a tendency to use the word interfaith among Protestant circles and to use the word interreligious among Catholics. In addition, the term interfaith has historically often referred to interaction between two religious groups, such as Jewish–Christian or Christian–Muslim dialogue. While the term interfaith is widely used in the USA, multifaith has been more frequently used in the UK and in Australia in the late twentieth century, implying that diversity of faiths is something that should be welcomed, in the same way that the term multiculturalism advanced a respect for cultural diversity (Beckford and Gilliat 1998: 4). The terms interfaith, interreligious and multifaith are often used interchangeably, however, for the purposes of this study the term multifaith is preferable as it affirms a commitment to promoting religious pluralism, and also differentiates this inquiry from research on bilateral interfaith relations, which have been the focus of extensive scholarship. This book, however, is primarily concerned with interactions among multiple communities of faith, with one another and with state and non-state actors, for peace-building purposes.

A. Halafoff, *The Multifaith Movement: Global Risks and Cosmopolitan Solutions*,
DOI 10.1007/978-94-007-5210-8_1, © Springer Science+Business Media Dordrecht 2013

were far from passive in their responses to the impact of these events, initiating multifaith and educational activities to dispel negative stereotypes and attitudes propagated by the media and political leaders. The State Government of Victoria and Victoria Police also supported multifaith peacebuilding initiatives and prioritised engagement with religious leaders and communities as part of their social inclusion and community building strategies (HREOC 2004: 43–62; Cahill et al. 2004: 84–85; Halafoff 2006: 3, 9–12; Bouma et al. 2007: 5–6, 22–26, 43–60, 65–68). Indeed, the Victorian Government placed multiculturalism and a commitment to working in partnership with culturally and religiously diverse communities at the heart of its counter-terrorism policies during this period (State Government of Victoria 2005: 3).

A rise in multifaith engagement also occurred in the USA after the events of September 11 (Eck 2001: xiii–xix; Brodeur 2005: 42; McCarthy 2007: 85; Niebuhr 2008: xxii, 5–7, 10–11) and the number of multifaith and multi-actor peacebuilding networks, including both religious and state actors, also increased in the UK as a result of September 11 and the 7 and 21 July 2005 London bombings (Braybrooke 2007: 1, 13; Pearce quoted in Bharat and Bharat 2007: 245–246).

These twenty-first century developments form part of a long history of multifaith initiatives that well predate the events of September 11, 2001. The first Parliament of the World's Religions (PWR),[2] held in Chicago in 1893, is commonly described as the beginning of the multifaith movement, and the second PWR,[3] held in Chicago 100 years later, as signifying the movement's 'coming of age' (Braybrooke 1992: 7–8). The period from the 1960s to the 1980s heralded a new era of social movements, including anti-war, women's and environmental movements, which arose to defend the 'lifeworld' from the negative effects of capitalist modernity and to advance equal rights for all (Habermas 1981: 35). William Sims Bainbridge's (1997: 3) defines social movements as 'collective human attempts to create or to block change' and religious movements as 'a relatively organized attempt by a number of people to cause or prevent change in a religious organization or in religious aspects of life'. Fred Kniss and Paul D. Numrich (2007: 227) describe the multifaith movement in particular as 'a decentralized social movement of individuals, groups and organizations seeking to foster mutual respect and understanding across religions in order to achieve positive individual, social, cultural, and civic change'. The multifaith movement is made up of numerous local, national and global multifaith organisations, networks and actors, who meet at local, regional and global multifaith conferences, festivals and events. As will be explained in more detail throughout this book, the multifaith movement has always been committed to social change on issues such as

---

[2] The 1893 Parliament of the World's Religions (PWR) was originally titled the World's Parliament of Religions (WPR). The Council for the Parliament of the World's Religions (CPWR) was established to coordinate the 1993 PWR and future PWRs. CPWR is now simply called the Parliament of the World's Religions (PWR). Parliament of the World's Religions (PWR) has been used throughout the text to describe all WPR, CPWR and PWR events in order to avoid confusion.

[3] The 1993 PWR, commonly described as the second PWR, was actually the third. The second, much smaller PWR was held in Chicago in 1933, convened by the World Fellowship of Faiths (WFF) (Braybrooke 1992: 39).

protecting the environment, nuclear disarmament, poverty alleviation, peacebuilding and post-conflict reconstruction. This commitment aligns the multifaith movement with other ultramodern[4] social movements, which emerged at the turn of the twenty-first century.

Global multifaith engagement, particularly multifaith engagement in the USA, expanded dramatically in the 1990s well before September 11. This was evidenced by the 1993 PWR and the formation of a number of major multifaith organisations such: as the United Religions Initiative (URI); the Interfaith Centre of New York (ICNY); and the Tanenbaum Centre for Interreligious Understanding (TCIU) (Eck 2001: 370; Kirkwood 2007: xiv). As Marc Gopin (2000: 4) stated:

> … while the fractionating character of religious revivalism is more noticeable and sometimes more violent, there is a quiet revolution in integration taking place as well … never before in history … have so many leaders and adherents been inspired to work for a truly inclusive vision that is multicultural and multireligious.

While Diana L. Eck (2005: 21–26) described initial fears that September 11 would provide a 'cataclysmic setback' to multifaith relations, it had the opposite effect of becoming a stimulus for multifaith engagement, particularly in Western societies (Eck 2001: xiii–xix; Bouma et al. 2007: 61–66, 106; Kirkwood 2007: v–vi; Niebuhr 2008: 5–7, 10–11). In addition, as described above, since September 11, state actors in Australia and the UK have increasingly initiated and supported multifaith activities with a focus on social inclusion and countering radicalisation (Brodeur 2005: 42; Halafoff 2006: 11–12, 2007; Bouma et al. 2007: 69–74, 111–112; Braybrooke 2007: 1, 13; Bouma 2008: 13; Weller 2008: 198–199). Therefore, religious peacebuilding efforts in Western societies including the USA, the UK and Australia have, according to Cynthia Sampson's (1997: 304) prediction, become 'increasingly intentional and systematic' in response to this crisis event.

A Missing Peace?

Despite this rise of multifaith and multi-actor peacebuilding networks at the turn of the twenty-first century, they have received scant attention in the sociology of religion literature.[5] The growth of social movements confronting the global issues of human rights, peace, social justice and sustainability from the 1960s onward

---

[4] Sociologist of religion Jean-Paul Willaime (2006: 78) coined the term 'ultramodernity' in 1998. It is used throughout this book in preference to other terms such as postmodernity or late modernity, which commonly describe the period from the 1960s onward. A more detailed description of Willaime's concept of ultramodernity is provided in Chap. 2.

[5] Religious and multifaith peacebuilding initiatives have, however, been examined in detail within the field of peace theory. These case studies have typically focused on situations of post-conflict reconstruction in non-Western societies in Africa (Johnston 1994a: 177–207; Kraybill 1994: 208–257; Sampson 1994: 88–118; Nyang and Johnston 2003: 210–230; Botman 2004: 243–260;

has been extensively documented in the sociological literature, yet the multifaith movement remains hardly mentioned (Beckford 2003: 109, 138). According to James A. Beckford (2003: 127), sociological studies of religion have tended 'to emphasize marginal, deviant or sensational aspects of religion and show relatively little interest in the "normal" range of religious beliefs, actions and organisations'. In particular, sociologists have been preoccupied with studies of fundamentalism and how these movements, while critical of the global spread of capitalism, have used some of the advances of globalisation (such as global communication systems) to their advantage (Beckford 2003: 127, 115). Therefore, Beckford (2003: 136, 138) challenges sociologists of religion 'to demonstrate that globalisation … is still associated with interesting aspects of religion other than fundamentalism' and suggests the growth of interfaith networks as one such under-researched example. Beckford (2003: 109–110) cites Richard H. Roberts's (2002) account of the 1993 PWR as evidence of the search among religious organisations for 'common ground' as a way to deal collectively with threats and problems such as poverty, gender inequity, environmental degradation and human rights abuses.

In addition, James V. Spickard (2006: 169–181) has recently outlined five major sociological narratives that explain religion's place in contemporary societies. They depict religion as: (1) in decline (*secularisation*); (2) weakening nationally but strengthening locally (*religious reorganisation*); (3) becoming more individualised (*religious individualisation*); (4) a competitive consumer culture of religious markets, firms and goods (*rational-choice 'theory' of religious markets*); or (5) a rise of 'conservative' fundamentalist movements (*the 'Good Old Way'*). However, religion's capacity to act as a peacebuilding force, as evidenced by the rise of the multifaith movement, is completely overlooked in Spickard's otherwise comprehensive typology.

This study takes up Beckford's challenge, and addresses this omission, by examining the ultramodern rise of multifaith engagement from the perspective of social movement theory and cosmopolitan theory. In particular it investigates how multifaith initiatives have been implemented as cosmopolitan strategies to counter global risks—such as terrorism and climate change—and advance common security in ultramodern Western societies. It therefore provides a missing narrative within the sociological literature, which is comprised of cosmopolitan peacebuilding religious responses

---

Nurayn Ashafa and Movel Wuye 2006: 21–24; LoWilla 2006: 25–28; Smock 2006: 17–20); Asia (Wooster 1994: 153–177; Embree 2003: 33–75; Seneviratne 2003: 76–90; Morris 2004: 191–212; Philpott and Cox 2006: 5–8); Central and South America (Nichols 1994: 62–87); former Yugoslavia (Steele 2002: 73–88, 2003: 124–177; Johnston and Eastvold 2004: 213–242); Macedonia (Mojzes 2006: 29–34); the Middle East (Young 2002: 63–72; Gopin 2003: 91–101; D'Souza 2004: 169–190; White 2006a: 9–12, 2006b: 13–16); and Northern Ireland (Liechty 2002: 89–102; Grant 2004: 261–278). The development of global multifaith organisations such as the Appeal of Conscience Foundation (Schneier 2002: 105–114), the United Religions Initiative (Gibbs 2002: 115–126), the World Congress of Faiths (Braybrooke 1996) and Religions for Peace (Klaes 2004: 199–224) have also been examined in these case studies. Religious peacebuilding theory is discussed in more detail in Chap. 4.

aimed at collaboratively countering global risks. In addition, by documenting these peacebuilding aspects of the ultramodern resurgence of religion, it contributes new evidence to further challenge the secularisation thesis.

By the mid-2000s, there was relatively little empirical research and peer-reviewed scholarship documenting these developments (Braybrooke 1992, 1996; Eck 2001, 2005; Boehle 2002; Gibbs 2002; Schneier 2002; Cahill et al. 2004; Klaes 2004; Ahmed and Forst 2005; Brodeur 2005; Brodeur and Patel 2005). However, in recent years there have been many more publications examining the post–September 11 rise of multifaith activity in the USA (Lohre 2007; McCarthy 2007; Niebuhr 2008), the UK (Braybrooke 2007; Weller 2008), Australia (Halafoff 2006, 2007; Bouma et al. 2007) and globally (Bharat and Bharat 2007; Kirkwood 2007: v–vi). While the majority of these studies have described the success of these multifaith and multi-actor peacebuilding networks as peacebuilding strategies, questions remain regarding the efficacy of these initiatives, particularly around the precise role that multifaith engagement plays in countering global risks such as terrorism (Garfinkel 2004: 2; Tyndale quoted in Bharat and Bharat 2007: 275). In addition, concerns have been raised over the growing proximity between religious and state actors in the UK as multifaith initiatives have increasingly been implemented as social cohesion strategies following the September 11 and London bombings (Pearce quoted in Bharat and Bharat 2007: 245–246).

By drawing on 56 interviews with expert professionals in the field of multifaith relations conducted for this study, and by comparing previously published material with this new data, this book identifies four principle aims and six characteristics of the multifaith movement, examines the benefits and challenges of multifaith engagement and explains the role of multifaith initiatives in countering processes of radicalisation. Finally, by building upon cosmopolitan theories, it proposes a new theoretical framework called *netpeace*. *Netpeace* recognises the interconnectedness of global problems and solutions and the capacity of multi-actor peacebuilding networks—in which religious actors engage both critically *and* collaboratively with state actors—to overcome the most pressing risks of our times. This study can thereby assist in building new models of activism and governance, as outmoded, oppositional frameworks of modernity are being replaced by new ultramodern, cosmopolitan possibilities, founded on a *politics of understanding*, modelled by the multifaith movement and by multi-actor peacebuilding networks.

References

Ahmed, Akbar, and Brian Forst (eds.). 2005. *After terror: Promoting dialogue among civilizations*. Cambridge: Polity Press.

Bainbridge, William Sims. 1997. *The sociology of religious movements*. New York: Routledge.

Bauman, Zygmunt. 2006. *Liquid fear*. Cambridge: Polity Press.

Beck, Ulrich. 2006. *The cosmopolitan vision*. Cambridge: Polity Press.

Beckford, James A. 2003. *Social theory and religion*. Cambridge: Cambridge University Press.

Beckford, James A., and Sophie Gilliat. 1998. *Religion in prison: Equal rites in a multi-faith society*. Cambridge: Cambridge University Press.

Bharat, Sandy, and Jael Bharat. 2007. *A global guide to interfaith: Reflections from around the world*. Winchester: O Books.

Boehle, Josef. 2002. Inter-religious cooperation and global change: From a clash of civilisations to a dialogue of civilisations. *Pacific Review* 14(3): 227–234.

Botman, H.Russel. 2004. Truth and reconciliation: The South African case. In *Religion and peacebuilding*, ed. Harold Coward and Gordon S. Smith, 243–260. Albany: State University of New York Press.

Bouma, Gary D. 2008. The challenge of religious revitalization and religious diversity to social cohesion in secular societies. In *Religious diversity and civil society: A comparative analysis*, ed. Brian S. Turner, 13–25. Oxford: The Bardwell Press.

Bouma, Gary D., Sharon Pickering, Anna Halafoff, and Hass Dellal. 2007. *Managing the impact of global crisis events on community relations in multicultural Australia*. Brisbane: Multicultural Affairs Queensland.

Braybrooke, Marcus. 1992. *Pilgrimage of hope: One hundred years of global interfaith dialogue*. London: SCM Press Ltd.

Braybrooke, Marcus. 1996. *A wider vision: A history of the world congress of faiths*. Oxford: Oneworld.

Braybrooke, Marcus. 2007. *Interfaith witness in a changing world: The world congress of faiths, 1996–2006*. Abingdon: Braybrooke Press.

Brodeur, Patrice. 2005. From the margins to the centers of power: The increasing relevance of the global interfaith movement. *Cross Currents* 55(1): 42–53.

Brodeur, Patrice, and Eboo Patel. 2006. Introduction: Building the interfaith youth movement. In *Building the interfaith youth movement: Beyond dialogue to action*, ed. Patel Eboo and Brodeur Patrice, 1–14. Oxford: Rowman and Littlefield Publishers, Inc.

Cahill, Desmond, Gary D. Bouma, Dellal Hass, and Michael Leahy. 2004. *Religion, cultural diversity and safeguarding Australia*. Canberra: Department of Immigration, Multicultural and Indigenous Affairs.

D'Souza, Diane. 2004. Creating spaces: Interreligious initiatives for peace. In *Religion and peacebuilding*, ed. Harold Coward and Gordon S. Smith, 169–190. Albany: State University of New York Press.

Eck, Diana L. 2001. *A new religious America: How a "Christian Country" has become the world's most religiously diverse nation*. New York: HarperOne.

Eck, Diana L. 2005. Dialogue and the echo boom of terror: Religious women's voices after 9/11. In *After terror: Promoting dialogue among civilizations*, ed. Akbar Ahmed and Brian Forst, 21–28. Cambridge: Polity Press.

Embree, Ainslie. 2003. Kashmir: Has religion a role to play in making peace? In *Faith-based diplomacy: Trumping realpolitik*, ed. Douglas Johnston, 33–75. Oxford: Oxford University Press.

Garfinkel, Renee. 2004. What works? Evaluating interfaith dialogue programs. USIP Special Report 123. Washington, DC: United States Institute of Peace.

Gibbs, Charles. 2002. The United Religions Initiative at work. In *Interfaith dialogue and peacebuilding*, ed. David R. Smock, 115–126. Washington, DC: United States Institute of Peace Press.

Gopin, Marc. 2000. *Between Eden and Armageddon: The future of world religions, violence, and peacemaking*. Oxford: Oxford University Press.

Gopin, Marc. 2003. Judaism and peacebuilding in the context of Middle East conflict. In *Faith-based diplomacy: Trumping realpolitik*, ed. Douglas Johnston, 91–101. Oxford: Oxford University Press.

Grant, Patrick. 2004. Northern Ireland: Religion and the peace process. In *Religion and peacebuilding*, ed. Harold Coward and Gordon S. Smith, 261–278. Albany: State University of New York Press.

Habermas, Jürgen. 1981. New social movements. *Telos* 49: 33–37.

Halafoff, Anna. 2006. UnAustralian values. In *Cultural Studies Association of Australasia Annual Conference, UNAustralia*. University of Canberra, Canberra, 6–8 December 2006 (electronic resource).

Halafoff, Anna. 2007. Advancing Australian "shared security": Secular-religious peacebuilding networks. In *Australian Sociological Association (TASA) and the Sociological Association of Aotearoa New Zealand (SAANZ) Joint Conference, Public Sociologies: Lessons and Trans-Tasman Comparisons*. University of Auckland, Auckland, 4–7 December 2007 (CD-Rom).

Human Rights and Equal Opportunity Commission (HREOC). 2004. Isma` – Listen: National consultations on eliminating prejudice against Arab and Muslim Australians. Sydney: Human Rights and Equal Opportunity Commission.

Johnston, Douglas. 1994a. The churches and apartheid in South Africa. In *Religion, the missing dimension of statecraft*, ed. Douglas Johnston and Cynthia Sampson, 177–207. Oxford: Oxford University Press.

Johnston, Douglas M., and Jonathon Eastvold. 2004. History unrequited: Religion as provocateur and peacemaker in the Bosnian conflict. In *Religion and peacebuilding*, ed. Harold Coward and Gordon S. Smith, 213–242. Albany: State University of New York Press.

Kirkwood, Peter. 2007. *The quiet revolution: The emergence of interfaith consciousness*. Sydney: ABC Books.

Klaes, Norbert. 2004. Peace and multireligious co-operation: The World Conference of Religions for Peace (WCRP). In *War and peace in world religions*, ed. Perry Schmidt-Leukel, 199–224. London: SCM Press.

Kniss, Fred, and Paul D. Numrich. 2007. *Sacred assemblies and civic engagement: How religion matters for America's newest immigrants*. New Brunswick: Rutgers University Press.

Kraybill, Ron. 1994. Transition from Rhodesia to Zimbabwe: The role of religious actors. In *Religion, the missing dimension of statecraft*, ed. Douglas Johnston and Cynthia Sampson, 208–257. Oxford: Oxford University Press.

Liechty, Joseph. 2002. Mitigation in Northern Ireland: A strategy for living in peace when truth claims clash. In *Interfaith dialogue and peacebuilding*, ed. David R. Smock, 89–102. Washington, DC: United States Institute of Peace Press.

Lohre, Kathryn. 2007. Women's interfaith initiatives in the United States Post 9/11. *Interreligious Insight* 5(2): 11–23.

LoWilla, Emmanuel. 2006. Intrafaith and interfaith dialogue in southern Sudan. In *Religious contributions to peacemaking: When religion brings peace, not war*, ed. David R. Smock, 25–28. Washington, DC: United States Institute of Peace.

McCarthy, Kate. 2007. *Interfaith encounters in America*. Piscataway: Rutgers University Press.

Mojzes, Paul. 2006. Peacemaking through interreligious dialogue in Macedonia. In *Religious contributions to peacemaking: When religion brings peace, not war*, ed. David R. Smock, 29–34. Washington, DC: United States Institute of Peace.

Morris, Catherine. 2004. Case studies in religion and peacebuilding: Cambodia. In *Religion and peacebuilding*, ed. Harold Coward and Gordon S. Smith, 191–212. Albany: State University of New York Press.

Nichols, Bruce. 1994. Religious conciliation between the Sandinistas and the East Coast Indians of Nicaragua. In *Religion, the missing dimension of statecraft*, ed. Douglas Johnston and Cynthia Sampson, 153–176. Oxford: Oxford University Press.

Niebuhr, Gustav. 2008. *Beyond tolerance: Searching for interfaith understanding in America*. New York: Viking.

Nurayn Ashafa, Muhammad, and James Movel Wuye. 2006. Training peacemakers: Religious youth leaders in Nigeria. In *Religious contributions to peacemaking: When religion brings peace, not war*, ed. David R. Smock, 21–24. Washington, DC: United States Institute of Peace.

Nyang, Sulayman, and Douglas Johnston. 2003. Conflict resolution as a normative value in Islamic law: Application to the Republic of Sudan. In *Faith-based diplomacy: Trumping realpolitik*, ed. Douglas Johnston, 210–230. Oxford: Oxford University Press.

Philpott, Daniel, and Brian Cox. 2006. What faith based diplomacy can offer in Kashmir. In *Religious contributions to peacemaking: When religion brings peace, not war*, ed. David R. Smock, 5–8. Washington, DC: United States Institute of Peace.

Roberts, Richard H. 2002. *Religion, theology and the human sciences*. Cambridge: Cambridge University Press.

Sampson, Cynthia. 1994. "To make real the bond between us all": Quaker conciliation during the Nigerian Civil War. In *Religion, the missing dimension of statecraft*, ed. Douglas Johnston and Cynthia Sampson, 88–118. Oxford: Oxford University Press.

Sampson, Cynthia. 1997. Religion and peacebuilding. In *Peacemaking in international conflict: Methods and techniques*, ed. I. William Zartman and J. Lewis Rasmussen, 273–318. Washington, DC: United States Institute of Peace Press.

Schneier, Arthur. 2002. Religion and interfaith conflict: Appeal of conscience foundation. In *Interfaith dialogue and peacebuilding*, ed. David R. Smock, 105–114. Washington, DC: United States Institute of Peace Press.

Seneviratne, H.L. 2003. Religion and conflict: The case of Buddhism in Sri Lanka. In *Faith-based diplomacy: Trumping realpolitik*, ed. Douglas Johnston, 76–90. Oxford: Oxford University Press.

Smock, David R. 2006. Mediating between Christians and Muslims in Plateau State, Nigeria. In *Religious contributions to peacemaking: When religion brings peace, not war*, ed. David R. Smock, 17–20. Washington, DC: United States Institute of Peace.

Spickard, James V. 2006. Narrative versus theory in the sociology of religion: Five stories of religion's place in the late modern world. In *Theorising religion: Classical and contemporary debates*, ed. James A. Beckford and John Walliss, 169–181. Aldershot: Ashgate.

State Government of Victoria. 2005. *Protecting our community: Attacking the causes of terrorism*. Melbourne: State Government of Victoria.

Steele, David. 2002. Contributions of interfaith dialogue to peacebuilding in the former Yugoslavia. In *Interfaith dialogue and peacebuilding*, ed. David R. Smock, 73–88. Washington, DC: United States Institute of Peace Press.

Steele, David. 2003. Christianity in Bosnia-Herzegovina and Kosovo: From ethnic captive to reconciling agent. In *Faith-based diplomacy: Trumping realpolitik*, ed. Douglas Johnston, 124–177. Oxford: Oxford University Press.

Weller, Paul. 2008. *Religious diversity in the UK: Contours and issues*. London: Continuum.

White, Canon Andrew. 2006a. Bringing religious leaders together in Israel/Palestine. In *Religious contributions to peacemaking: When religion brings peace, not war*, ed. David R. Smock, 9–12. Washington, DC: United States Institute of Peace.

White, Canon Andrew. 2006b. Establishing the premier interfaith organization in Iraq. In *Religious contributions to peacemaking: When religion brings peace, not war*, ed. David R. Smock, 13–16. Washington, DC: United States Institute of Peace.

Willaime, Jean-Paul. 2006. Religion in ultramodernity. In *Theorising religion: Classical and contemporary debates*, ed. James A. Beckford and John Walliss, 77–89. Aldershot: Ashgate.

Wooster, Henry. 1994. Faith at the ramparts: The Philippine Catholic Church and the 1986 revolution. In *Religion, the missing dimension of statecraft*, ed. Douglas Johnston and Cynthia Sampson, 153–176. Oxford: Oxford University Press.

Young, Ronald. 2002. American Jews, Christians, and Muslims working together for peace in the Middle East. In *Interfaith dialogue and peacebuilding*, ed. David R. Smock, 63–72. Washington, DC: United States Institute of Peace Press.

Chapter 2
Social Movements, Cosmopolitanism and Multifaith Engagement

This chapter examines the ultramodern rise of multifaith engagement from the perspective of social movement theory and cosmopolitan theory. It argues that the rise of the multifaith movement and of multi-actor peacebuilding networks in ultramodernity, alongside other social movements of this period, provides a missing sociological narrative of cosmopolitan peacebuilding religious responses aimed at collaboratively countering global risks.

Religion and Social Problems

The vast majority of sociologists of religion, due to their preoccupation with secularisation theory, showed relatively little interest in religious responses to the emerging problems posed by industrialisation and capitalism for much of the twentieth century (Beckford 1990: 4). According to Charles Taylor (2009: xviii–xx), the term 'secular' was originally used in Western Christian societies to denote the lower, profane realms in contrast to the higher, sacred realms of existence. During the Enlightenment period in eighteenth century France, Enlightenment thinkers rejected the authority of the church and sought to replace it with critical reason and science as the guiding principles of the modern era (Marty and Appleby 1992: 11–13). The term secular became associated with rationality, whereas religion was increasingly viewed as irrational and superfluous. This view of religion as disruptive and problematic led to the exclusion of religion from the public sphere and to an understanding of secularism as the separation of church and state in Western societies (Taylor 2009: xviii–xx).

Enlightenment thinkers held the assumption that religion would eventually decline and cease to be a public force and that whatever religions were to remain in modern societies would be reasonable and tolerant. These views led to the development of theories of secularisation among sociologists of religion, such as Max Weber, Emile Durkheim, Thomas Luckmann and Niklas Luhmann, who assigned an increasingly privatised and thereby marginalised role to religion in modern societies

A. Halafoff, *The Multifaith Movement: Global Risks and Cosmopolitan Solutions*,
DOI 10.1007/978-94-007-5210-8_2,

(Casanova 1994: 5–6, 17–19, 35). However, religions, far from disappearing from public life, have increased their influence in the public sphere throughout the world in the latter half of the twentieth century. The Satyagraha movement in India; the Civil Rights Movement in the USA; the Iranian and Nicaraguan revolutions of 1979; the Solidarity movement in Poland; the spread of liberation theology through Latin America, Asia and Africa; conflicts in Northern Ireland and former Yugoslavia; the Salman Rushdie affair in the UK; and the rise of the Christian Right's influence on American politics provide evidence of this phenomenon (Casanova 1994: 3; Bainbridge 1997: 331–339). In addition, the more liberal, 'reasonable and tolerant' forms of religion, such as the multifaith movement, while undoubtedly increasing their presence in ultramodern public life, have been challenged by a simultaneous rise in exclusive and conservative forms of religion and identity politics (Marty and Appleby 1992: 11–13; Kaldor 1999: 6). Therefore, by the end of the twentieth century religions were described as not only playing a more public role but also an increasingly ambivalent one by promoting both cultures of violence and cultures of peace in ultramodern societies (Casanova 1994: 4; Kaldor 1999: 6, 9; Appleby 2000, 2003: 240; Halafoff and Conley Tyler 2005).

Pluralism, Multiculturalism and Rising Religious Diversity

A period of intense religious conflict, resulting in the repression of religious diversity as evident in the Spanish Inquisition and the European Wars of Religion, preceded the 1648 so-called Peace of Westphalia. Concurrently, during the sixteenth and seventeenth centuries the principle of religious tolerance was enshrined in law in Holland, France, Maryland (USA) and England to protect religious minorities from persecution (Bouma 1999: 11–12; Habermas 2003: 2). However, from 1648 until the nineteenth century a hegemonic approach to managing religious diversity was established throughout most of Europe, such that one religious group was chosen to unify each emerging nation-state (Bouma 1999: 11–12). The imposition of these nation-building projects around the world often came at the expense of pre-existing cultural and religious communities as national governments typically implemented settlement policies that displaced Indigenous communities and established 'minorities' thereby eliminating traditional forms of governance (Kymlicka and Straehle 1999: 72–75).

Following the end of the Second World War and the collapse of the Japanese and British empires, the steady process of decolonisation, coupled with the 'human rights revolution' centred on a commitment to equality of all peoples, led to rising demands for justice, autonomy, equitable participation and self-organisation among Indigenous, cultural and religious groups (Habermas 1998: 313; Kymlicka and Straehle 1999: 74–75; Fraser 2001: 25, 27; Kaldor 2003a: 144–145; Kymlicka and Banting 2006: 300). This period also led to a rise in immigration from previous colonies to Western countries and consequently to the creation of increasingly multicultural and multifaith societies, particularly in the UK, the USA, Canada,

Australia and New Zealand (Bouma 1999: 14, 19). As Gary D. Bouma (1999: 14) states, 'the fact and experience of diversity preceded the institutionalisation of diversity', and as a result societies were forced to choose between repressive or tolerant policies. This eventually led to the legitimation of a pluralist worldview in Western societies, evident in policies of multiculturalism, as diverse cultural and religious groups acted within the democratic system to introduce rights for previously excluded minorities (Bouma 1999: 20–22; Habermas 2003: 8).

During the 1970s and 1980s, as a result of policies of multiculturalism, immigrants were encouraged to maintain some of their cultural practices and identities and political institutions were reformed to accommodate them. In some societies Indigenous communities and national minorities were accorded self-governance powers to establish their own political, economic and educational institutions. As a result of these developments the multifaith movement expanded in Western societies as diverse cultural and religious groups strengthened their participation in the ultra-modern public sphere during this period (Eck 2001; Halafoff 2006: 6–7; Weller 2008: 179–180). However, while a growing respect for cultural pluralism characterised Western societies in the 1970s and 1980s, undercurrents of cultural and religious exclusivity remained, evident in majority cultures' frequently hostile attitudes to Indigenous and immigrant communities acquiring rights and autonomy (Kymlicka 1997: 73–74, 76; Bouma 1999: 24; Jayaraman 2000: 151).

Capitalist Globalisation and Its Discontents

Processes of decolonisation and globalisation led not only to an increase in rights accorded to immigrant and Indigenous communities, but also to a global rise of critiques of Western capitalism. According to sociologist of religion Jean-Paul Willaime (2006: 78) the term 'ultramodernity', which he coined in 1998, best describes our current era as '(a) we have not left modernity behind and (b) we are actually in a stage of radicalisation of modernity'. Willaime aligned his term ultra-modernity with Marcel Gauchet's (2002: xv) observation that we live in a time of 'major discontinuity which is compatible with an underlying continuity'. The major discontinuity lies in a shift 'from a logic of certainty to uncertainty' wherein the modernist belief in progress has become subject to considerable doubt and where 'nothing escapes close critical examination' (Willaime 2006: 78–79).

Willaime (2006: 78–79) explained how the modernist belief in progress has been increasingly questioned and a period of radical reflexivity categorised the ultramodern era. While capitalist modernity promised to deliver economic benefits and equal rights for all, by the mid to late twentieth century it was becoming increasingly clear, especially with the spread of global communication systems, that capitalism had fallen well short of providing these benefits except to a very small proportion of the world's population, largely at the expense of the lifeworld and the majority of its citizens.

In the ultramodern period, globalisation became increasingly viewed as a process of global 'marketisation and Americanisation' that threatened to destroy the environment, cultural and religious identities, values, and livelihoods (Beckford 2003: 11). Pressing concerns about the survival of humanity meshed well with religious discourses of end times and religious responses to social problems elicited radical narratives of overturning existing orders and re-establishing new orders in their place (Beckford 1990: 10). As a result of these transformations religions came to play a central mobilising role among social movements of people questing for self-determination, political participation, and equitable and sustainable development, seeking to defend the lifeworld against state and market penetration (Casanova 1994: 4–5, 228; Habermas 1981: 35, 1987: 396; Hegedus 1989; Beckford 1990: 6–8, 11). These religious movements, violent and non-violent, frequently evoked theological rhetorics of justice to question the legitimacy of state and market forces. Islamic movements spoke of empowering the 'disinherited', liberation theology of liberating the 'poor', and the 'velvet' revolution of 'the power of the powerless' (Casanova 1994: 4–5).

Concurrently, dramatic advances in information and communications technologies in the 1980s led to a dawning 'global circumstance' and the realisation of the interconnectedness of global problems and their solutions (Robertson 1985 cited in Beckford 1990: 7; Kaldor 1999: 3). According to Jürgen Habermas (1998: 318), the process of globalisation 'sharpens our awareness of the growing interdependence of our social arenas, of shared risks, and the joint networks of collective fates'. However, while an increased awareness of interconnectedness created a perception of 'oneness' among an emerging global citizenry, it also heightened differences, thereby threatening ontological security (Kaldor 1999: 2–4, 6; Beckford 2003: 109). On the one hand, this led to a rise of social movements and international Non-Governmental Organisations (NGOs) and UN agencies—the so-called 'tamed' social movements and networks—in the 1980s and 1990s, which embodied 'a growing global consciousness' and 'sense of a common humanity', and on the other a rise of 'new wars' and fundamentalist movements (Kaldor 2003a: 144–145).

Social Movements and New Mazeways

Non-violent social movements, including anti-nuclear, peace, women's, environmental and multifaith movements, not only resisted attacks on the lifeworld, but they also sought to create 'new forms of cooperation and community' to replace the competitiveness of consumerism (Habermas 1981: 35). These new 'mazeways' were comprised of non-violent collaborative frameworks that sought to replace existing mechanisms of profit-driven resource development with equitable development for the common good (Hargrove 1988: 41S quoting Wallace 1956). 'Mazeways' was a term invented by Anthony F. C. Wallace (1956) to describe certain patterns of behaviour, which Barbara Hargrove (1988: 41) in turn adopted to describe the 'new and more satisfying mazeways' created by ultramodern social movements.

According to Hargrove (1988: 44), the three principal qualities of these mazeways are that they offer: (1) a sense of community, (2) opportunities for collectively effected social change, and (3) a new emphasis on personal development.

Mohandas Karamchand Gandhi and his Satyagraha movement, inspired by Hindu and Christian principles, and the Reverend Martin Luther King Jr. and the Civil Rights Movement, whose 'ritual core' lay in African-American churches, were pioneers of these new mazeways. They sought change not only by non-violently seeking independence for India and equal rights for African-Americans but also by critiquing the British Empire and American society more broadly, thereby providing new visions of global responsibility and economic justice (Hargrove 1988: 45 citing Harding 1987; Bainbridge 1997: 333–339). The Civil Rights Movement inspired the rise of non-violent social movements, including Indigenous, feminist, environmental and peace movements of the 1970s and 1980s. In addition, New Religious Movements (NRMs) attracted many followers in Western societies during this era (Hargrove 1988: 44–45). The post–Vatican II Catholic Church was also described by José Casanova (1994, 2001: 433) as one of the few public voices that questioned the global spread of capitalism and demanded a 'humanization and moralization of market economies', and a fairer distribution of resources. The proliferation of social movements in the 1980s was unprecedented and led to the development of a '*new ethic of [global] responsibility*' (Hegedus 1989: 33) and a '"planetarisation" of practices' (Hegedus 1989: 19) as social movements built 'transnational publics' (Fraser 2005: 72), mobilising global opinions and actions, which called into question nation-state frameworks (Kaldor 2003b: 583; Fraser 2005: 72).

As discussed in Chap. 1, a significant rise of multifaith engagement occurred, alongside the rise of many other social movements, in the 1980s and 1990s (Eck 2001: 370; Kirkwood 2007: xiv). The multifaith movement shared much in common with the social movements of this period and contributed to the creation of new collaborative mazeways that non-violently and collectively effected social change and began to build genuinely peaceful and inclusive societies. In addition, the multifaith movement created a new framework in which religious diversity was no longer viewed as problematic but rather as a resource that could be drawn upon to confront global risks such as poverty, nuclear war and environmental degradation, and to advance common security, both locally and globally, as will be discussed in more detail in subsequent chapters.

New Wars and the Rise of Fundamentalisms

However, alongside the rise of non-violent social movements, particularly after the end of the Cold War, a series of 'new wars' erupted in which the boundaries between war, organised crime and human rights violations were blurred and in which the new actors were not states, but cultural or religious exclusivist movements claiming power based on identity politics (Kaldor 1999: 1–2, 6). Growing fears of losing national and/or religious identity and power resulted in a global reassertion of ethnic and religious identities and '*introverted* forms of nationalism', fostering aggressive intolerances (Beck 2006: 4).

Among the major actors in these new wars were so-called fundamentalist religious movements. According to Martin E. Marty and R. Scott Appleby (1992: 3), fundamentalism describes 'a pattern of belief and behaviour' that has emerged in all the major faith traditions since the 1970s. Religious fundamentalist movements, especially Christian and Muslim movements, have formed in response to capitalist modernity; however, fundamentalists do not necessarily reject modernity entirely, as they are adept at utilising modern technology to facilitate their goals. Yet fundamentalists do object to the assertion that human reason is superior to the will of God/Spirit, which they believe provides the most authoritative guide to inspire humans to their highest potential. Fundamentalists believe that humanity has lost its way and fallen into moral decay and materialism by disavowing such guidance in the pursuit of freedom. Consequently, they seek to restore security with the belief that society would benefit from being steered by religious leaders, and thereby ensuring that they can attain—or retain—privileges and power for themselves. Fundamentalists have felt threatened by the global spread of Western capitalism and also of liberal movements within their own religious groups who have promoted pluralism and implemented changes to tradition. They have fought these changes, seeking instead to create their own world order (Hargrove 1988: 47; Marty and Appleby 1992: 15–17, 19; Bouma 2006: 103).

The dramatic increase in fundamentalist movements throughout the Muslim world in the 1970s and 1980s arose under conditions of severe economic hardship and social oppression. While many fundamentalists themselves are well educated and well off, they are concerned with the 'moral, social, political, and economic failures' of their societies, attributing these failures to Western intervention (Marty and Appleby 1992: 175–176). Fundamentalist movements in postcolonial Islamic societies can thereby be understood as 'both products and agents of social change', expressing Muslim peoples' right to self-determination (An-Na'im 2003: 25, 27). Fundamentalists fight modernity not irrationally but rather with 'a different modality of rationalism'. Fundamentalist movements are 'protest movements' and 'community-building movements' that seek to create 'a new sociopolitical recipe for cultural transformation' similar to '*any* social movement' (Marty and Appleby 1992: 32). They are not only critics, but also activists proposing changes grounded in religious worldviews (Marty and Appleby 1992: 24, 33–34, 173, 177). According to Marty and Appleby (1992: 34–35), '[f]undamentalists do not intend to impose archaic practices and lifestyles … By selecting elements of tradition and modernity, fundamentalists seek to remake the world' in their own image.

As religious revitalisation typically occurs after a period of laxity in religious practice and ethics, fundamentalism can be seen as a corrective measure, based on the view that society and even modern religious institutions are corrupt and immoral, and asserting the need to apply heightened standards and stricter codes of practice to cure personal and societal ills. By promoting purity, such groups tend to isolate themselves from the mainstream in order to protect themselves against contamination (Bouma 2006: 103). According to Bouma (2006: 103), a growing distance from the broader society can result in 'mutual ignorance and fear', leading to an increase in the potential for public condemnation, repression and violence. This violence can be directed toward another religious group in the form of religious vilification and harassment or perpetuated by a religious group against the broader society, such as attacks on abortion clinics and homosexual people. In addition, Bouma (2006: 158–159) explains that it is wrong to assume that all fundamentalists pose a threat to society or to conflate fundamentalism with religious revitalisation as the energy within such movements can be harnessed and channelled into non-violent political processes to effect positive social change. However, it is when such avenues are blocked that violence is more likely to ensue.

September 11, Islamophobia and Critiques of Multiculturalism

While the end of the Cold War and the rise of new collaborative cosmopolitan maze-ways in the 1980s and 1990s presented an opportunity to strengthen global governance and peacebuilding initiatives, unfortunately these hopes were thwarted by the events of September 11 (Kaldor 2003a: 148). Instead, the terrorist attacks against the USA evoked a Hobbesian response with former President George Bush's Government in the role of global hegemon imposing its own self-interest upon the world in the name of 'a new liberal global order', contravening the UN Security Council and the UN Charter of Human Rights (Beck 2006: 146, 168–169, 181–182). According to Ulrich Beck (2005: 294, 159, 17), the events of September 11 were used by the Bush Government to legitimate attempts to spread the 'American way of life' and American values as 'the one road to modernity', exploiting the rhetoric of peace, global justice and human rights to legitimate hegemonic aspirations, while violating the self-same principles they claimed to protect. The Bush Government and its allies believed that '[t]he only way forward [wa]s Christian/Western universalism' and that all other alternatives were to be excluded (Beck 2005: 53). Those who dared to criticise the validity of their truth claims were deemed unpatriotic. In this way, by globalising a culture of fear and intimidation, the Bush Government and its Western allies sought to silence voices of dissent and critique (Beck 2005: 53, 297; Lawrence 2006). Under the guise of counter-terrorism, 'a lawless space' opened, in which human rights violations were justified and a 'permanent state of emergency' was imposed to legitimate USA foreign policy (Beck 2005: 140 citing Agamben 2003). In so doing, *Pax Americana* failed to recognise the reality of multiple [ultra] modernities and, worse still, that the USA's global domination was a primary cause of global terrorism (Beck 2006: 160).

The events of September 11 and subsequent terrorist attacks on the 12 October 2002 in Bali and on the 7 and 21 July 2005 in London, together with the divisive rhetoric emanating from the Bush Government and its allies, had the deleterious effect of creating a wave of Islamophobia and migrantophobia throughout Western societies (Eck 2001: xiii–xix; Halafoff 2006: 3, 9; Bouma et al. 2007: 5–6, 48–53,

65–68; Niebuhr 2008: 5–7, 10–11). Will Kymlicka and Keith Banting (2006: 281) note how attitudes towards immigrants have swung between periods of openness and periods of 'backlash and retrenchment' in response to local and international events and concerns. As described above, during the 1970s and 1980s policies of multiculturalism and pluralism received broad community support. However, by the 1990s, processes of globalisation and the demise of the welfare state had already begun to exacerbate existing prejudices against immigrant communities. Fears abounded that an influx of immigrants would undermine solidarity, and thereby pose a threat to social cohesion and economic security as immigrants would either take jobs away from locals or become a welfare burden on the state. Despite the fact that ultramodern global labour markets depend on immigrants, following September 11 and the London bombings, Western governments hardened their immigration policies and multiculturalism was widely criticised, particularly within the UK and the EU, for contributing to ghettoisation and cultural relativism, thus hindering processes of integration and threatening the stability of ultramodern societies (Kymlicka and Banting 2006: 300; Turner 2008: 1–2; Taylor 2009: xiii–xiv; Levey 2009: 3).

In addition, the global war on terror waged by the USA and its allies 'squeeze[d] the space for global civil society' (Kaldor 2003a: 148). The anti-globalisation movement postponed or cancelled protests (Kaldor 2003a: 154) and women's and environmental initiatives ceased to receive public funding. However, the global peace movement expanded its circle to include more religious communities, especially Islamic groups, and mass demonstrations in opposition to the war in Iraq were held throughout the world (Kaldor 2003a: 154; Beck 2006: 118). As described in the previous chapter, the multifaith movement also increased dramatically in size and number during this period. Indeed, the multifaith movement was among the only social movements that actually enjoyed growing state support, particularly in the UK and Australia, as multifaith initiatives began to be included in strategies to counter extremism and advance social cohesion (Halafoff 2006: 10–12; Braybrooke 2007: 1, 13; Pearce quoted in Bharat and Bharat 2007: 245–246; Bouma et al. 2007: 6, 22–26, 55, 57–60; Halafoff and Wright-Neville 2009). Therefore, the multifaith movement and the growth of multi-actor peacebuilding networks, in which religious actors have played a crucial role alongside state and NGO actors in responding to the global risk of terrorism, were among the few cosmopolitan spaces remaining in Western societies during the early 2000s.

Public Religion

At the turn of the twenty-first century two competing narratives emerged *within* religious communities between the push for: (1) religious homogeneity, and (2) religious pluralism. Rising critiques of the spread of capitalist modernity described above, be they peaceful or violent, contributed to a global resurgence of religion at the end of the twentieth century, thereby challenging theories of secularisation. Whether exclusive or plural, these movements are all 'part and parcel of the [ultra]modern political agenda', constituting 'multiple [ultra]modernities' based on reflexive principles which are shared among modernities' advocates and critics (Eisenstadt 2000: 3, 20).

In the late twentieth century, as religious actors reasserted the relevance of religious values in the public and political sphere, refusing to accept the privatised and thus marginalised role accorded to them by secularisation theories, so-called 'invisible and privatised religion' (Beckford 1990: 8 citing Luckmann 1967) became more '*visible*' (Beckford 1990: 9) and deprivatised (Casanova 1994: 3–6, 17–19 citing Luckmann 1967). Casanova (1994: 5–6) has argued that secularisation is not a myth, as a process of functional differentiation and separation of the so-called secular spheres—primarily state and economic function systems—from religious institutions and norms no doubt occurred in Western societies during the modern era. However, religions have re-entered the political sphere and the religious sphere has become repoliticised in ultramodernity (Casanova 1994: 19). This demonstrates that, firstly, religions have not disappeared, as many sociologists had predicted, but rather that 'religions are here to stay', and, secondly, that religion will continue to play an important public, as well as private, role in the ultramodern era (Casanova 1994: 6–7). Consequently, Casanova (1994: 7) called for 'better theories of the intermeshing of public and private spheres' relating to religion, politics and economics and applied a Habermasian cosmopolitan framework in order to better understand the increasingly public role of religion in the 1990s.

While Habermas's early work largely excluded religion, in the mid-1990s Casanova (1994) argued that Habermas's (1987) theory of communicative action could well be applied to the dynamics of ultramodern religious social movements. Following a Habermasian discursive model, expanded upon by Seyla Benhabib (1992a), Casanova (1994: 217) explained that the concept of public religion is compatible with liberal democracy because '[a] discursive or agonic space ... open to all citizens', including religious actors, introduces 'intersubjective norms into the private sphere (analogous to the feminist dictum "the personal is political") and morality into the public sphere of state and economy (the principle of the "common good" as a normative criterion)'. According to Casanova (1994: 220):

> As churches [religions] transfer the defence of their particularistic privilege (*libertas ecclesae*) to the human person and accept the principle of religious freedom as a universal human right, they are for the first time in a position to enter the public sphere anew, this time to defend the institutionalisation of modern universal rights, the creation of a modern public sphere, and the establishment of democratic regimes.

Therefore, religion's role in the ultramodern public sphere is not simply one of 'antimodern religious critiques of modernity'. Rather, religions represent 'new types of immanent normative critiques of specific forms of institutionalisation of modernity' which have been made possible by the principles of modernity including the development of differentiated and deliberative structures. 'In other words', Casanova (1994: 221–222) stated, 'they are immanent critiques of particular forms of modernity from a modern [or ultramodern] religious point of view'. This reflexivity, applied to the spheres of politics and economics, also applies to the religious sphere itself, as religious actors elaborate on and reformulate religious traditions according to modern, and ultramodern, principles of human rights and sustainable development (Casanova 1994: 229). In this way 'religions force modern societies to confront the task of reconstructing reflexively and collectively their own normative foundations. By doing so, they aid in the process of practical rationalization of the traditional lifeworld and of its own normative traditions' (Casanova 1994: 229). Again, according to a Habermasian deliberative framework (1987), Casanova (1994: 231) explained how:

> [a]ccording to this model, modern social integration emerges in and through the discursive and agonistic participation of individuals, groups, social movements, and institutions in a public yet undifferentiated sphere of civil society where the collective construction and reconstruction, contestation, and affirmation of common normative structures—"the common good"—takes place. Unlike functionalist theories of normative societal integration, however, such a theory does not conceptualise modern civil societies as homogenous societal community sharing norms and values but, rather, as a space and a process of public societal interaction through which common norms cannot be presupposed as the premise and foundation of a modern social order but, rather, as the potential and always fragile outcome of a process of communicative interaction. Through such a process of communicative interaction in the public sphere of modern civil societies, normative traditions can be reflexively reconstructed—that is—rationalized—and the differentiated subsystems of modern societies can be made responsible to a publicly defined "common good".

In this sense, religions, by challenging the global inequities and environmental destruction wreaked by markets and states, can be seen to be 'on the side of human enlightenment', thereby furthering 'the unfinished project of modernity' (Casanova 1994: 234). Casanova (1994: 234) therefore concludes that religion could possibly and 'unintentionally help modernity save itself'.

Casanova's reading of Habermas's theory can be effectively applied to developing an understanding not only of the increasingly public role of religion in the ultramodern public sphere but also of the ultramodern rise of the multifaith movement and of multi-actor peacebuilding networks in which religious actors play a significant role. As will be explored in the following chapters, multifaith initiatives provide discursive spaces in which religious actors can be critical of state, market and religious forces, challenging cultures of violence and advancing cultures of peace in their stead. Within this framework, the multifaith movement, alongside other social movements, situated within the sphere of civil society, offers criticism from the grassroots up, by enabling religious actors to play an agonistic role as critics of states and markets. Moreover, the rise of multi-actor peacebuilding networks, in which religious and state actors collaborate on security issues, reveals that religions can act as *both* critics *and* partners of state actors, on matters of common security within a cosmopolitan, deliberative framework.

Ultramodern Cosmopolitan Governance

Theories of global governance, including cosmopolitan theory, rose to prominence in the late twentieth century, largely due to the realisation that traditional forms of nation-state governance provided inadequate responses to global issues such as growing inequalities and climate change (Munck 2005: 151). In addition, processes of globalisation, enabled by the growth of global communication systems, led to an awareness of global interdependence, which called for global cooperation rather than competition in the face of these crisis events (Bauman 2006: 96–97, 100). According to Beck (1999, 2005: 280), in this new 'world risk society', in which global risks know no borders, there is an increasing need for a global polity to collaboratively address risks at causal levels, thereby minimising future risks in addition to combating present ones. It is within this context that cosmopolitanism has re-emerged as a political philosophy that offers a methodology of global governance that can effectively respond to the most pressing risks of our time (Held 1995; Beck 2006).

While there has been an ultramodern trend toward conceptualising the world through a global framework, David Inglis and Roland Robertson (2005: 100–101, 104, 117) describe how, as a result of processes of colonial expansion, an '*ecumenical sensibility*' and '"cosmopolitan" manner of understanding one's place in the world' arose during the late Greek and early Roman period, in which the planet was viewed as an interconnected entity. Western cosmopolitanism originated in Greece with the Stoics, who conceived of themselves as cosmopolitan citizens; however, the origins of modern cosmopolitan theory can be attributed to the Prussian philosopher Immanuel Kant (1724–1804).

According to Kant's view of enlightenment, everyone is capable of developing 'higher' qualities; yet this can only take place in conditions of freedom and security where a base level of peace is guaranteed by law and by the state (Kant [1784b] 2006: 17, [1784a] 2006: 6–8). In this way, the cosmopolitan condition is primarily one of 'public security', a common security founded on the principle of 'cosmopolitan rights', which Kant ([1784a] 2006: 12, [1795] 2006: 84–85) described as equal rights for all. Kant ([1784b] 2006: 20–21, [1795] 2006: 93, [1784a] 2006: 11) claimed that it is the responsibility of each citizen, particularly religious scholars and intellectuals more generally, to continually critique and revise these laws, on the understanding that the process of individual and collective enlightenment is a gradual deliberative process. Over time an enlightened global community will no longer require laws to keep its members in line or policies to guide them. However, until such time as this occurs laws remain necessary, and these laws must always be balanced with granting freedom and rights for all, as long as they do not impede the rights of others. Despite the potential risks that this entails, Kant ([1784a] 2006: 8, 12, 14, [1784b] 2006: 22) argued that these conditions would more likely lead to collective enlightenment than oppressive regimes that forbid free expression and thereby thwart enlightening processes. An enlightened citizenry poses no threat to an enlightened state. Indeed, they will reinforce one another's collective processes of enlightenment. Conversely, an immature state threatened by its citizens will seek to oppress them and thereby stall the process of collective enlightenment. However, according to Kant's ([1784a] 2006: 10) view of '*antagonism*', this oppression cannot be maintained because resistance will inevitably procure new awareness and liberation over time.

Kant's emphasis on the importance of reflexivity at both the individual and collective level is of particular relevance in that the responsibility to make and revise laws and policies lie with the citizenry *in cooperation* with the state. Kant's cosmopolitanism emphasises the importance of equal rights for all and a belief that non-state actors, including religious actors, can collaborate with state actors by offering constructive criticism through deliberative processes as they strive collectively toward 'perpetual peace'. Therefore, Kant's cosmopolitanism offers an effective framework for responding to contemporary challenges as it is founded on an awareness of a global community in which all have equal rights and should have a voice in determining their future, enabled by collaborative, deliberative, democratic processes. According to Kant's cosmopolitanism, all citizens are equal bearers of human rights and democratic legitimacy arises as all members of a political community are viewed as consociates, who establish self-governance and are at once authors and subjects of the laws they create (Benhabib 2005: 768). However, not all people were included in the sovereign body during the eighteenth century: notably women, servants, slaves, non-Christians and non-whites were excluded, and famously referred to by Kant ([1797] 1996: 140 quoted in Benhabib 2005: 769) as 'mere auxiliaries to the commonwealth'. Kant's cosmopolitanism, therefore, needed to be reflexively examined and revised to meet twenty-first century developments and norms.

While Kant's *Towards Perpetual Peace* ([1795] 2006) described the cosmopolitan condition, it was not until after the Second World War that global cosmopolitan institution-building occurred, as witnessed in the 1948 United Nations (UN) Declaration of Human Rights and the subsequent Covenants of Rights in 1966 (Held 2003: 473). As a result of these developments, alongside processes of decolonisation, the rise of social movements and policies of multiculturalism (which were institutionalised in partnership between immigrant communities and state actors), the notion of citizenship—and cosmopolitan theory respectively—became progressively more inclusive. Indeed, the process of globalisation and an increased awareness of global risks, combined with a new awareness of diversity, contributed to the formation of ultramodern cosmopolitanism that, according to deliberative cosmopolitan principles, built upon and revised Kant's theories.

Ultramodern cosmopolitan governance is radically reflexive. It recognises the interdependence of all life and emphasises equal rights *alongside* respect for diversity. It is inclusive and deliberative, collaborative and multilateral, concentrated at local and global, as opposed to national, levels. Notably, Habermas's (1984, 1987, 2006, 2007) and Beck's (2006) ultramodern cosmopolitan theories display many of the above characteristics and Habermas's writings in particular have become gradually more respectful of diverse cultural and religious perspectives over time. It follows that ultramodern cosmopolitanism need no longer be viewed as an exclusive Western philosophy imposed upon non-Western societies (Munck 2005: 117), but rather as a framework that is constantly being refined, by multiple actors in increasingly culturally and religiously diverse societies, to be more inclusive over time.

While Mary Kaldor (1999: 89, 122) stated that terms such as 'anti-politics' and 'civil society' were frequently used to describe the social movements of the 1980s and 1990s, reflecting their disaffection with state-centred power and political processes, she also noted that '[c]ivil society needs a state' and local actors 'need to be consulted and treated as partners' by state authorities. Rather than pit civil society against the state, civil society (including religious actors) and state actors need to collaborate on issues of common concern.

More recently, Beck has also described the changing nature of relations between states and civil society, away from divisive to more inclusive frameworks. According to Beck (2006: 23, 35–36), the heightened awareness of global risks in our ultramodern era creates 'an unavoidable pressure to cooperate' and serves as a 'source of new commonalities and interaction networks'. Global risks 'explode self-referential systems and national and international political agendas, overturning their priorities and producing practical interconnections', often among previously indifferent or even hostile groups. In this way, globalisation has created a 'new space and framework for acting' whereby the realm of politics is no longer reserved for state actors but has expanded to include new players such as civil society advocacy movements (Beck 2005: 3–4). As these actors are no longer capable of achieving their goals independently they must instead form coalitions and paradoxical alliances, recognising that this cooperation must include the nation-state in its capacity to institutionalise cosmopolitan values such as a rights-based framework for stabilising differences (Beck 2005: 288–289). Beck (2006: 89) asserts that '[c]osmopolitan competence' rests on 'the art of translation and bridge-building' among multiple diverse actors. Indeed, Appleby (2003: 255) has described the emergence of a new 'secular–religious' model of diplomacy as a promising recent development, and has attributed 'the building of strong secular and religious networks and coalitions' as the key to its success, as such collaborations can draw upon expertise and resources from diverse sectors. Beckford (1990: 9, 11) similarly asserted the importance of cooperative responses to social problems through 'networks, campaigns, and movements', which challenge distinctions between public and private religion and the spheres of religion and politics. The ultramodern rise of multi-actor peacebuilding initiatives, which include religious and state actors, as briefly described in the introduction, provides some evidence of these developments in Western multifaith societies.

In addition, Beck (2006: 5–7, 161) asserts that the 'territorial either/or' theory of identity belongs to an outdated methodological nationalism of the first modernity. He argues that '[t]he diagnosis of the crisis is: too little cosmopolitan outlook; and the cure: *more* cosmopolitan sense of reality', which affirms respect for difference and equal rights for all, thereby challenging narrow nationalistic and religious extremist ideologies. Accordingly ultramodernity's 'both/and logic of inclusive differentiation' constructs a new model in which multiple identities and loyalties expand beyond the nation-state. Moreover, a growing awareness of global suffering and a corresponding '*cosmopolitan empathy*' and compulsion for action, as witnessed in global protests against the Iraq War, indicate that the friend/foe scheme of first modernity no longer holds in an increasingly globalised world. Beck (2006: 14) states that: 'the old differentiations between internal and external, national and international, us and them' have lost 'their validity, and a new cosmopolitan realism becomes essential to survival'.

Religion and the Ultramodern Public Sphere

Despite his inclusive rhetoric, Beck (2005: 306, 309) relegates religion to the past, refers to secularised cosmopolitanism as an ideal and declares that: 'Ultimately, cosmopolitanism is the secularized divine order after the divine order has come to an end'. In so doing, Beck completely neglects the positive contribution of religious actors in the ultramodern public sphere. As Casanova took it upon himself to extend Habermas's theory of communicative action in the mid-1990s, in a similar way sociologists of religion, including Robert A. Campbell and Willaime, have more recently applied Beck's theories to the study of ultramodern religious phenomena with a particular emphasis on reflexivity. According to Campbell (2006: 92 quoting McGuire 1997: 32), following a Weberian argument, theodicies provide 'paths of practical action' to address social and economic inequities, thus providing 'religious explanations that provide meaning for meaning-threatening experiences'. Campbell (2006: 96) quotes Beck (1999: 93), explaining that the reflexive nature of ultramodern societies creates 'the possibility and necessity to reinvent our political institutions and to invent new ways of conducting politics at social "sites" that we previously considered unpolitical'. Campbell (2006: 96, 99) argues that New Religious Movements can be viewed as such sites, providing theodicies during times of uncertainty.

Following a very similar argument to Casanova's (1994), Willaime (2006: 82–83) also cites Beck's (1992: 186) observation that in ultramodernity, technological, scientific and economic systems have more power than politics and, consequently, politics is in the process of being 'disentangled from the grand visions of man and society'. It is precisely at this juncture that religion has radically re-entered the public sphere. According to Willaime (2006: 79), in ultramodernity the so-called secular ideals of modernity that marginalised and criticised religion and 'set themselves up as new certainties' are being de-absolutised, resulting in 'the disenchantment of the disenchanters'. A period of *radical reflexivity* thereby categorises the ultramodern era in which social movements and diverse cultural and religious groups have played an increasingly critical role in the public sphere.

Religions, argues Willaime (2006: 86), have come 'to the rescue of democracies … to underline the importance and the dignity of political responsibility … and to make sure that actors in social and political life remain strongly active in attempts to keep democracy alive'.

Indeed, Habermas (2006: 1–4) himself now argues that in the complex world of *multiple [ultra]modernities* there is no longer any place for exclusive truth claims and politically imposed religious doctrines. The (plural) secular state guarantees religious freedom for all and in so doing enables religion to self-reflexively 'see itself through the eyes of others … thenceforth … renounce violence … and recourse to state power … to enforce their religious claims' (Habermas 2007: 10–11). In this way, ultramodern plural societies demand respect for all, enabling processes of deliberative democracy that provide a space for multiple, including religious, voices in the public sphere. Religious individuals and communities have a right to exert their influence in the deliberative public sphere alongside other citizens and groups, as '[e]veryone is permitted to realize her own ethos … within the limits of the equal ethical liberties of all' (Habermas 2005: 27–28). In addition, Habermas (2006: 8) acknowledges that religious persons cannot separate political views from their religious beliefs, given that concepts of justice are often religiously derived. Habermas (2006: 16, 20) thereby proposes a new multi-dimensional conceptualisation of reason, that no longer excludes religion and whose success rests on the ability of both non-religious and religious citizens to behave self-reflexively in the public sphere.

Moreover, Habermas (2007: 184, 15) states that only 'self-critical dialogue between cultures' can address the root causes of risks, such as terrorism, asserting that 'conflicts arise due to disruptions in communication, from misunderstandings and incomprehension, insincerity and deception'. According to Habermas (2007: 15–16, 18), a 'spiral of violence' begins with a disruption in communication that leads to mutual mistrust and communication breakdown. However, if there is a commitment between the parties involved in the conflict to work toward 'mutual understanding' it is possible to determine the cause of the conflict, to repair it and to prevent its reoccurrence. Habermas (2007: 18) thus describes his *Theory of Communicative Action* as it applies to contemporary conflicts:

> In struggling with the difficulties of understanding, participants in conversation must progressively broaden their original perspectives until they finally achieve congruence. Moreover, they can achieve such a "fusion of horizons" in virtue of their ability to assume the role of "speaker" and "hearer" through which they engage in a fundamental symmetry that all speech situations ultimately demand… And in the course of multiple perspective taking, a common horizon of background assumptions can develop in which both sides reach an interpretation that is neither ethnocentrically condescending nor a conversion, but something *intersubjectively* shared.

In addition, Benhabib builds upon Habermas's theory by describing the importance of dialogical models in bridging the divide between religious and state actors in the ultramodern public sphere. According to Benhabib (2002b: 44 citing Benhabib 2002a):

> We can intervene in this process of complex cultural negotiations as dialogue partners in a global civilization only insofar as we make an effort to understand the struggles of others whose idioms and terms may be unfamiliar to us, but which, by the same token, are also not so different from similar struggles at other times in our own cultures; through acts of strong hermeneutical generosity, we can still extend our moral imagination to view the world through the others' eyes.

Benhabib (2004a: 293) argues that 'creative resignification and renegotiation' of core commitments is necessary for religions to continue to provide 'hermeneutically plausible strands of meaning' in ultramodern societies. Benhabib (2004b, 2007: 454) labels these deliberations '"democratic iterations" … through which universalist rights claims and principles are contested and contextualised, invoked and revoked, posited and positioned throughout legal and political institutions, as well as in the associations of civil society'. Benhabib (1992b, 2004b, 2007: 455) also notes that it is vital that these democratic iterations be carried out according to the premise of a 'discourse ethic', which guarantees equality of participation.

The ultramodern rise of the multifaith movement and of multi-actor peacebuilding networks constitutes evidence of cosmopolitan responses aimed at countering risks in increasingly plural Western societies. The need to develop greater understanding—of diverse faiths, of the underlying causes of conflicts and of the nature of reality—is a central tenet of both the multifaith movement and ultramodern cosmopolitan theory. In addition, the non-violent, dialogical methods employed by multifaith actors to enact social change, addressing risks at the causal level in partnership with state actors, align the multifaith movement with cosmopolitan principles. However, relatively little research has been undertaken in this field and further investigation is required in order to substantiate this hypothesis. This new evidence is provided in the following chapters, in the form of actor perspectives from within the multifaith movement reflecting on the movement's role in social change.

A Cosmopolitanism Methodology

As this study is primarily concerned with developing a greater understanding of the ultramodern multifaith movement it therefore employs a cosmopolitan research methodology, drawing extensively on Beck's (2006: 72–96) 'methodological cosmopolitanism', in order to achieve this aim.

According to Beck (2006: 87–88), while social structures are becoming increasingly global and thereby cosmopolitan, social research remains largely focused on the national level. Beck poses the question, '[h]ow … is an empirical sociology of the global possible?' and answers by stating that sociologists 'can investigate the global locally'. Beck cites Robertson's (1992 in Robertson and Khondker 1998) theory of 'glocalisation' to illustrate his argument that global forces impact local contexts and can thereby be examined locally. Therefore, Beck (2006: 88–89) concludes that the global need not be investigated 'in a totally global fashion'. Instead '[w]e can develop a new, functional, historically sensitive empiricism focused on the ambivalent consequences of globalization in boundary-transcending and multi-local research networks'. Indeed, 'the extension, permeation and reconstruction of boundaries … can themselves become objects of social scientific inquiry' (Beck 2006: 90).

Beck (2006: 74, 91, 94) states that it is therefore possible to develop a new methodological cosmopolitanism that analyses, 'discloses, reconstructs and investigates the active and passive cosmopolitanization of the world' and 'the interconnections between cosmopolitan developments and movements, on the one hand, and the resistance and obstructions to which they give rise, on the other'. This is precisely the intention of this study: to investigate how multifaith initiatives have been implemented as cosmopolitan strategies to counter global risks in ultramodernity and also to examine the resistances the multifaith movement has encountered in this process.[1]

[1] Beck's focus on movements, in his definition of methodological cosmopolitanism, reflects an emphasis on looser social forms rather than institutions in cosmopolitan theory. This has informed the methodology of this study, which focuses on multifaith actors and the multifaith movement rather than religious organisations, as discussed in more detail below.

In terms of data collection, Beck (2006: 92–93, 75) suggests that these patterns of relations are best investigated through 'actor perspectives' and communication flows, declaring that the foundation of methodological cosmopolitanism must rest on going '[b]ack to the things themselves! Away from pure theories for their own sake! Away from books!'. Bouma and Rod Ling (2005: 177) similarly suggest that conducting semi-structured interviews can provide a 'window' into phenomena, by allowing interviewees to tell their own stories, to '"open up" and lead' the discussion, identifying the issues that are most important to them. Techniques of in-depth, semi-structured interviewing can thereby provide an effective method for understanding people and interpreting the motivations behind their actions (Minichiello et al. 2008: 1, 4).

A Glocal Approach

A defining feature of Beck's (2006) methodological cosmopolitanism is a notable shift in his approach to selecting contexts for sociological research. As modern national–national relations are in the process of being replaced by ultramodern local–global, national–global and global–global relational patterns, Beck (2006: 75–76, 87–90) recommends that methodology must evolve away from oppositional nation–nation comparisons to reflect these new developments. In short, as we are living in an increasingly globalised world it is impossible to accurately investigate local experiences without situating them within the global context. Following Beck's advice, this study incorporates a local–global focus, examining ultramodern multifaith engagement in the local context of Victoria, Australia within a broader 'global' framework.

Monash University scholars have conducted several recent studies in Victoria, which have indicated that multifaith initiatives have been successfully implemented by culturally and religiously diverse communities, in collaboration with state actors, as strategies to counter global risks such as terrorism (Halafoff 2006, 2007; Bouma et al. 2007; Halafoff and Wright-Neville 2009). Victoria was therefore chosen as the local focus of this research. However, establishing a 'global' context for the study was somewhat more challenging than choosing the local case study. Beck (2006: 88–89) himself notes that 'the global' cannot be investigated in a completely global fashion, yet research questions can be explored in multiple locations thereby providing a global overview. As Emile Durkheim ([1914] 1995: 91–92, 95) suggested, research is best confined to clearly defined types of societies that resemble one another rather than over all possible societies or societies that are very different. Following these recommendations three countries were chosen—Australia, the UK and the USA—to provide the 'global' context for this study.

The UK, USA and Australia are all societies in which diverse Indigenous spiritualities once flourished but which have now been transformed into predominantly Christian societies. More recently, these countries have become increasingly multicultural and multifaith societies as a result of the processes of globalisation. As the first Parliament of the World's Religions (PWR) was held in Chicago in the USA in 1893, and also as many of the initiatives of the emerging global multifaith movement subsequently occurred in the USA and UK (Braybrooke 1992), these countries were selected rather than other so-called Western multicultural and multi-faith societies such as Canada and New Zealand.

This study begins and ends in Melbourne, Australia, the place in which the author resides. It also includes the USA and the UK, cultural contexts that are relatively similar to Australia, with a long history of multifaith engagement. However, it recognises that Asian, so-called Eastern, religions, particularly Hinduism and Buddhism, have played a central role in the multifaith movement since its inception in 1893 (Braybrooke 1992; Eck 2001)[2] and that many non-Western societies have long histories and expertise in multifaith relations. It therefore has no intention of falsely elevating Western contributions to the multifaith movement above others; it simply begins in the author's local context. In future, ideally a team of global experts, from South-East Asia, Central Asia, Russia, Central and Eastern Europe, the Middle East, Africa, Central and South America, and the Pacific, could collaborate on a more inclusive study of multifaith initiatives in a genuinely cosmopolitan global context.

Three to four cities—with established multifaith organisations—in each country were chosen as focal points for the study: New York, Washington, Chicago and San Francisco in the USA; London, Oxford and Glasgow in the UK; and Melbourne, Sydney and Brisbane in Australia. Professional experts were identified from published studies of multifaith engagement and also from the author's insider knowledge of local and global multifaith organisations. As many of the leading figures in multifaith organisations are men, and are often in an older age bracket, the study sought to purposely balance the sample by including women and young people. It also sought to include participants from diverse religious traditions. That said, all participants were selected for their expertise in multifaith relations and not as representatives of religious organisations. A total of 56 semi-structured interviews being conducted throughout 2007–2008, 18 in Australia, 11 in the UK and 23 in the US with 30 men, 23 women and including 8 young people.[3] Twelve participants were interviewed in the State of Victoria and their comments have been included in both the 'global' overview and the local case study. As all participants consented to having their comments identified, tags appear throughout the following chapters wherever respondents' remarks are included. Tags include the actor's surname, the year of the interview and the country in which the participant resides i.e. <Patel 2007, USA>.[4]

It is also important to stress that, in accordance with methodological cosmopolitanism, this is not a three nation-state comparative study but rather a glocal inquiry

[2] The influence of Hindu and Buddhist leaders on the multifaith movement is discussed in more detail in Chap. 3.

[3] A complete list of participants is included in Appendix 1.

[4] As actors were selected as professional experts participating in the multifaith movement, and not as representatives of religious organisations, it would be misleading to identify them according to their religious affiliation, although from participants' titles and comments in many cases it is made quite obvious.

exploring both global and local contexts. Firstly, in Chaps. 3, 4, 5, 6, and 7, a 'global' overview of the rise of the multifaith movement in ultramodernity, multifaith responses to global risks and the benefits and challenges of multifaith engagement, is provided by drawing on previously published material and actor perspectives gathered specifically for this study. Then, in Chap. 8, the local Victorian case study is presented. This chapter provides a brief history of multiculturalism and multifaith engagement in Victoria, drawing on secondary data in the form of reports, policy documents, monographs, and newspaper and journal articles. It also includes a summary of Victorian participants' responses gathered for this study and of issues raised within the 'global' overview that have been reflexively applied to the Victorian context. As a result insights gained from the 'global' context have enabled the Victorian context to be viewed with new eyes, so to speak, and new issues have emerged that previously haven't been noted by local scholars in Victorian studies.

Strengths and Limitations of an Insider Approach

This book focuses on the development of the multifaith movement primarily from the perspective of key participants in the movement. As outlined above the participants are diverse and include actors from different faiths, local communities and national contexts, namely Australia, the UK and the US. Consequently, on the surface, an insider approach was utilised in this study, which brings the researchers', and in this case also the actors-participants', experiences and beliefs to the foreground of the inquiry. However, the boundary between insiders and outsiders are not so clearly defined in our ultramodern era, and this certainly applies to the study of the multifaith movement (Knott 2009).

The multifaith movement includes many so-called scholar-practitioners, namely scholars, who are active participants in multifaith organisations and networks. The author also falls into this category, having been active within the multifaith movement since the mid-1990s. Kim Knott (2009: 260–261 citing Pike 1967: 37) describes how there has been a long-held debate among scholars of religion regarding whether an objective, outsider, *emic* perspective is more desirable that a more informed, insider, *etic* perspective when studying religion and/or religious movements. Instead of framing actors and observers simply as insiders and outsiders, Knott (2009: 262) lists Buford Junker and Raymond L. Gold's (1958: 217) four categories of (1) 'complete observer' (outsider), (2) 'observer as participant', (3) 'participant as observer' and (4) 'complete participant' (insider). Knott (2009: 263, 267) explains that scholarly participants can adopt the role of observer while conducting research in order to take a more critical stance while retaining the benefits of an insider's knowledge. This can provide an added benefit as such scholars can play a 'bridge-building' role by making the religious movement, or group and its practices, more comprehensible for outsiders. In addition, 'the both/and position' of the scholar-practitioner enables a deeper level of reflexivity of the phenomenon in question than does outsider scholarship (Knott 2009: 269 citing Pearson 2002).

Following this argument, this research can best be described as 'participant as observer' research, which seeks to reflexively gain a greater understanding of the multifaith movement in order to communicate this information to other scholars, practitioners and policy makers, both within and beyond the movement.

In addition, in so far as drawing on the views of expert professionals in the field of multifaith relations risked presenting a biased positive description of multifaith initiatives, the critical analysis of the movement was enhanced by specifically asking participants to describe the challenges of multifaith engagement, thereby providing a critique of the multifaith movement and of multi-actor peacebuilding networks from the so-called 'inside'. Therefore, as described by Knott above, employing research methods that focused on gathering actors' perspectives provided more meaningful understandings of the multifaith movement drawn from the most knowledgeable of sources, as experts in the field of multifaith relations provided insights regarding the benefits and difficulties of multifaith engagement based on first-hand experiences. Presenting this analysis to scholars outside of the multifaith movement, such as at sociology and religious studies conferences, also provided an opportunity to gain feedback from a critical audience.

While the vast majority of previously material published by scholars and scholar-practitioners on the multifaith movement is largely positive, this book includes criticisms levied against the movement from scholars, scholar-practitioners and actors-practitioners interviewed for this study. By raising concerns regarding the multifaith movement, it demonstrates that a 'participant as observer' *etic* approach can reflexively and critically examine the subject matter in question. Indeed this is a vital component of a cosmopolitan methodology, as according to Beck (2006: 75) the process of cosmopolitanisation, 'followed to its logical conclusion, is … concerned with how to create new political forms capable of solving the problems of cosmopolitanisation'. This book provides a reflexive study of the multifaith movement, with the hope that these findings will assist in the refinement of existing multifaith practices and policies, locally and globally, according to cosmopolitan principles. In the same way as religious actors can play a role as *both* critics *and* partners of state authorities, encouraging them to improve their practices, scholar-practitioners through critical research can seek to play a positive role in social change.

Given that all of the interviewees in this study are active in the multifaith movement, and are positively disposed to multifaith engagement, a potential limitation of this book is that these committed participants may have a tendency to overestimate the influence of their movement and its contribution to common security. While it incorporates some of the views of prominent critics of the multifaith movement, including Peter A. Huff (2000) and Geneive Abdo (2008), further research investigating state actors' and the general publics' perception of multifaith engagement is necessary in order to provide a more complete analysis of the multifaith movements' benefits and difficulties in future.

Finally, Knott (2009: 269 citing Collins 2002) concludes, that the 'insider/outsider dichotomy is an unhelpful consequence of a modernist view of self and society' and that distinctions between outsiders and insiders are no longer relevant.

According to Peter J. Collins, it is preferable to frame 'everyone as co-participants' and co-constructors 'of the story'. These observations resonate well with the overall framework of an ultramodern cosmopolitan methodology. Every actor, scholar and scholar-practitioner, whose views have been included in this study, be they an advocate or critic of the multifaith movement, have participated in its development and its findings will be of interest to all co-constructors of the global multifaith movement, be they religious or non-religious persons, faith leaders, donors and/or state actors.

Conclusions

The rise of the multifaith movement in ultramodernity is best understood by situating these developments in the broader context of the resurgence of religion at the turn of the twenty-first century. While secularisation theory predicted the demise of religion, instead religious actors have increasingly played a prominent role in the ultramodern public sphere, most notably as critics of the spread of global capitalism. Processes of capitalist globalisation not only threatened traditional ways of life, but also alerted humanity to the interconnectedness of global problems and their solutions. In response to the threats posed by global capitalism, religious movements, including the multifaith movement, arose alongside other social movements of this period in defence of the lifeworld and its citizens, advocating new collaborative cosmopolitan mazeways to advance common human and environmental security.

In addition, global communication systems and the global spread of people resulted in increasingly culturally and religiously diverse societies. Processes of decolonisation and self-determination among minority groups led to the development of policies of multiculturalism, which institutionalised respect for diversity and enabled a greater level of participation of minorities in the public sphere. Human rights and multicultural policies were developed according to cosmopolitan principles, such that laws were refined in consultation with diverse actors, and inequitable policies were replaced with more inclusive measures. These processes of local and global ultramodern cosmopolitanisation, however, were widely resisted among interest groups who felt their power and privileges were threatened by these new developments.

By the mid-1990s, the optimistic cosmopolitan moment, created by the end of the Cold War and the plethora of social movements that sought more inclusive, non-violent, multilateral forms of governance, was replaced by a regressive decade categorised by the rise of conservative governments and fundamentalist religious movements that routinely employed direct and structural violence in order to impose their regimes upon citizens. The environmental movement and women's movement were all but silenced during this period. However, the peace movement and the multifaith movement gathered strength and momentum, especially following September 11 and the wars in Afghanistan and Iraq. As religion frequently played a central role in the public sphere in discourse around these conflicts, religious peacebuilders united in multifaith activities to develop greater understanding of diverse communities and the underlying causes of these tensions. In addition, multifaith initiatives received state support in Australia and the UK in the form of social cohesion and counter-terrorism strategies. In this way, the multifaith movement employed a dialogical framework to non-violently address risks and advance common security in multifaith societies. According to cosmopolitan principles, religious peacebuilders, from diverse traditions acted as both critics *and* partners of state actors, advising on policies to counter the underlying causes of terrorism and to build more genuinely inclusive and peaceful societies.

Therefore, rather than view the tensions in ultramodern societies as reflective of a battle of civil society versus the state (Kaldor 1999: 89) or a clash of civilisations (Huntington 1993, 2003), the rise of the multifaith movement and of multi-actor peacebuilding networks indicate that the real clash exists between cosmopolitan and anti-cosmopolitan actors both within, and outside of, all faith traditions. While anti-cosmopolitans seek to impose their will and policies upon others, cosmopolitans seek to create a public sphere through dialogical means in which all actors, be they religious or non-religious, have a role to play in governance and in refining policies. In this way, they extend and refine modern principles of democracy to be more truly inclusive and participatory. Cosmopolitans do not reject modernity. However, they reject all that is unjust about it, recognising that we—comprising the entire lifeworld—are in a process of constant development that is not so much linear but rather, like a pendulum, swings between more progressive and regressive qualities and periods. It follows, therefore, that despite *and* as a result of religions' capacity to incite both structural and direct violence, religions have played a cosmopolitan peacebuilding role in ultramodern societies, as evidenced by the increase in multifaith initiatives at the turn of the twenty-first century. Therefore, the rise of the multifaith movement and of multi-actor peacebuilding networks in ultramodernity, alongside other social movements of this period, provides a missing narrative within the sociological literature comprising cosmopolitan peacebuilding religious efforts to collaboratively counter global risks.

While situating contemporary developments within a historical context, this book aims primarily to investigate precisely how multifaith initiatives have been implemented as cosmopolitan strategies to counter global risks such as terrorism and climate change, and to advance common security in ultramodern Western societies. The majority of existing research demonstrates the success of multifaith engagement (Eck 2001, 2005; Cahill et al. 2004; Ahmed and Forst 2005; Brodeur 2005; Brodeur and Patel 2006; Halafoff 2006, 2007; Bouma et al. 2007; Lohre 2007; McCarthy 2007; Niebuhr 2008; Braybrooke 2007; Bharat and Bharat 2007; Kirkwood 2007; Halafoff and Wright-Neville 2009), as outlined in the introduction, some concerns have been raised regarding the growing proximity between religious and state actors and whether religious groups have been able to maintain their critical role in the public sphere (Beckford 1990: 13; Pearce quoted in Bharat and Bharat 2007: 245–246). There is a pressing need to examine the tensions and challenges of religious–state collaboration in greater detail, particularly the distribution of power and resources, and possible ways of remedying them (Beckford 2003: 99).

In so doing, the findings of this study can assist faith communities and state actors to refine existing multifaith practices and policies, at the local, national and global levels, as part of social inclusion strategies.

References

Abdo, Geneive. 2008. False prophets. *Foreign Policy*, July/August: 51–53.

Agamben, Georgio. 2003. Der Gewahrsam-Ausnahmezustand als Weltordnung. *Frankfurter Allgemeine Zeitung*, April 19.

Ahmed, Akbar, and Brian Forst (eds.). 2005. *After terror: Promoting dialogue among civilizations*. Cambridge: Polity Press.

An-Na'im, Abdullahi Ahmed. 2003. Islamic fundamentalism and social change: Neither the "end of history" nor a "clash of civilisations". In *The freedom to do god's will: Religious fundamentalism and social change*, ed. ter Haar Gerrie and J.Busuttil James, 25–48. London/New York: Routledge.

Appleby, R.Scott. 2000. *The ambivalence of the sacred: Religion, violence, and reconciliation*. Maryland: Rowman and Littlefield Publishers, Inc.

Appleby, R.Scott. 2003. Retrieving the missing dimension of statecraft: Religious faith in the service of peacebuilding. In *Faith-based diplomacy: Trumping realpolitik*, ed. Douglas Johnston, 231–258. Oxford: Oxford University Press.

Bainbridge, William Sims. 1997. *The sociology of religious movements*. New York: Routledge.

Bauman, Zygmunt. 2006. *Liquid fear*. Cambridge: Polity Press.

Beck, Ulrich. 1992. *Risk society. Towards a new modernity*. London: Sage Publications.

Beck, Ulrich. 1999. *World risk society*. Cambridge: Polity Press.

Beck, Ulrich. 2005. *Power in the global age: A new global political economy*. Cambridge: Polity Press.

Beck, Ulrich. 2006. *The cosmopolitan vision*. Cambridge: Polity Press.

Beckford, James A. 1990. The sociology of religion and social problems. *Sociological Analysis* 51(1): 1–14.

Beckford, James A. 2003. *Social theory and religion*. Cambridge: Cambridge University Press.

Benhabib, Seyla. 1992a. Models of public space: Hannah Arendt, the liberal tradition and Jürgen Habermas. In *Habermas and the public sphere*, ed. Craig Calhoun. Cambridge: MIT Press.

Benhabib, Seyla. 1992b. *Situating the self gender, community and postmodernism in contemporary ethics*. New York/London: Routledge/Kegan and Paul.

Benhabib, Seyla. 2002a. *The claims of culture: Equality and diversity*. Princeton: Princeton University Press.

Benhabib, Seyla. 2002b. Unholy wars. *Constellations* 9(1): 34–45.

Benhabib, Seyla. 2004a. On culture, public reason, and deliberation: Response to Pensky and Peritz. *Constellations* 11(2): 291–299.

Benhabib, Seyla. 2004b. *The rights of others: Aliens, citizens and residents*, The John Robert Seeley Memorial Lectures. Cambridge: Cambridge University Press.

Benhabib, Seyla. 2005. Beyond interventionism and indifference: Culture, deliberation and pluralism. *Philosophy and Social Criticism* 31: 753–771.

Benhabib, Seyla. 2007. Democratic exclusions and democratic iterations: Dilemmas of "just membership" and prospects of cosmopolitan federalism. *European Journal of Political Theory* 6(4): 445–462.

Bharat, Sandy, and Jael Bharat. 2007. *A global guide to interfaith: Reflections from around the world*. Winchester: O Books.

Bouma, Gary D. 1999. From hegemony to pluralism: Managing religious diversity in modernity and post-modernity. In *Managing religious diversity: From threat to promise*, ed. Gary D. Bouma, 7–27. Melbourne: Australian Association for the Study of Religions.

Bouma, Gary D. 2006. *Australian soul: Religion and spirituality in the twenty-first century*. Cambridge: Cambridge University Press.

Bouma, Gary D., and Rod Ling. 2005. *The research process*, 5th ed. Oxford: Oxford University Press.

Bouma, Gary D., Sharon Pickering, Anna Halafoff, and Hass Dellal. 2007. *Managing the impact of global crisis events on community relations in multicultural Australia*. Brisbane: Multicultural Affairs Queensland.

Braybrooke, Marcus. 1992. *Pilgrimage of hope: One hundred years of global interfaith dialogue*. London: SCM Press Ltd.

Braybrooke, Marcus. 2007. *Interfaith witness in a changing world: The world congress of faiths, 1996–2006*. Abingdon: Braybrooke Press.

Brodeur, Patrice. 2005. From the margins to the centers of power: The increasing relevance of the global interfaith movement. *Cross Currents* 55(1): 42–53.

Brodeur, Patrice, and Eboo Patel. 2006. Introduction: Building the interfaith youth movement. In *Building the interfaith youth movement: Beyond dialogue to action*, ed. Patel Eboo and Brodeur Patrice, 1–14. Oxford: Rowman and Littlefield Publishers, Inc.

Cahill, Desmond, Gary D. Bouma, Dellal Hass, and Michael Leahy. 2004. *Religion, cultural diversity and safeguarding Australia*. Canberra: Department of Immigration, Multicultural and Indigenous Affairs.

Campbell, Robert A. 2006. Theodicy, distribution of risk, and reflexive modernisation: Explaining the cultural significance of new religious movements. In *Theorising religion: Classical and contemporary debates*, ed. James A. Beckford and John Walliss, 90–104. Aldershot: Ashgate.

Casanova, José. 1994. *Public religions in the modern world*. Chicago: University of Chicago Press.

Casanova, José. 2001. Religion, the new millennium, and globalization. *Sociology of Religion* 62(4): 423–431.

Collins, Peter J. 2002. Connecting anthropology and Quakerism. In *Theorising faith: The insider/outsider problem in the study of ritual*, ed. Elisabeth Arweck and Martin Stringer, 77–95. Birmingham: Birmingham University Press.

Durkheim, Emile. 1914. *The elementary forms of religious life*. Trans. Karen E. Fields (1995). New York: The Free Press.

Eck, Diana L. 2001. *A new religious America: How a "Christian Country" has become the world's most religiously diverse nation*. New York: HarperOne.

Eck, Diana L. 2005. Dialogue and the echo boom of terror: Religious women's voices after 9/11. In *After terror: Promoting dialogue among civilizations*, ed. Akbar Ahmed and Brian Forst, 21–28. Cambridge: Polity Press.

Eisenstadt, S.N. 2000. Multiple modernities. *Daedalus* 129(1): 1–29.

Fraser, Nancy. 2001. Recognition without ethics? *Theory Culture and Society* 18(2–3): 21–42.

Fraser, Nancy. 2005. Reframing justice in a globalizing world. *New Left Review* 36 Nov/Dec: 69–88.

Gauchet, Marcel. 2002. *La Démocratie Contre Elle-Même*. Paris: Gallimard.

Gold, Raymond L. 1958. Roles in sociological field observations. *Social Forces* 36: 217–223.

Habermas, Jürgen. 1981. New social movements. *Telos* 49: 33–37.

Habermas, Jürgen. 1984. *The theory of communicative action: Vol. 1 Reason and the rationalization of society*. Cambridge: Polity Press.

Habermas, Jürgen. 1987. *The theory of communicative action: Vol. 2 Lifeworld and system: A critique of functionalist reason*. Cambridge: Polity Press.

Habermas, Jürgen. 1998. Learning by disaster? A diagnostic look back on the short 20th century. *Constellations* 5(3): 307–320.

Habermas, Jürgen. 2003. Intolerance and discrimination. *International Journal of Constitutional Law* 1(1): 2–12.

Habermas, Jürgen. 2005. Equal treatment of cultures and the limits of postmodern liberalism. *The Journal of Political Philosophy* 13(1): 1–28.

Habermas, Jürgen. 2006. Religion in the public sphere. *European Journal of Philosophy* 14(1): 1–25.

Habermas, Jürgen. 2007. *The divided west*. Edited and translated by Cronin Ciaran (2007). Cambridge: Polity Press.

Halafoff, Anna. 2006. UnAustralian values. In *Cultural Studies Association of Australasia Annual Conference, UNAustralia*. University of Canberra, Canberra, 6–8 December 2006 (electronic resource).

Halafoff, Anna. 2007. Advancing Australian "shared security": Secular-religious peacebuilding networks. In *Australian Sociological Association (TASA) and the Sociological Association of Aotearoa New Zealand (SAANZ) Joint Conference, Public Sociologies: Lessons and Trans-Tasman Comparisons*. University of Auckland, Auckland, 4–7 December 2007 (CD-Rom).

Halafoff, Anna, and Conley Tyler Melissa. 2005. Rethinking religion: Transforming cultures of violence to cultures of peace. In *UNESCO Paris and International Outlook Conference, Religion in Peace and Conflict: Responding to Militancy and Fundamentalism*. UNESCO, Paris, 12–14 April 2005, pp. 365–371.

Halafoff, Anna, and David Wright-Neville. 2009. A missing peace? The role of religious actors in countering terrorism. *Studies of Conflict and Terrorism* 32(11): 921–932.

Harding, Vincent. 1987. We must keep going: Martin Luther King and the future of America. *Fellowship*, January/February: 3–15.

Hargrove, Barbara. 1988. Religion, development, and changing paradigms. *Sociological Analysis* 49 Supplement: Presidential Issue: 33S–48S.

Hegedus, Zsuzsa. 1989. Social movements and social change in self-creative society: New civil initiatives in the international arena. *International Sociology* 4(1): 19–36.

Held, David. 1995. *Democracy and the global order: From the modern state to cosmopolitan governance*. Stanford: Stanford University Press.

Held, David. 2003. Cosmopolitanism: Globalisation tamed? *Review of International Studies* 29: 465–480.

Huff, Peter A. 2000. The challenge of fundamentalism for interreligious dialogue. *Cross Currents Spring* 50(1–2): 94–102.

Huntington, Samuel P. 1993. The clash of civilizations? *Foreign Affairs* 72(3): 22–49.

Huntington, Samuel P. 2003. *The clash of civilizations and the remaking of the world order*. London: Simon & Schuster.

Inglis, David, and Roland Robertson. 2005. The ecumenical analytic: "Globalization", reflexivity and the revolution in Greek historiography. *European Journal of Social Theory* 8(2): 99–122.

Jayaraman, Raja. 2000. Inclusion and exclusion: An analysis of the Australian immigration history and ethnic relations. *Journal of Popular Culture* Summer: 135–155.

Kaldor, Mary. 1999. *New & old wars: Organized violence in a global era*. Cambridge: Polity.

Kaldor, Mary. 2003a. *Global civil society: An answer to war*. Cambridge: Polity.

Kaldor, Mary. 2003b. The idea of global civil society. *International Affairs* 79(3): 583–593.

Kant, Immanuel. 1784a. Idea for a universal history from a cosmopolitan perspective. In *Toward perpetual peace and other writings on politics, peace, and history*. Edited by Pauline Kleingeld and translated by David L. Colclasure (2006). New Haven/London: Yale University Press.

Kant, Immanuel. 1784b. An answer to the question: What is enlightenment?. In *Toward perpetual peace and other writings on politics, peace, and history*. Edited by Pauline Kleingeld and translated by David L. Colclasure (2006). New Haven/London: Yale University Press.

Kant, Immanuel. 1795. Toward perpetual peace: A philosophical sketch. In *Toward perpetual peace and other writings on politics, peace, and history.* Edited by Pauline Kleingeld and translated by David L. Colclasure (2006). New Haven/London: Yale University Press.

Kant, Immanuel. 1797. *The metaphysics of morals*. Edited and translated by Mary Gregor (1996). Cambridge: Cambridge University Press.

Kirkwood, Peter. 2007. *The quiet revolution: The emergence of interfaith consciousness*. Sydney: ABC Books.

Knott, Kim. 2009. Insider/outsider perspectives. In *The Routledge companion to the study of religion*, ed. Hinnells John, 259–273. Hoboken: Routledge.

Kymlicka, Will. 1997. Do we need a liberal theory of minority rights? Reply to Carens, Young, Parekh and Forst. *Constellations* 4(1): 72–87.

Kymlicka, Will, and Keith Banting. 2006. Immigration, multiculturalism, and the welfare state. *Ethics and International Affairs* 20(3): 281–304.

Kymlicka, Will, and Christine Straehle. 1999. Cosmopolitanism, nation-states, and minority nationalism: A critical review of recent literature. *European Journal of Philosophy* 7(1): 65–88.

Lawrence, Carmen. 2006. *Fear and politics*. Melbourne: Scribe.

Levey, Geoffrey Brahm. 2009. Secularism and religion in a multicultural age. In *Secularism, religion and multicultural citizenship*, ed. Levey Geoffrey Brahm and Modood Tariq, 1–24. Cambridge: Cambridge University Press.

Lohre, Kathryn. 2007. Women's interfaith initiatives in the United States Post 9/11. *Interreligious Insight* 5(2): 11–23.

Luckmann, Thomas. 1967. *The invisible religion*. London: Macmillan.

Marty, Martin E., and R.Scott Appleby. 1992. *The glory and the power: The fundamentalist challenge to the modern world*. Boston: Beacon.

McCarthy, Kate. 2007. *Interfaith encounters in America*. Piscataway: Rutgers University Press.

McGuire, Meredith. 1997. *Religion: The social contract*. Belmont: Wadsworth.

Minichiello, Victor, Rosalie Aroni, and Terrence Hays. 2008. *In-depth interviewing*, 3rd ed. Sydney: Pearson Education Australia.

Munck, Ronaldo. 2005. *Globalization and social exclusion: A transformationalist perspective*. Bloomfield: Kumarian Press, Inc.

Niebuhr, Gustav. 2008. *Beyond tolerance: Searching for interfaith understanding in America*. New York: Viking.

Pearson, Jo. 2002. "Going native in reverse": The insider as researcher in British Wicca. In *Theorising faith: The insider/outsider problem in the study of ritual*, ed. Elisabeth Arweck and Martin Stringer, 97–113. Birmingham: Birmingham University Press.

Pike, Kenneth. 1967. *Language in relation to a unified theory of the structure of human behaviour*, 2nd ed. The Hague: Mouton.

Robertson, Roland. 1985. The sacred and the world system. In *The sacred in a secular age: Toward revision in the scientific study of religion*, ed. Phillip E. Hammond, 347–358. Berkeley: University of California Press.

Robertson, Roland. 1992. *Globalization: Social theory and global culture*. London: Sage.

Robertson, Roland, and Habib Haque Khondker. 1998. Discourses of globalization: Preliminary considerations. *International Sociology* 13(1): 25–40.

Taylor, Charles. 2009. Foreword. What is secularism? In *Secularism, religion and multicultural citizenship*, ed. Levey Geoffrey Brahm and Modood Tariq, xi–xxii. Cambridge: Cambridge University Press.

Turner, Brian S. 2008. Introduction. In *Religious diversity and civil society: A comparative analysis*, ed. Brian S. Turner, 1–12. Oxford: Bardwell Press.

Wallace, Anthony F.C. 1956. Revitalization movements. *American Anthropology* 58: 264–281.

Weller, Paul. 2008. *Religious diversity in the UK: Contours and issues*. London: Continuum.

Willaime, Jean-Paul. 2006. Religion in ultramodernity. In *Theorising religion: Classical and contemporary debates*, ed. James A. Beckford and John Walliss, 77–89. Aldershot: Ashgate.

Chapter 3
The Rise of the Multifaith Movement: 1893–1992

This chapter begins with a brief overview of the multifaith movement from the 1893 Parliament of the World's Religions (PWR) until the Second World War (WWII), derived from secondary sources. It then examines the causes and motives behind the rise of multifaith engagement from the 1960s until the early 1990s, by drawing on previously published material and actor perspectives gathered specifically for this study. Finally, building upon Patrice Brodeur's (2005) analysis, it identifies four principal aims and six characteristics of the ultramodern multifaith movement.

The 1893 Parliament of the World's Religions to the Second World War (WWII)[1]

The 1893 PWR is widely acknowledged as the beginning of the global multifaith movement (Braybrooke 1992: 7–8). The 1893 PWR was held as part of a World Columbian Exposition celebrating Christopher Columbus's 'discovery' of America and has been widely and rightly criticised as a flawed model of multifaith relations due to its Christian bias and 'civilizing mission' (Braybrooke 1992: 8–9, 18, 27, 39–42). Judith Snodgrass (2003: 1) describes how the first PWR 'was an aggressively Christian event, born of American Protestant Christian confidence in its superiority and organized around unquestioned Christian assumptions of the nature and function of religion.' However, the conflicting aims of the 1893 PWR are well illustrated in the divergent attitudes of its organisers. While Rev. John Henry Barrows (1893: 1581 quoted in Braybrooke 1992: 15) advocated a Christian Dominionist agenda by

[1] This book provides a relatively short account of the first PWR, as it focuses mainly on the ultra-modern multifaith movement, although its origins are crucial in identifying its main aims. As participants in this study were questioned about multifaith activities in contemporary societies, they made little mention of the movement's origins. Instead, discussions mostly began with events that occurred following WWII.

A. Halafoff, *The Multifaith Movement: Global Risks and Cosmopolitan Solutions*,
DOI 10.1007/978-94-007-5210-8_3,

marking the PWR as ‘a new era of Christian triumph’, Charles Carroll Bonney (1894: 73–78 quoted in Braybrooke 1992: 12–13) and Rev. Jenkin Lloyd Jones intended for the PWR to emphasise the ‘common essentials of all religions’ and shared a genuine wish to develop interreligious understanding.

The international gathering of the 1893 PWR was made possible by increased opportunities for travel and communication, which continued to escalate throughout the twentieth century, thus further enabling the global expansion of the multifaith movement (Braybrooke 1992: 22, 309). The Committee (quoted in Barrows 1893: 10), which organised the first PWR, stated ‘that the influence of Religion tends to advance the general welfare, and is the most vital force in the social order of every people’. They called representatives of diverse faiths together to aid them in ‘presenting to the world… the religious harmonies and unities of humanity, and also in showing forth the moral and spiritual agencies which are at the root of human progress’. These representatives hailed from Brazil, Canada, China, England, Egypt, France, Germany, Greece, India, Japan, New Zealand, Russia, Scotland, Sri Lanka, Sweden, Switzerland, Syria, Turkey and the USA and included adherents of Buddhism, Christianity, Confucianism, Hinduism, Islam, Judaism, Shintoism, Taoism and Zoroastrianism (Barrows 1893: 70).

The 1893 PWR intended : ‘To show… important truths the various Religions hold and teach in common’; ‘[t]o promote and deepen the spirit of human brotherhood… through friendly conference and mutual good understanding, while not seeking to foster the temper of indifferentism, and not striving to achieve any formal or outward unity’; and ‘[t]o set forth… what are deemed the important distinctive truths held and taught by each Religion’; ‘[t]o discover what light Religion has to throw on the great problems of the present age, especially the important questions connected with Temperance, Labor, Education, Wealth and Poverty’; and ‘[t]o bring the nations of the earth into a more friendly fellowship in the hope of securing permanent international peace’ (Barrows 1893: 18).

A number of Jewish leaders participated in the first PWR including the Orthodox Rabbi Henry Pereira Mendes and Reform Jewish Rabbis Hecht, Emil Hirsch and Kaufmann Kohler. The high level of representation and enthusiastic participation of Jewish leaders at the 1893 PWR is said to have established a tradition of ecumenical relations among Catholics, Protestants and Jews in America (Braybrooke 1992: 29–30).[2]

In addition, due to the spread of the British and European colonial expansion, a fascination with Asian religions and philosophies was prevalent in certain segments of Western societies in the mid-late nineteenth century (Croucher 1989: 6–1; Braybrooke 1996: 10; McCarthy 2007: 15). Since the seventeenth century, distorted accounts of Asian religions from Jesuit missionaries to China, Tibet and Japan

[2]This section draws on Barrows’ 1983 account of the PWR, alongside discussions and critiques of his description, notably Braybrooke’s (1992), Eck’s (2001) and Snodgrass’s (2003). The PWR representatives’ names are spelled differently in each of these monographs. Braybrooke’s and Eck’s spelling has been used for consistency, as this section is based primarily on their research interpreting the first PWR and its effects on the contemporary multifaith movement, while recognising that the accuracy of this spelling might be debatable.

reached Europe. By the turn of the twentieth century a vast amount of texts, artefacts and information on Asian cultural and religious practices had been gathered and sent to London and Paris in particular (Baumann 2001: 7). Martin Baumann (2001: 7) explains how '[t]he discovery of the Asian religion[s] was… essentially treated as a textual object, being located in books, Oriental libraries, and institutes of the West'. Therefore, while Ralph Waldo Emerson, Henry David Thoreau and the Theosophical Society had all been influential in introducing Americans to Hindu and Buddhist thought, the 1893 PWR provided the first opportunity for Americans to have direct contact with teachers from Asia (Eck 2001: 96–97, 180–184).

These teachers, in addition to providing first-hand explanations of their religious and philosophical traditions, utilised the PWR as a platform to challenge Christian Dominionism and exclusivity propagated by British, European and American missionaries. The Indian Swami Vivekananda, in particular, questioned the PWR's 'Christian triumphalism' (Braybrooke 1992: 25). Three Buddhists who attended the 1893 Parliament, Sri Lankan Anagarika Dharmapala, Japanese Zen Master the Right Rev. Soyen Shaku and Japanese Harai Ryuge Kinzo, also publicly challenged the 'presumptive universalism of Christianity' in their lectures. Dharmapala spoke on the eightfold path, emphasising that Buddha's teachings well preceded Christ's. He also described Buddhism is a 'scientific religion' containing 'a comprehensive system of ethics', which had influenced Greek thought well before Christ's birth (Barrows 1893: 829–831, 862–880, 1288–1290: Eck 2001: 182–185). Soyen spoke on the 'law of cause and effect' disputing the notion of a creator God, and Harai highlighted the shortfalls in Christian ethics, with illustrations of human rights abuses of Japanese by Christian missionaries and the persecution of Japanese communities in the Hawaiian islands and in San Francisco (Barrows 1893: 444–450, 829–831; Eck 2001: 182–185). Indeed, Snodgrass (2003: 2–3) describes how the Japanese representatives' aim was to challenge the 'Western presupposition of cultural superiority and protest the lowly position assigned to the Japanese in the hierarchy of evolutionary development'. The first PWR occurred at a time of 'Buddhist revival', in which its leaders argued that Japanese Buddhism was 'the most appropriate religion for the modern world' and that it offered an antidote to Western materialism. The 1893 PWR also offered an opportunity for Japanese Buddhists to 'intervene in the Western discourse on Buddhism' in order to 'modify Western perceptions' (Snodgrass 2003: 14–15).

One of the few Muslim participants at the first PWR was American Mohammed Russell Alexander Webb, who had converted to Islam while posted as America's consul general in the Philippines. Webb publicly acknowledged the negative stereotypes associated with Islam in America yet also articulated his confidence that once Americans had a true understanding of Islam they would learn to appreciate it (Barrows 1893: 989–996; Eck 2001: 234–235). The relatively small Muslim presence at the 1893 PWR clearly illustrates that the first bridges to be built in global multifaith engagement were largely among Hindus, Buddhists, Jews and Christians. Finally, Indigenous people were excluded from the main assembly of the 1893 PWR (Brodeur 2005: 44) and it was not until a century later that Indigenous and Muslim participants began to play a prominent role in multifaith initiatives in Western societies.

Despite its many flaws the 1893 PWR is widely believed to have established 'a normative model' for multifaith encounters conducted in a spirit of openness and respect for diversity, with a new emphasis on non-proselytising and on promoting understanding between faith traditions (McCarthy 2007: 18; Brodeur 2005: 43). As Swami Vivekananda (quoted in Bharat and Bharat 2007: 5) stated at the conclusion of the first PWR:

> The Parliament of Religions has proved to the world that holiness, purity and charity are not the exclusive possessions of any church in the world, and that every system has produced men and women of the most exalted character.

Even Barrows (Barrows 1893: vii, 4) concluded that contact with 'learned minds… inspired a new reverence' for diverse religious thought and that religion's 'spirit of mutual love, [and] of cosmopolitan fraternity' was 'disclosed and largely augmented' at the first PWR. He also noted religions' capacity as a peacebuilding force when he exclaimed:

> Striking the noble chord of universal human brotherhood, the promoters of the World's First Parliament of Religions have evoked a starry music which will yet drown the miserable discords of earth. (Barrows 1893: viii)

Following the 1893 PWR, multifaith congresses and conferences were held in the USA, the UK and Europe and several multifaith organisations were established including: the International Council of Unitarian and other Liberal Religious Thinkers and Workers in the USA in 1900, which eventually became the International Association for Religious Freedom (IARF) in 1969; the World Fellowship of Faiths (WFF) in the USA in 1924; and the World Congress of Faiths (WCF) in the UK in 1934 (Braybrooke 1992: 49–52, 114, 66–67). While the First World War (WWI) and WWII restricted global multifaith engagement, several multifaith congresses were convened in America and Europe by the IARF before WWI and by the IARF and the WCF between WWI and WWII (Braybrooke 1992: 49–52, 67–72).

The Christian ecumenical movement also arose at the turn of the twentieth century.[3] The first World Missionary Conference (WMC) was held in Edinburgh in 1910 and The International Missionary Council was formed as a result of this gathering. The second WMC was held in Jerusalem in 1928, during which the common values of diverse religions began to be acknowledged. The second WMC was gravely concerned with the rise of secularism and called for other religions to join with Christians in response to this common threat (Pratt 2010: 33–34). However, it is important to note that the multifaith movement's aims of developing mutual respect between religions, and uniting religions in response to common risks, preceded this development within the ecumenical movement.

Throughout the history of the multifaith movement, especially during its earliest period, beyond the impact of any external event, there has been an underlying driver,

---

[3] For a detailed account of the ecumenical movement see Pratt, Douglas (2010) *The Church and other Faiths: The World Council of Churches, the Vatican, and Interreligious Dialogue*. Bern: Peter Lang.

a spirit of inquiry, which has brought leaders and people of faith together to discuss their philosophies and theologies, to obtain greater understanding not only of diverse faith traditions but also of the nature of reality (Braybrooke 1992: 3, 2007: 25; Eck 2001: 377). Indeed, a fascination with the theological and philosophical aspects of religions remained a prominent theme within the multifaith movement throughout the first half of the twentieth century (Braybrooke 1992: 7–72). Moreover, from its inception, participants in the multifaith movement have sought to challenge misconceptions and false views of their traditions in order to advance a greater respect for their teachings. Consequently, *developing understanding of diverse faiths and the nature of reality* must be highlighted as one of the most important components of the multifaith movement. This emphasis on the exchange of theological, philosophical and mystical understandings of the world within the multifaith movement was particularly evident at the 1893 PWR up until WWII.

In addition, while the 1893 PWR was intended at least in part as a celebration of Columbus's Christian 'triumph' in America, the Hindu and Buddhist participants alerted the Parliament to the brutality of colonisation and the rights of all communities of faith to maintain and to practice their own traditions. Thereby the suffering experienced by colonised communities provided the impetus for multifaith engagement, challenging Christian triumphalism and affirming respect for religious diversity and the need for processes of reconciliation. It follows that from the 1893 PWR onward the multifaith movement has been committed to *challenging exclusivity and normalising pluralism.*[4]

Finally, from its inception the multifaith movement has also sought to *address global risks and injustices*, facilitating processes of reconciliation and collaborative action for the common good. This was evident in the 1893 PWR's Declaration which emphasised not only the need for more understanding among religions, but also of the need for common action in response to social problems. This commitment to peacebuilding within the multifaith movement strengthened after WWII, as evident in the discussion below.

Post–Second World War to the 1993 Parliament of the World's Religions

At the end of WWII the IARF resumed its multifaith congresses and conferences in the USA, the UK and Europe (Braybrooke 1992: 55–56). The first World Council of Churches' (WCC) Assembly[5] was held in 1948, and although its focus was on 'theological reflection and social action' it didn't address the issue of Christianity's

[4] Eboo Patel <2007, US> stressed the importance of 'normalising pluralism' when interviewed for this study.

[5] For a detailed account of the WCC and its effect on dialogue between diverse faiths see Pratt, Douglas (2010). *The Church and other Faiths: The World Council of Churches, the Vatican, and Interreligious Dialogue*. Bern: Peter Lang.

relationship with diverse religions, but rather 'the presumption of evangelical witness' and missionary focus was still predominant at this time (Pratt 2010: 38).

In response to the atrocities of WWII the imperative to address global risks and injustices intensified within the multifaith movement alongside other social movements of this period. After WWII multifaith activities were focused largely on bilateral initiatives of Jewish–Christian relations in response to the tragedy of the Holocaust (Braybrooke 1992: 175–215; Niebuhr 2008: 126–127). Jewish–Christian dialogue enabled communities to confront and address gross injustices committed against Jews and to unite in common action to prevent the recurrence of such atrocities. Many participants in this study confirmed that subsequent to WWII multifaith engagement focused largely on Jewish–Christian relations <Voll 2007, USA; Dupuche 2008, AUS; Shashoua 2008, UK; Summers 2008, AUS>. The WCC and the Second Vatican Council (Vatican II)[6] deplored anti-Semitism and declared their abhorrence for the genocide of Jewish people that occurred during the Holocaust (Pratt 2010: 44; Braybrooke 1992: 197–198). Vatican II was a pivotal document that sought to legitimise religious pluralism, within and beyond the Catholic Church, among diverse religious traditions. From the 1960s onwards, bilateral peacebuilding initiatives between Christians and Muslims and trilateral initiatives among Muslims, Christians and Jews began to occur in Western societies (Braybrooke 1992: 216–226; Baldock 1997: 194–195: Pratt 2012: 46–47). In 1967 the WCC and the Vatican held a conference in Kandy, Sri Lanka, and issued a statement on *Christians in Dialogue with Men of Other Faiths*, that stressed the importance of dialogue and friendship among people of diverse religious views (Pratt 2010: 53). Another important development, in the early ultramodern period, was the founding of The Temple of Understanding (ToU), which facilitated many multifaith events from the 1960s onward. However its attempts to build a multifaith centre in Maryland, an initiative that received substantial global support, were never realised (Braybrooke 1992: 95–108).

These developments, particularly within Christian organisations such as the WCC and the Vatican, led to theological reflections on how to deal with religious diversity.[7] Notably, Alan Race (1983) categorised Christian responses to different religions according to three types: Exclusivism, Inclusivism and Pluralism.[8] More recently Paul F. Knitter (2009) has expanded upon these three classifications. Knitter describes an exclusivist approach as a 'Replacement Model', in which Christianity is seen to eventually replace all other religious traditions, as the one and only right way

[6] For a detailed account of Vatican II and its effect on dialogue between diverse faiths see Pratt, Douglas (2010). *The Church and other Faiths: The World Council of Churches, the Vatican, and Interreligious Dialogue*. Bern: Peter Lang.

[7] As this is a sociological rather than a theological study, while there is some mention of theological theories in this chapter, a detailed theological exploration of multifaith relations is beyond the scope of this inquiry.

[8] For a detailed account of Race's Christian Theology of Religions see Race, Alan (1983). *Christians and Religious Pluralism: Patterns in the Christian Theology of Religions*. London: SCM Press Ltd.

to salvation. In this model dialogue is primarily aimed at conversion. The inclusivist approach, the 'Fulfilment Model', recognises the validity of other religions, yet believes that they are mere preparations for the only true Gospel as revealed through Christ. Pluralism, Knitter's 'Mutuality Model', affirms diversity, and strives for parity among religious groups. According to Knitter, pluralism is the most preferable model as it allows for genuine dialogical understanding to develop between religions, as no one religion claims superiority over others. A fourth approach, particularism, which Knitter refers to as the 'Acceptance Model', stresses the differences between religions and makes allowances for religious truth claims. Knitter warns that that this type of multifaith engagement is problematic as it risks becoming a new type of Replacement Model, which can lead to 'holy competition' among diverse religious groups. Participants in this study frequently referred to both exclusivist and pluralist approaches to religious diversity more generally, and not only from a Christian perspective, as described in the following sections and chapters. However, they made little mention of particularism or inclusivism, as described by Race and Knitter. When the term inclusivism was mentioned, it was again used more generally and positively, often aligned with pluralism, or practices and policies of social inclusion aimed to promote respect for cultural and religious diversity. A detailed discussion of the benefits of shifting from exclusivism to pluralism, as described by participants, is contained in Chap. 7.

From the 1960s onward, a new concern over peace and nuclear disarmament also arose within the ultramodern multifaith movement in response to the atrocities committed in Hiroshima and Nagasaki (Braybrooke 1992: 52, 56, 59). The Japanese Buddhist movement Rissho Kosei Kai joined the IARF in 1969, and in 1970 the IARF gathered for the first time in Japan. During the Cold War, the nuclear threat became a major focus of multifaith engagement and numerous multifaith initiatives were coordinated to protest against the Vietnam War in the 1960s and 1970s. This led to the establishment of the World Conference of Religions for Peace (WCRP, now Religions for Peace (RfP)) in 1970, corresponding with the rise of the global peace movement (Brodeur 2005: 45–46). Indeed, the themes of the first WCRP conference held in Kyoto in 1970 were disarmament, human rights and development, and the WCRP stressed the need for religious leaders to condemn the use of religion to justify violence (Braybrooke 1992: 141, 133–134).

Participants in this study affirmed these statements, recounting how, during the 1960s, multifaith organisations were formed, as were other social movements, to combat global inequities and to campaign for human rights <Jones 2008, AUS; Toh 2008, AUS>. The WCRP, with its focus on nuclear disarmament, global warming, economic and social justice, was described as a leader in the field of multifaith peacebuilding particularly in the 1970s and 1980s <Jones 2008, AUS>. While a chapter of the WCRP was established in Australia in 1970 immediately following the first WCRP World Assembly in Kyoto, it was not until 1987, when the decision was made to hold the 1989 fifth WCRP World Assembly in Melbourne at Monash University, that the WCRP began to play an influential role in Australia (Baldock 1997: 196). As addressing global risks and injustices emerged as the new central theme of the ultramodern multifaith movement, a significant shift occurred within multifaith engagement from dialogue to common action. Jeremy Jones <2008, AUS>, Co-Chair of the Australian National Dialogue of Christians, Muslims and Jews, describes these developments below:

> … there was a time I guess it was probably in the 60s more than the 80s, when the atmospherics were very much is the world going to survive, or is everybody going to blow each other out of the sky … there was a parallel path and one was dialogue and the other was common activity, faith-driven common activity … [it] might have been made easier by the fact that there was interfaith dialogue taking place, but it wasn't the same … <Jones 2008, AUS>

Participants also explained how a new concern with addressing economic inequities emerged within the multifaith movement during the 1980s, evident in the foundation of the Inter Faith Network for the UK (IFNUK) <Braybrooke 2007, UK; Pearce 2007, UK>. Rev. Marcus Braybrooke <2007, UK>, President of the World Congress of Faiths (WCF), which had been the major multifaith organisation in the UK until the 1980s, described the WCF as 'a fellowship of enthusiasts' largely focused on developing greater theological and philosophical understanding. However, the IFNUK included a broader base of leaders from diverse faith communities who recognised the importance of developing both greater understanding of diverse faiths and the need to actively respond to common issues, such as growing economic inequalities. Maurice Glasman <2007, UK>, Director of the Faith and Citizenship Program at the London Metropolitan University, recalled how religious communities in the UK became increasingly concerned with the economic pressures affecting families and young people during this period and began 'to realise their mutual support for matters of resisting the market'. As states became weaker and markets became stronger, religious organisations played an increasingly critical role in the public sphere by responding to local and global problems of growing inequality, commodification and atomisation produced by market forces. In addition, faith-based and multifaith organisations became increasingly involved in aid and development to counter poverty and address the growing gaps between rich and poor <Toh 2008, AUS>.

A new awareness of the global environmental crisis, and the role that religious and spiritual traditions can play in either inflaming or ameliorating this problem, was also steadily building alongside other social movements in the 1960s and 1970s. As religious and multifaith organisations began to focus much of their attention on social problems including civil rights, the Vietnam War, poverty and gender inequality, extending this concern to the rights of nonhuman life emerged as a continuation of this pattern (Nash 1996: 220; Keller and Kearns 2007: 2; Tucker 2007: 496). Buddhist philosophy also played a central role in the environmental movement from the 1960s onwards, particularly due to the doctrines of interdependent arising, impermanence, non-violence and respect for all beings (Rockefeller 1992: 156; Nash 1996: 215). Greater awareness of the environmental crisis also led Western societies to turn to Indigenous, especially Native American, traditions for inspiration and guidance on how best to live in harmony with the natural environment (Braybrooke 1992: 242; Rockefeller and Elder 1992: 6; Nash 1996: 214). From the 1970s onwards, particularly during the early 1990s, when the global environmental crisis was considered the greatest threat not only to humanity but also to all life on earth, environmental issues became a key focus of the multifaith movement (Rockefeller and Elder 1992: 1; Braybrooke 1992: 148–149). The North American Coalition on Religion and Ecology (NACRE) was formed at this time (Rockefeller and Elder 1992: 1, 10–11) and the National Religious Partnership for the Environment (NRPE) was founded in the late 1980s comprising members from Evangelical Christian, Catholic, Orthodox, Historic African-American churches and Jewish peak bodies. The NRPE also established the Interfaith Climate Change Network (ICCN) throughout the USA (Kearns 2007: 98, 100–101) and a rise of interest in faith-based ecological activism was also evidenced by the formation of groups such as Earth Ministry and GreenFaith during this period (McCarthy 2007: 58–61; Kearns 2007: 103).

Participants in this study confirmed that environmental issues became a key focus for multifaith organisations in the early 1990s, principally in the USA, as illustrated by the comments of Laurel Kearns <2008, USA>, Associate Professor of Sociology of Religion and Environmental Studies at Drew University, and Rev. Fletcher Harper <2008, USA>, Executive Director of GreenFaith, below:

> … the 1990s really was a time when a lot of environmental news was coming out; we began learning about global warming in the beginning of the 90s and that's where I watched a lot of interfaith work start, as people started really realising the enormity of it, the impact it would have … <Kearns 2008, USA>

> … during the 1990s … there has been a growing awareness of serious challenges to human wellbeing and ecological wellbeing due to human activity … increasing numbers of religious leaders are aware of this and see this as something that they are morally called to respond to. <Harper 2008, USA>

Whereas scholars had observed that Buddhist philosophy played a significant role in multifaith responses to environmental issues, participants in this study made no mention of this development. However, Sylvie Shaw <2007, AUS>, Lecturer in Religion and Spirituality Studies at the University of Queensland, did describe how during the early 1990s, the multifaith movement, alongside the New Age movement, looked toward Native American and also Hindu traditions for inspiration and guidance on how best to live in harmony with the natural environment:

> When the Rio meeting happened, the first UN meeting, there were some Indians who came out of the jungle from the Amazon, and they said, "you white people, you people from the West, have to listen to us. If you don't listen, it will be too late". There was another group of people from the very high mountains of Colombia, and they saw in 1990, their glaciers beginning to melt, and the whole climate beginning to change, and [together with the BBC] they [made a] documentary … around the same time, 91, 92 of the Rio [Summit] … and it was all about the Indians [who] had this notion of little brother and big brother. And we were the little brother, and we were causing the mother to [be] really sick. Now, those two messages … with the New Age and the growing interest in Indigenous cultures … there was this message that went out saying … if you don't do something, it will be too late … in the late 80s, early 90s. There was a real interest in Indigenous cultures, and a kind of embracing of "maybe there's a different worldview, a different way" … But at the same time, people began to practise, even in the pick and mix New Age spirituality, there was an awareness about the Earth, and an awareness about organics, and an awareness about biodynamics … in poverty, you can't grow vegies, you can't afford the seeds, and people like Vandana Shiva through her Hindu practice were raising those things as a spiritual practice, "look after the environment", as spiritual practice. <Shaw 2007, AUS>

In addition, Eboo Patel <2007, USA>, Executive Director of the Interfaith Youth Core, explained how during the early 1990s, an international awareness of global issues led to a rise of social movements and a plethora of international conferences focused on areas of common concern, including environmental, women's and human rights issues. According to Patel <2007, USA>, these initiatives formed 'the beginning of an architecture for global living'. The multifaith movement responded accordingly, cementing its focus on more practical issues of ethics, human rights and environmental sustainability <Knitter 2007, USA>.

A radical reflexivity and the imperative to address global risks and injustices within the multifaith movement aligns it with many social movements of the same period, demonstrating that multifaith alliances were formed among liberal multifaith actors and organisations focused on global issues such as poverty, justice, racism and peace in the ultramodern era (McCarthy 2007: 57). The multifaith movement owe a huge legacy to the new mazeways created by civil rights, women's and peace movements for informing multifaith practices, especially regarding issues of identity and social justice. However, as religions are typically viewed as perpetuating structures of domination and social hierarchy, there has been little understanding within the sociological literature of the positive role that the multifaith movement has played alongside other social movements of this time (McCarthy 2007: 8–10). This study hopes to address this omission.

Theological and Philosophical Drivers of Multifaith Action

While participants in this study did not link rising interest in environmental issues with an interest in Buddhist philosophy, they recounted how a renewed interest in 'East–West' philosophical exchange, particularly regarding contemplative traditions within Christianity, Hinduism and Buddhism, was enabled by the rise of social movements and increased opportunities for travel in the 1960s and 1970s <Keyes 2007, UK; Murdoch 2008, UK; Dupuche 2008, AUS>. Alison Murdoch <2008, UK>, Director of the Foundation for Developing Compassion and Wisdom, described the counter-culture movement of this period as being made up of 'people who were in the role of rejecting society… who were really deeply re-evaluating the cultures that they grew up in' and who looked towards Asian religions for alternatives. This rise of interest in Hinduism and Buddhism was enabled by increased global mobility, as young people travelled to India and religious leaders from India and Tibet, such as the Dalai Lama, began regularly teaching in the West. Catholic communities also frequently instigated this dialogue as Vatican II encouraged a new openness to Asian contemplative traditions, as evidenced in the World Day of Prayer for Peace in Assisi in 1986 at which Pope John Paul II and the Dalai Lama were both present <Dupuche 2008, AUS>.

The International Association of Sufism was also established in 1983 in Marin County, near San Francisco and was among the institutions that initiated and participated in multifaith activities with a specifically mystical focus at this time

<Kianfar 2007, USA>. According to Paul F. Knitter <2007, USA>, Paul Tillich Professor of Theology at the Union Theological Seminary, the main themes of this East–West dialogue, and also of Jewish–Christian dialogue in the 1960s to the early 1990s, were 'religious themes, theological themes… coming to talk together about whether there are any commonalities in the understanding of the nature of ultimate reality, on involvement in the world, on the nature of the individual [and] the after-life'. Fr. John Dupuche <2008, AUS>, Chair of the Catholic Interfaith Committee of the Catholic Archdiocese of Melbourne, also stressed that East–West dialogue 'was done irrespective of any crisis situation. It was done because it was very interesting'.

In particular, the principle of interdependence derived from Hindu and Buddhist religions and Indigenous ways of knowing played a significant role in the multifaith movement in the late twentieth century (Braybrooke 1992: 107). Theological and philosophical concepts, such as interdependence and altruism, have informed the need for collaboration between faith traditions to address global risks and to reflexively challenge injustices both within and beyond religious traditions. Knitter (1995: 54–55) was among the first scholars who called for religions to assume an active role in taking responsibility for confronting global issues such as the unjust distribution of wealth and environmental degradation. As Knitter (1995: 71) stated, religions have a common view that 'self-seeking, conflictive individualism can be transformed into… compassionate, cooperative mutuality'. Steven C. Rockefeller (1997: 54) similarly acknowledged that a realisation of the interdependence of all life awakens a commitment not only to cease causing harm and suffering to others but also to seek new participatory and cooperative methods of collaboratively addressing global crises. According to Rockefeller (1992: 147, 154), while aspects of biblical traditions, and one could add also Hindu and Buddhist traditions and some New Religious Movements, have generated 'anthropocentric, dualistic, hierarchical, and patriarchal ideas and attitudes that are problematic from an ecological as well as a democratic perspective', concurrently all faith traditions offer instructions on how to shift from the self-centred desire to compete, control and consume to a more cooperative, compassionate and creative ethic of living. John Hick (1985: 29, 34) also described a process of 'salvation or liberation or enlightenment' common to diverse faith traditions as 'the transformation of human existence from self-centeredness to Reality-centredness', moving away from 'greed, cruelty, pride and selfishness' toward actualising 'our highest good' (Hick 2001: 16–17). Similarly, William Vendley and David Little (1994: 307), described how religious narratives typically 'engage in some sort of questioning about what is wrong with the present state of affairs (pathology) and about what religious means should be applied to remedy that condition (soteriology)'. They suggested that this paradigm needs also to be applied reflexively to religious traditions themselves, by employing a self-critical attitude to transform religious narratives that justify direct and structural violence into peacebuilding narratives (Vendley and Little 1994: 308, 312–313).

The principles of altruism, founded on a realisation of the interdependence of all life coupled with a commitment toward developing one's highest qualities, are principles that are common to many diverse faith traditions and that have informed the multifaith movement since its inception, and particularly at the end of the twentieth century.

The actors' and scholars' perspectives described above are therefore consistent with the assertion that developing understanding of diverse faiths and the nature of reality must be highlighted as one of the most important components of the multifaith movement. This emphasis on the exchange of theological, philosophical and mystical understandings of the world within the multifaith movement was particularly evident at the 1893 PWR and up until WWII. While there is no doubt that the imperative to address global risks and injustices assumed a more prominent position within the multifaith movement in the mid to late twentieth century, these perspectives provide evidence that the need to develop understanding of diverse faiths and the nature of reality re-emerged as a central focus of the multifaith movement from the 1960s through to the 1990s.

Building upon several scholars' observations as described above, the multifaith movement can therefore be described as having a 'mutual mission' (Hick 1985: 44) of: (1) developing understanding of diverse faiths and the nature of reality; and (2) addressing global risks and injustices through collaborative action—and that these two forces continually inform one another (Hick 1985: 44; Wuthnow 2005: 303; Bharat and Bharat 2007: 4, 116). If we can understand the interdependent nature of our reality, then we are far less likely to seek self-centred gain at the expense of others' happiness. We are also more likely to choose cooperation over competition as a means to address global risks and to avoid future collective misfortune (Braybrooke 1992: 1; Rockefeller 1997: 59). Working together creates opportunities for personal contact and the development of friendships and long-term relationships, which deepen understanding especially over time (Wuthnow 2005: 304; Bharat and Bharat 2007: 244: McCarthy 2007: 123–124, 120). In addition, by emphasising the need to recognise the differences among religions, while concurrently affirming a common commitment to peace and human rights, multifaith movements continue to challenge exclusive religious narratives and to rethink theological understanding towards attaining the common good (Braybrooke 1992: 1). Therefore, it can be said that theological and philosophical principles underpin multifaith action, and have informed the creation of new cosmopolitan mazeways that facilitate global understanding and cooperation in the face of impending risks and crisis events affecting the entire lifeworld.

Globalisation and Religious Diversity

Another contributing factor behind the growth of the multifaith movement in ultramodernity was the rise in immigration to Western societies during the 1960s and 1970s (Eck 2001: 1–4; Bouma 2006: 52–53, 64; Weller 2008: 32–42). As briefly described in Chap. 2, this increased movement of people, due to the processes of globalisation, created plural, multicultural and multifaith societies as microcosms of a culturally and religiously diverse world. Consequently, a commitment to pluralism and multiculturalism, which promoted a positive attitude toward cultural diversity, emerged across increasingly multicultural and multifaith Western societies (Eck 2001;

Halafoff 2006: 6–7; Weller 2008: 179–180). These developments restructured the focus of multifaith engagement in Western societies after WWII from the predominance of Catholics, Protestants and Jews to the inclusion of Hindus, Buddhists, Sikhs and Muslims (McCarthy 2007: 7).

While increasingly multifaith societies, and policies of pluralism and multiculturalism within them, no doubt encouraged and broadened multifaith engagement, the multifaith movement was ahead of its time, in challenging exclusivity and normalising pluralism well before the dramatic rise of migration that occurred in the 1960s and 1970s. The multifaith movement also continued to highlight the need for promoting understanding between faith traditions during a period when the broader focus was largely on affirming cultural rather than religious diversity. Indeed, the WCF played a leading role in introducing the teaching of world religions into schools in the UK in the 1970s and 1980s, replacing the previous focus on Christianity, recognising that it was becoming not only an increasingly multicultural but also multifaith society (Braybrooke 1992: 85–86).

Many participants in this study affirmed that the dramatic rise in immigration to Western societies during the 1960s and 1970s produced a corresponding increase in multifaith engagement and consequently a growing respect for religious diversity <Ficca 2007, USA; Mogra 2007, UK; Patel 2007, USA; Aly 2008, AUS; Murdoch 2008, UK>. Rev. Dirk Ficca <2007, USA>, Executive Director of the Council for a Parliament of the World's Religions, and Shaykh Ibrahim Mogra <2007, UK>, Chair of the Interfaith Relations Committee at the Muslim Council of Britain, described how living in increasingly diverse societies created the impetus for multifaith initiatives:

> … for the first time in history, since the 60s, large, diverse, ethnic, cultural and religious communities are living next door to each other in metropolitan areas in ways that have never happened before … In your school, at the supermarket, in every aspect of most major cities' cultural life, people of different traditions are bumping into each other, so there's a need to find a way to live together. <Ficca 2007, USA>

> I think there has been ongoing migration of non-Christian religious communities into what we call the West, and clearly when such communities move into any part of the UK … they become visible, they make friendships, they go to work or take their children to school … so that initial interaction … feeds the need for people to want to get to know each other in a better way. <Mogra 2007, UK>

Participants also recalled how a shift in policy that occurred in the 1960s and 1970s, from assimilation to pluralism and multiculturalism, led to an increase in multifaith initiatives in Western societies <Voll 2007, USA; Blundell 2008, AUS; Dellal 2008, AUS; Lacey 2008, AUS; Postma 2008, AUS>. According to John O. Voll <2007, USA>, Associate Director of the Prince Alwaleed Bin Talal Center for Muslim-Christian Understanding at Georgetown University, this 'kind of enforced cosmopolitanism' reached a critical mass in the USA by the 1990s, permeating not only the larger cities but also the smaller towns:

> In the pre-1965 period, in the old immigration diaspora, the goal of American policy and American society and people coming here was to assimilate. The hope was that at least by the second generation or the third generation, nobody could tell that you were Iranian. But increasingly, in the 1970s … you have a transition from that to an emphasis on the virtue of

> diversity and the importance of pluralism. And so you have, then, this transformation that people become indigenised, that you can be an American who is Muslim. You don't have to be an American who looks like a white Anglo-Saxon Protestant anymore. So ... that kind of globalisation creates, then, a cosmopolitanism that makes people be more aware of the fact that even right next door they're dealing with somebody different. <Voll 2007, USA>

Several Australian participants similarly recounted how multiculturalism assumed a central place in government policies in the 1980s and that by the 1990s these policies began to acknowledge religious alongside cultural diversity <Blundell 2008, AUS; Dellal 2008, AUS; Lacey 2008, AUS; Postma 2008, AUS>. As a result, multifaith engagement in Australia was said to increase as a flow-on effect of multiculturalism <Postma 2008, AUS>.

Chapter 2 described how dramatic advances in information and communications technologies in the 1980s led to a dawning 'global circumstance' and the realisation of the interconnectedness of global problems and their solutions (Robertson 1985 cited in Beckford 1990: 7; Kaldor 1999: 3; Habermas 1998: 318), which enabled a *cosmopolitan empathy* to develop among global citizens (Beck 2006: 5–6). Many participants in this study confirmed and extended these arguments, describing how increased mobility coupled with growing global communication systems contributed to the rise of multifaith engagement in ultramodernity. According to Patel <2007, USA>, not only was the 'interactional' nature of ultramodernity enabled by the increased movement of people, it was also aided by the growth of global communication systems. Ficca <2007, USA> described this process as leading to a 'more deep weaving of our systems' and a heightened sense of interconnectivity. Many participants explained how this unprecedented access to information increased contact between people and facilitated understanding of increasingly diverse local communities <Murdoch 2008, UK; Ozalp 2008, AUS; Shashoua 2008, UK; Woodlock 2008, AUS; Young 2008, AUS>. As Stephen Shashoua <2008, UK>, Director of the Three Faiths Forum (TFF), illustrated below, it also awakened a sense of global empathy and a corresponding need to know one's new neighbours:

> ... viewing the global neighbourhood through the new technologies we were feeling that the world was much closer, realising the neighbours ... from across the world were actually, they were right next to us ... poverty around the world, [was] always very high on the list but now a more direct relationship with those specific countries, and also with that global understanding of other [contexts], led to ... an increased curiosity of knowing the neighbour that lived within your locality, so I think the global led to the local in that way. <Shashoua 2008, UK>

Multi-actor Peacebuilding Networks

Toward the end of the twentieth century, the processes of globalisation and the increase of interest in religion led to a new awareness among non-religious organisations of the need to partner with religious actors in response to common concerns. This new emphasis on collaboratively countering global risks resulted in the formation of *multi-actor peacebuilding networks* in which faith-based actors played an increasingly significant role alongside non-religious actors such as state, UN, NGO and

Inter-Governmental Organisation (IGO) actors, on issues of common security. In an increasingly interdependent world, issues such as climate change, HIV-AIDS and economic inequalities required global solutions in which faith communities and their theologies and philosophies had an important role to play (Eck 2001: 380). In the mid-1970s the WCRP opened an office opposite the United Nations and thereafter became increasingly involved in UN activities (Braybrooke 1992: 161). Significant initiatives of this period included a World Day of Prayer for Peace, hosted by the Vatican in Assisi in 1986 (Braybrooke 1992: 141) and sponsored by the World Wildlife Fund (WWF) (Rockefeller and Elder 1992: 10–11). The Global Forum was also founded by the ToU and the Global Committee of Parliamentarians on Population and Development, which held meetings in Tarrytown, New York State (1985), Oxford (1988) and Moscow (1990) that brought together high-level religious and parliamentary leaders, including Mother Teresa, the Dalai Lama, Javier Perez de Cuellar, Sheikh Ahmad Kuftaro and Mikhail Gorbachev alongside scientists, journalists, business leaders and artists to address common threats to human and environmental security (Braybrooke 1992: 109–110).

As Patel <2007, USA> remarked, the world 'has always been diverse, let's not kid ourselves, it's just not always been this interactional'. These actor perspectives thus demonstrate that increased contact, facilitated by the processes of decolonisation and globalisation, including global communication systems, enabled the rise of the multifaith movement in ultramodernity. As Western societies became increasingly culturally and religiously diverse this heightened the need to develop understanding of diverse faiths and the nature of reality and to challenge exclusivity and normalise pluralism. Established multifaith organisations were well placed to undertake these activities and many new multifaith bodies began to form in the late 1980s and early 1990s. In addition, the increased awareness of the interconnected nature of reality that dawned on humanity as a consequence of the processes of globalisation and the rise of interest in Hindu, Buddhist and Indigenous philosophies during this period led to a cosmopolitan awakening, and the creation of new collaborative mazeways that built bridges between previously separated communities aimed at addressing common concerns. These scholar and actor perspectives also show that a rise of multi-actor peacebuilding networks in which religious individuals and institutions have partnered with state and global actors to address global risks and injustices occurred at the end of the twentieth century. These collaborative networks formed pockets of cosmopolitanism in action and thereby provide evidence of an awakening cosmopolitan consciousness across diverse, including religious, sectors in ultramodern societies.

Conclusions

Brodeur's (2005) typology of multifaith engagement provides a starting point for examining the rise of the multifaith movement in ultramodernity. While the findings of this study mostly align with Brodeur's arguments, it expands on some of his main points and also includes some new aims and characteristics of the multifaith movement by drawing on scholars' and actors' perspectives examined above. Brodeur (2005: 43) identified six major characteristics of the global interfaith movement in his paper, *From the Margins to the Centers of Power: The Increasing Relevance of the Global Interfaith Movement*, as follows:

1. It emerged from a singular social location, Chicago, in 1893. Following WWII it spread to an interconnected set of social locations in the West and then throughout the world.
2. Its 'uniqueness lies predominantly at the perceptual level' as dialogue enables mistrust and fear to develop into 'deep spiritual transformation and new levels of trust' which are needed to address the common issues facing humanity.
3. The exponential growth of the movement is a consequence of 'a revolution in information technology' that has produced a 'networked culture'.
4. This 'network culture shapes the diversity of forms (methodologies) and contents (goals) of every interreligious organization'.
5. It is 'glocal in nature'—integrating local and global variables.
6. It is increasingly being noticed by 'traditional centres of power', thus heightening its relevance.

While the multifaith movement originated in Chicago and most of the pre-WWII initiatives took place in the USA, the UK and Europe, the Hindu and Buddhist participants from India, Sri Lanka and Japan at the 1893 PWR were instrumental in the movement's foundation. Therefore, the multifaith movement can be described as having been born out of East–West interaction rather than out of an entirely Western, American context. Indeed, there are parallel narratives of the rise of multifaith engagement in Asian societies, such as India, Japan and Indonesia, which are unfortunately beyond the scope of this study.

The 1893 PWR also highlighted the brutality of colonisation and the rights of all communities of faith to maintain and to practice their own traditions. Following WWII and the collapse of the British Empire, the steady process of decolonisation and the rise of self-determination movements, within Indigenous and culturally and religiously diverse groups, had a significant influence on the multifaith movement. Therefore an emphasis on addressing inequalities needs to be included among the multifaith movement's central aims.

While Brodeur's argument that shifting perceptions from fear to trust can lead to common action on global issues is accurate, understanding must first be developed for these changes in perception to occur. Consequently, this study suggests that developing understanding—of our differences and of reality—is the foundation of multifaith collaboration. In addition, in order to build trust and a peaceful world, injustices need to be addressed, and cultures of exclusivity and violence, whether direct or structural, need to be challenged. This must involve a radical reflexivity, and therefore the multifaith movement can be described as at once a spiritual and political project, with a dual commitment to developing understanding and collaborative action for the common good.

The network culture that Brodeur rightly describes as infusing all aspects of multifaith movements' methodologies and goals is founded not only on new technology but also on a growing consciousness of interdependence grounded in Indigenous, Hindu and Buddhist philosophies, which have had a significant influence on the multifaith movement in the ultramodern period. In an increasingly globalised world no one is immune to common threats. This fact has led to a new awareness of our interdependence and the need for collective, collaborative action in order to confront our common crises. This new mazeway of thinking and being is at the heart of the ultramodern multifaith movement and aligns it with cosmopolitan strategies to counter global risks and to advance common security.

The glocal nature of the multifaith movement that Brodeur describes is also reflected in this study's findings, as many of its participants are committed to working on local and global issues concurrently, this point is explored in more detail in Chap. 6. Finally, the rise of interest among state actors and NGOs, described by participants in this study, concurs with Brodeur's claim that the multifaith movement is being noticed by 'traditional centres of power' and thereby increasing in relevance. This development intensified throughout the 1990s, particularly following the events of September 11, 2001, as will be discussed in the following chapters.

Building on Brodeur's (2005) characteristics of the multifaith movement, the global multifaith movement, comprising numerous local and global multifaith organisations and networks, arose through interaction between primarily Hindu, Buddhist, Jewish and Christian actors at the turn of the twentieth century and has four principal aims of:

1. *developing understanding of diverse faiths and of the nature of reality;*
2. *challenging exclusivity and normalising pluralism;*
3. *addressing global risks and injustices; and*
4. *creating multi-actor peacebuilding networks for common security.*

The first three aims of the multifaith movement have been present since the 1893 PWR. At this time, due to a fascination with Asian religions and philosophies, the primary aim of multifaith movement was developing understanding of diverse faiths and also of the nature of reality. In addition, at the 1893 PWR, the Hindu and Buddhist participants from Asia challenged Christian Dominionism and, together with American Jewish, Christian and Muslim leaders, began to establish a normative framework of multifaith relations of non-proselytising and mutual respect. Consequently they began to normalise pluralism—engendering a positive attitude toward cultural and religious diversity. This also established a commitment within the multifaith movement to reflexively challenge cultures of exclusivity within faith traditions and in the broader society. Moreover, the 1983 PWR's Declaration provides evidence that a collaborative approach to addressing global risks and injustices was also a concern among the multifaith movement at its inception.

This aim of addressing global risks and injustices became more prominent throughout the twentieth century in response to crisis events such as the Holocaust and the nuclear bombing of Hiroshima and Nagasaki. In response to these crises the scope of the multifaith movement expanded, Jewish and Japanese actors began to play a more prominent role, and the multifaith movement began to establish peacebuilding networks with UN and NGO actors. The multifaith movement also began to place more emphasis on collaborative action than on dialogue.

An increase in immigration to Western societies in the 1960s and 1970s also highlighted the aim of challenging exclusivity and normalising pluralism during this period. Increased opportunities for travel and global communication systems assisted contact and communication among diverse communities and contributed to the ultramodern rise of multifaith engagement. In addition, a growing awareness of an increasingly interconnected and interdependent world resulting from the processes of globalisation led to the formation of multi-actor peacebuilding networks, which enabled religious actors to collaborate with state, NGO and UN actors on issues of common human and environmental security.

Therefore, the imperative of developing understanding of diverse faiths and also of the nature of reality has remained the primary aim of the multifaith movement throughout their history and has informed the subsequent aims of challenging exclusivity and normalising pluralism, addressing global risks and injustices and building multi-actor peacebuilding networks.

From these observations the multifaith movement displays six primary characteristics. The multifaith movement is *responsive, preventive, creative, collaborative, radically reflexive* and *deliberative.* Multifaith actors, organisations and networks consistently *respond* to their context, and particularly to local and global crisis events. They seek to *prevent* further crises, and to *create* new conditions within which future risks can be avoided. Their methods are *collaborative*, promoting a *radical reflexivity* in order to overcome conditions of suffering and to establish peace through *deliberative* processes. In line with Habermas's (1984, 1987, 2007) *Theory of Communicative Action*, the multifaith movement seeks to arrive at mutual understanding through communicative processes in order to address the root causes of problems and to effectively enact social change. Therefore, the rise of the multifaith movement in ultramodernity provides evidence of cosmopolitan religious responses aimed at countering global risks and advancing common security. This process began to occur at the turn of the twentieth century. However, it was not until the turn of the twenty-first century that the multifaith movement began to increase its public presence significantly, alongside anti-cosmopolitan religious movements, as a result of processes of globalisation. Indeed, the clash between cosmopolitan and anti-cosmopolitan actors emerged as one of the greatest global challenges of the 1990s, as will be discussed in the following chapter.

References

Baldock, John. 1997. Responses to religious plurality in Australia. In *Many religions, all Australian: Religious settlement, identity and cultural diversity*, ed. Gary D. Bouma, 193–204. Melbourne: The Christian Research Association.

Barrows, John Henry (ed.). 1893. *The world's parliament of religions*. Chicago: The Parliament Publishing Co.

Baumann, Martin. 2001. Global Buddhism: Developmental periods, regional histories, and a new analytical perspective. *Journal of Global Buddhism* 2: 1–43.

Beck, Ulrich. 2006. *The cosmopolitan vision*. Cambridge: Polity Press.

Beckford, James A. 1990. The sociology of religion and social problems. *Sociological Analysis* 51(1): 1–14.

Bharat, Sandy, and Jael Bharat. 2007. *A global guide to interfaith: Reflections from around the world*. Winchester: O Books.

Bonney, Charles Carroll. 1894. The genesis of the world's religious congresses of 1893. *New Church Review* 1: 73–78.

Bouma, Gary D. 2006. *Australian soul: Religion and spirituality in the twenty-first century*. Cambridge: Cambridge University Press.

Braybrooke, Marcus. 1992. *Pilgrimage of hope: One hundred years of global interfaith dialogue*. London: SCM Press Ltd.

Braybrooke, Marcus. 1996. *A wider vision: A history of the world congress of faiths*. Oxford: Oneworld.

Braybrooke, Marcus. 2007. *Interfaith witness in a changing world: The world congress of faiths, 1996–2006*. Abingdon: Braybrooke Press.

Brodeur, Patrice. 2005. From the margins to the centers of power: The increasing relevance of the global interfaith movement. *Cross Currents* 55(1): 42–53.

Croucher, P. 1989. *A history of Buddhism in Australia 1848–1988*. Kensington: New South Wales University Press.

Eck, Diana L. 2001. *A new religious America: How a "Christian Country" has become the world's most religiously diverse nation*. New York: HarperOne.

Habermas, Jürgen. 1984. *The theory of communicative action: Vol. 1 Reason and the rationalization of society*. Cambridge: Polity Press.

Habermas, Jürgen. 1987. *The theory of communicative action: Vol. 2 Lifeworld and system: A critique of functionalist reason*. Cambridge: Polity Press.

Habermas, Jürgen. 1998. Learning by disaster? A diagnostic look back on the short 20th century. *Constellations* 5(3): 307–320.

Habermas, Jürgen. 2007. *The divided west*. Edited and translated by Cronin, Ciaran (2007). Cambridge: Polity Press.

Halafoff, Anna. 2006. UnAustralian values. In *Cultural Studies Association of Australasia Annual Conference, UNAustralia*. University of Canberra, Canberra, 6–8 December 2006 (electronic resource).

Hick, John. 1985. *Problems of religious pluralism*. Basingstoke/London: Macmillan.

Hick, John. 2001. *Dialogues in the philosophy of religion*. Basingstoke/New York: Palgrave.

Kaldor, Mary. 1999. *New & old wars: Organized violence in a global era*. Cambridge: Polity.

Kearns, Laurel. 2007. Cooking the truth: Faith, science, the market, and global warming. In *Ecospirit: Religions and philosophies for the earth*, ed. Laurel Kearns and Catherine Keller, 97–124. New York: Fordham University Press.

Kearns, Laurel, and Catherine Keller. 2007. Preface. In *Ecospirit: Religions and philosophies for the earth*, ed. Laurel Kearns and Catherine Keller, xi–xvi. New York: Fordham University Press.

Knitter, Paul F. 1995. *One earth many religions: Multifaith dialogue and global responsibility*. Maryknoll: Orbis Books.

Knitter, Paul F. 2009. Theories and theologies of interreligious relations. Unpublished Keynote Address, *Interfaith Relations in the 21st Century: A Post-Parliament Reflection*. Monash University, Melbourne, 10 December.

McCarthy, Kate. 2007. *Interfaith encounters in America*. Piscataway: Rutgers University Press.

Nash, Roderick. 1996. The greening of religion. In *This sacred earth: Religion, nature and environment*, ed. Roger S. Gottlieb, 194–229. New York/London: Routledge.

Niebuhr, Gustav. 2008. *Beyond tolerance: Searching for interfaith understanding in America*. New York: Viking.

Pratt, Douglas. 2010. *The church and other faiths: The World Council of Churches, the Vatican, and interreligious dialogue*. Bern: Peter Lang.

Race, Alan. 1983. *Christians and religious pluralism: Patterns in the Christian theology of religions*. London: SCM Press Ltd.

Robertson, Roland. 1985. The sacred and the world system. In *The sacred in a secular age: Toward revision in the scientific study of religion*, ed. Phillip E. Hammond, 347–358. Berkeley: University of California Press.

Rockefeller, Steven C. 1992. Faith and community in an ecological age. In *An interfaith dialogue, spirit and nature: Why the environment is a religious issue*, ed. Steven C. Rockefeller and John C. Elder, 139–172. Boston: Beacon.

Rockefeller, Steven C. 1997. The wisdom of reverence for life. In *The greening of faith: God, the environment, and the good life*, ed. John E. Carroll, Paul Brockelman, and Mary Westfall, 44–66. Hanover/London: University Press of New England.

Rockefeller, Steven C., and John C. Elder. 1992. Introduction. In *An interfaith dialogue, spirit and nature: Why the environment is a religious issue*, ed. Steven C. Rockefeller and John C. Elder, 1–14. Boston: Beacon.

Snodgrass, Judith. 2003. *Presenting Japanese Buddhism to the west: Orientalism, occidentalism, and the Columbian exposition*. Chapel Hill/London: The University of North Carolina Press.

Tucker, Mary Evelyn. 2007. Ethics and ecology: A primary challenge of the dialogue of civilizations. In *Ecospirit: Religions and philosophies for the earth*, ed. Laurel Kearns and Catherine Keller, 495–503. New York: Fordham University Press.

Vendley, William, and David Little. 1994. Implications for religious communities: Buddhism, Islam, Hinduism, and Christianity. In *Religion, the missing dimension of statecraft*, ed. Douglas Johnston and Cynthia Sampson, 306–315. Oxford: Oxford University Press.

Weller, Paul. 2008. *Religious diversity in the UK: Contours and issues*. London: Continuum.

Wuthnow, Robert. 2005. *America and the challenges of religious diversity*. Princeton/Oxford: Princeton University Press.

Chapter 4
Multifaith Engagement in the 1990s

This chapter focuses on multifaith activities in the 1990s, beginning with the 1993 Parliament of the World's Religions (PWR). It then examines the effect that the end of the Cold War had on religious communities and the rise of religious, multifaith and multi-actor peacebuilding initiatives during this period. Finally it explores the increased involvement of Muslims in the multifaith movement, in response to crises events such as the First Gulf War.

The 1993 Parliament of the World's Religions

Following on from the increase in multifaith activity from the 1960s through to the 1980s, there was a dramatic rise of multifaith engagement in the early 1990s (Baldock 1997: 197; Kirkwood 2007: xiv; Eck 2001: 370). In 1988, the IARF, the ToU, WCF and WCRP formed the International Interfaith Organisations' Coordinating Committee to begin planning the 1993 centenary of the 1893 Parliament of the World's Religions (PWR) (Bharat and Bharat 2007: 102; Braybrooke 1992: 301–302). This event was held in Bangalore, India, while a larger celebration was organised in the USA by the Council for a Parliament of the World's Religions (Braybrooke 1992: 303–304). In 1993 over 7,000 people from diverse faith traditions including Baha'is, Buddhists, Christians, Hindus, Jains, Jews, Muslims, Sikhs, Taoists, Wiccans, Zoroastrians, and Indigenous peoples from all over the world, assembled in Chicago to participate in the PWR (Eck 2001: 366–368). Much of the discussion focused on the signing of a 'Global Ethic' drafted by theologian Hans Küng, which emphasised the need for common action and global responsibility among faith-based actors and communities (Eck 2001: 368–369). Whereas the 1893 PWR was seen as the beginning of the global multifaith movement, the 1993 PWR is said to have signified its 'coming of age' (Braybrooke 1992: 7–8).

Many participants in this study confirmed that the 1990s were a time of increased multifaith activity, as evidenced in the renewal and/or foundation of many of the world's largest multifaith organisations <Knitter 2007, USA; Patel 2007, USA>

A. Halafoff, *The Multifaith Movement: Global Risks and Cosmopolitan Solutions*, DOI 10.1007/978-94-007-5210-8_4, © Springer Science+Business Media Dordrecht 2013

including the Tanenbaum Centre for Interreligious Understanding (TCIU) <Dubensky 2007, USA>, the United Religions Initiative (URI) <Gibbs 2007, USA>, the International Interfaith Centre at Oxford (IIC) <Braybrooke 2007, UK> and the Interfaith Centre of New York (ICNY) <Breyer 2007, USA>. Patel <2007, USA> also described how the WCRP grew substantially under the new leadership of William F. Vendley during this period. Participants cited the 1993 PWR as the real beginning of a global multifaith movement <Knitter 2007, USA; Patel 2007, USA>, in so far as this event raised the profile <Braybrooke 2007, UK> and visibility <Gibbs 2007, USA> of international multifaith engagement.

The End of the Cold War

However, the euphoria and optimism of the early 1990s, epitomised by the global gathering of religious leaders at the 1993 Parliament, was soon to be overshadowed by other international events. Chapter 2 described how, alongside the rise of non-violent social movements, especially after the end of the Cold War, a series of 'new wars' erupted in which the new actors were not states, but rather cultural and/or religious anti-cosmopolitan movements claiming power based on identity politics (Kaldor 1999: 1–2, 6). While an increased awareness of interconnectedness created a perception of 'oneness' among an emerging global citizenry, it also heightened differences, thereby threatening ontological security (Kaldor 1999: 2–4, 6; Beckford 2003: 109). Growing fears around losing identity and power as a result of processes of globalisation resulted in a global reassertion of '*introverted* forms of nationalism', of ethnic and religious identities, fostering aggressive intolerances (Beck 2006: 4). As a result, a global resurgence of religion and a rise of religious fundamentalisms categorised the turn of the twenty-first century (Marty and Appleby 1992). The fifth WCRP Assembly Declaration (1989: 4 quoted in Braybrooke 1992: 156) foresaw these events by ending with the words: '"Lead us from fear to trust". Lead us from common terror to common security'. This statement reflected both growing concerns regarding the global rise of religious extremism and the recognition that religions could play a positive role in countering religiously motivated violence.

Participants in this study explained how access to global communication systems enabled increased contact and thereby understanding to develop between culturally and religiously diverse communities. However, it also increased tensions among people of diverse faiths and cultures as a result of a growing awareness of inequalities, which contributed to the ultramodern rise of terrorism <Marshall 2007, USA; Ozalp 2008, AUS>. According to Katherine Marshall <2007, USA>, Senior Fellow at the Berkley Center for Religion, Peace and World Affairs at Georgetown University, 'in a society where poor people see vividly through the internet or through television, the lifestyles of the other … it fuels the sense of unfairness and anger'. Poverty, she argued, in itself does not breed terrorism: 'most terrorists are not poor, and the vast majority of poor people are not terrorists'. However, an awareness of inequality, together with oppression, in particular repression of free speech and high unemployment—especially evident in poorly governed societies with large proportions of young people—both fostered and enabled processes of radicalisation.

In addition, several participants echoed the views of scholars, linking rising critiques of the spread of modernity and of capitalist globalisation with a global resurgence of religion at the end of the twentieth century (Habermas 1981: 35, 1987: 396; Hegedus 1989; Beckford 1990: 6–8, 10–11; Casanova 1994: 4–5, 228). According to Mogra <2007, USA>, religious communities, including immigrant communities in Western multifaith societies, asserted their opposition to materialist values and defended their traditions, having witnessed 'the abandoning of religion and particularly Christianity in the developed world' and feeling 'that they didn't want to go down a similar path'. Joseph Camilleri <2008, AUS>, Director of the Centre for Dialogue at La Trobe University, similarly explained how diverse religious groups have questioned the benefits of Western capitalism, arguing that their religious traditions offer better ways of building more equitable and sustainable societies:

> … there has been … over the last several decades … an increasing questioning … of the value of modernity: is it all that it's cracked up to be? And many people have been at the receiving end of so-called modernity in ways that have not led to the satisfaction of their needs, either material needs or for that matter psycho-social needs, and so there's been a tendency to return, to look for value in tradition. And again religion plays a very important role for those who seek something to return to their traditional roots, and that's true of the Christian world, the Muslim world, the Hindu world and many other parts of the world. So, we now have a serious debate, between the proponents of tradition and modernity in the world and religion is quite central to that kind of debate and discussion. <Camilleri 2008, AUS>

As stated in the previous chapter, this questioning of the benefits of Western capitalism and looking to religion for alternative worldviews was evident in the counter-culture movements that turned to Hinduism and Buddhism in the 1960s and 1970s <Murdoch 2008, UK>. Evangelical Christian movements were also described as reflexively resisting aspects of the market that were eroding family values. As Chris Seiple <2007, USA>, President of the Institute for Global Engagement, noted: 'conservative, Evangelical Americans … Neither one wants [the rock star] Madonna on their satellite dish coming into their kids [lives]. They want to raise kids who respect their elders and honour God'. In addition, Rev. Chloe Breyer <2007, USA>, Executive Director of the Interfaith Centre of New York, citing author Karen Armstrong, described fundamentalist movements as resisting the global spread of Western capitalism and secularisation as an 'activist response' against materialism, attributing the rise of fundamentalism at the end of the twentieth century to 'a way of defining self and community over and against that'.

Participants confirmed that whereas in the 1970s and 1980s the primary marker of identity was culture, by the 1990s it had shifted to religion <Voll 2007, USA>; and they suggested a number of diverse reasons for this occurrence. Ficca <2007, USA> described how the processes of globalisation, particularly increased mobility, influenced the global rise of religious identity. He argued that 'as we become more mobile we're not so tied to place or nationality' and that religion is one form of identity which people 'can carry with them'. For this reason, while the twentieth century was defined by the 'rubrics' of 'race and nationalism', Ficca <2007, USA> posited 'religion and transnational institutions' as 'the driving forces of the twenty-first century'. Josh Cass <2008, UK>, an interfaith youth worker at Encounter in London, similarly saw 'the decline in the nation-state' and the welfare state in particular as being responsible for people 'seeking to identify themselves through other means'. As 'religion is one of the things that have replaced those institutions', it was to religion that people were increasingly turning for support and consequently as a marker of their identity <Cass 2008, UK>. In addition, Seiple <2007, USA> described globalisation as causing 'a spiritual and psychological vacuum' which has caused people, in their quest for meaning, to turn to religion. Waleed Aly <2008, AUS>, Lecturer in Politics at the Global Terrorism Research Centre, Monash University, however, was more sceptical about the rise in religious identification being linked to a return to religious traditions. He argued that what we are witnessing in ultramodernity is 'a new kind of religiosity' that is 'very much more concerned with reactionary identity politics than it is to do with a genuine increase in spirituality'. Regardless of the underlying reasons, according to Janet Penn <2007, USA>, Executive Director of Interfaith Action Inc., 'it was the rise of religious identity in general' that then led to an increase in multifaith engagement at the end of the twentieth century.

It is also important to note that since the 1990s a new emphasis on youth engagement developed within the multifaith movement, evident in a rise of youth programs within the major multifaith organisations and the creation of specifically youth-oriented organisations such as the Interfaith Youth Core (IFYC) founded in Chicago in 1999 (Brodeur and Patel 2006: 4; Bharat and Bharat 2007: 190; Patel 2007).

These actor perspectives therefore demonstrate that the multifaith movement has increased its presence in the public sphere and expanded its membership as a result of the resurgence of religions and religious identity at the turn of the twenty-first century. They also offer further evidence that disillusionment with capitalist globalisation, particularly concerns regarding growing economic inequalities and a decline of morality, was the primary reason for the rise of religious social movements, be they cosmopolitan or anti-cosmopolitan, in ultramodernity.

Religious and Interreligious Peacebuilding

Religious peacebuilders Douglas Johnston and Sampson (1994) have argued that due to the growing public role of religions during the 1990s state actors could no longer afford to ignore religious dimensions in a world in which religion played an increasingly prominent role in both perpetuating *and* ameliorating conflict. As described above, following the end of the Cold War conflicts arose derived largely from clashes of cultural and/or religious communal identity. Rivalry between nationalities or religions was exacerbated by economic competition and rising expectations regarding quality of life fuelled by the processes of globalisation (Johnston 1994a: 3; Sampson 1997: 274). Conventional diplomacy, geared as it was toward resolving conflicts between nation-states, was unprepared to deal with these new conflicts, which centred on principles of self-determination, freedom and justice. In addition, as existing international law discouraged outside nations and international organisations from becoming involved in conflicts within nation-states, they were ill prepared to deal with these 'new wars' (Johnston 1994a: 3). This created a vacuum in which religious organisations, among other civil society actors, became involved in conflict resolution, mediation and 'track II (nonofficial) diplomacy', effecting non-violent social change 'from the middle' (Johnston 1994a: 4).

According to religious peacebuilding theory, there are several factors that predispose religions and religious leaders to peacebuilding and conflict prevention, amelioration and resolution: religious communities have extensive networks for communication and action; injustice can give rise to conflicts and religions provide mandates for non-violent resistance to injustice; in situations where there is state corruption or collapse religious institutions and leaders provide moral authority and have the trust and respect of the people; processes of reconciliation are often informed by religious concepts; and religious actors are engaged with communities at the grassroots level (Sampson 1997: 275; Little and Appleby 2004: 3). Faith-based peacemaking draws on religious texts and narratives of peace, justice, repentance and forgiveness to aid the peacebuilding process. Faith-based peacebuilding can be undertaken within single faith communities as well as between faith communities (Smock 2006: 37–38). Religious peacebuilding has also been described as including education, conflict resolution and reconciliation, and sociopolitical change through non-violent means (Sampson 1997: 274). In addition, religious peacebuilders, who advocate non-violence and pluralism, are present within all major religious traditions (Appleby 2003: 251).

Religious peacebuilders played a prominent role within the multifaith movement and in the formation of multi-actor peacebuilding networks at the end of the twentieth century. Interreligious peacebuilders sought to transform exclusive attitudes into more pluralist perspectives and to provide detailed methodologies for the peaceful resolution of conflict based on peace theory, which was heavily influenced by theological and philosophical principles derived from faith traditions (Abu-Nimer 2001: 686, 701). Religious traditions provide detailed methodologies for personal and collective peace realisation in so far as most religions advocate the importance of virtues and ethics and of cultivating one's good qualities. As mentioned in the previous chapter, many religions also advocate the need for transforming a self-centred, adversarial individualism or group dynamics into cooperative, compassionate mutuality and global responsibility (Knitter 1995; Hick 1985, 2001). It is this reflexive nature of religion, particularly its emphasis on taking personal responsibility, which lies at the foundation of religious peacebuilding and conflict transformation (Sampson 1997: 276). It is also an undervalued aspect of religions. Reflexivity, applied to self and society, is not solely a product of ultramodernity, as some sociologists have recently argued; rather, it is a quality inherent to many religious and spiritual traditions that well predate modern and ultramodern eras.

While all of the major religions proclaim peace as a worthy pursuit and ultimate goal at both the individual and collective social level, there are many conflicting theories of how this common goal can best be achieved (Schmidt-Leukel 2004: 3–4). There is a prevalent view, frequently expressed at multifaith events, that religions in their pure forms advocate only peace and that they have been misused for political ends. However, Perry Schmidt-Leukel (2004) argues that there must be religious predispositions towards conflict, or it would not be possible to exploit religions for political purposes. According to Schmidt-Leukel (2004: 3–7), the claim of superiority inherent in all major religions and therefore the existence of 'mutual superiority claims' render 'mutual supersession' and therefore predisposition to conflict inevitable. In addition, most religions also justify the use of violence and war in order to protect or defend one's religion and religious values from external threats. This conviction of undertaking a holy duty and its corresponding absence of guilt or moral dilemma is what makes religious violence especially dangerous and problematic. Mark Juergensmeyer (2003: 124–125) warns that simplifying religious violence as purely a political strategy negates this symbolic aspect of religious violence and in particular its long association with what he describes as 'Cosmic War'. According to Juergensmeyer (2003: 158–183), when 'life struggles' are merged with cosmic struggles and a cause has been sacralised, violence becomes legitimised. It follows that enemies are demonised and therefore dehumanised. Multiple theologies not only lay the ground for Cosmic War, but they also proclaim that its proponents will ultimately be victorious and rewarded. Martyrdom offers hope and restores pride to the suffering and the oppressed by exalting and ennobling the defiant. Consequently, the triumph sought by Cosmic War over the forces of evil is one that is not easily abandoned. Juergensmeyer (2003: 149–150) argues that what makes religious violence particularly savage and relentless is that its perpetrators have placed religious images of divine struggle and Cosmic War in the service of worldly political battles. For this reason, acts of religious terrorism serve not only as tactics in a political strategy but also as evocations of a much larger spiritual confrontation.

In addition to legitimising direct violence, whether in the form of war or terrorism, religious traditions are often hierarchical, patriarchal, didactic and discriminatory, thereby legitimising cultures of structural violence directed against Indigenous people, women, homosexual people, children, 'other' religious and cultural groups, and all forms of nonhuman life (Appleby 2003: 237; Halafoff and Conley Tyler 2005). Scholars who highlight the ambivalent nature of religion, rather than positing religion as either entirely problematic or peaceful, argue that it is precisely religions' role in promoting these cultures of violence, be they direct or structural, that predisposes religious actors to advance cultures of peace in their stead (Johnston 1994b: 332; Appleby 2003: 240; Halafoff and Conley Tyler 2005). These religious peacebuilders not only have the potential to transform their own faith traditions, but they can also be valuable allies for state actors in collaboratively addressing issues of common security. Therefore, by developing an understanding of how religion legitimates violence, rather than denying that it does, religious peacebuilders are better equipped to address the root causes of social problems. By challenging the aspects of religion that promote cultures of violence, multifaith peacebuilders occupy an ideal position to offer an alternative role for religion, one that valorises religious diversity, and affirms a commitment to non-violent methods of conflict transformation and the highest peacebuilding principles of their traditions (Appleby 2003: 240).

Many participants in this study affirmed these observations, that the end of the Cold War stimulated a new interest in religions' role in conflict and peacebuilding, and thus in multifaith engagement <Patel 2007, USA; Marshall 2007, USA; Vendley 2007, USA; Abu-Nimer 2008, USA; Camilleri 2008, AUS>. William F. Vendley <2007, USA>, Secretary General of Religions for Peace, claimed that the end of the Cold War had an even greater impact than September 11 on the process of 'religion re-emerging in the domain of political science, in the domain of statecraft', because during the Cold War period religion was 'largely submerged' and consequently had no place in government departments, think-tanks or in political science. According to Vendley <2007, USA>, it was the USSR's demise that 'brought not simply ethnicity, but religion, which is just about 2 cm below the soil of even the most secular nationalism … to the fore'. Camilleri <2008, AUS> agreed that with the collapse of Communism, 'the lid was taken off [religion] but in the taking off of the lid that also brought a number of simmering or latent conflicts to the surface'. Mohammed Abu-Nimer <2008, USA>, Director of the Peacebuilding and Development Institute at the American University, also stated that the end of the Cold War increased the visibility of religious and ethnic identities, previously subsumed under Soviet rule, and that as religion was increasingly perceived as 'a provocateur of conflict', its role in conflict resolution and peacebuilding became increasingly prominent. Therefore, a clash between religious extremists and peacebuilders emerged in the 1990s <Braybrooke 2007, US>. Harper <2008, USA> explained how consequently leaders within the multifaith movement chose to emphasise the constructive role of religion, thus challenging prevalent discourses in which religion was largely associated with conflict and fundamentalism, which in turn led to a rise in multifaith engagement:

> … over the previous 30 years and certainly the previous 20 to 25 years … many ascendant religious groups, often but not always religiously conservative, had contributed toward sectarian strife and … the polarising of relationships between people, and … there are a large majority of people of faith who want their religious tradition and their community to play a positive role in both mediating and lessening conflict … so … some of the increase of activity is related to the stepping forward of many people of goodwill from a range of religious traditions who want to see their religion play a constructive role rather than one that might tend to increase tension. <Harper 2008, USA>

As David R. Smock <2007, USA>, Vice-President of the Centre for Mediation and Conflict Resolution at the United States Institute of Peace, explained, 'in places where religion is one of the sources of conflict… it's particularly incumbent upon religious actors to be peacemakers'. Participants also recalled how a new emphasis on second track diplomacy and the power of religious actors to influence the dynamic of conflict began to emerge in the 1990s <Abu-Nimer 2008, USA>, evident in the research undertaken by Johnston (ed. 1993; with Sampson eds. 1994), which was described by many participants as a highly significant and undervalued body of work <Braybrooke 2007, UK; Marshall 2007, USA; Tippett 2007, USA; Von Hippel 2007, USA>.

While the rise of religiously motivated extremism and terrorism after the end of the Cold War has been thoroughly examined by scholars, the corresponding rise of religiously motivated peacebuilding initiatives and of the multifaith movement has received relatively little attention within the discipline of sociology. These actor perspectives thereby provide some much needed evidence not only of heightened multifaith engagement in the 1990s, but also that multifaith peacebuilding initiatives were implemented as ultramodern cosmopolitan strategies to counter growing anti-cosmopolitan sentiments during the 1990s.

Multi-actor Peacebuilding Networks

A rise of multi-actor peacebuilding networks, alongside the increase of multifaith networks, occurred in the 1990s (Bharat and Bharat 2007: 243). A ground-breaking initiative of this period was the World Faiths Development Dialogue (WFDD), established in 1998 by James Wolfensohn, the then President of the World Bank, and the then Archbishop of Canterbury, George Carey, to create partnerships between faith and development actors to address the problems of poverty (Bharat and Bharat 2007: 247; Wolfensohn 2004: xii; Marshall and Keough 2004: 3). The 1999 PWR in Cape Town, attended by over 7,000 people, also released *A Call to the Guiding Institutions* such as the UN and global IGOs to play a role in building peaceful, just and sustainable societies (Braybrooke 2007: 9). The Millennium World Peace Summit of Religious and Spiritual Leaders was also convened on August 27, 2000 at the United Nations in New York (Eck 2001: 380; Smock 2002: 3). Several major multi-actor peacebuilding events also took place at the turn of the twenty-first century, including the creation of a Faith Zone and *A Shared Act of Reflection and Commitment by Faith Communities* at the Palace of Westminster. The UK Government, the Archbishop of Canterbury's Office and the Interfaith Network of the UK coordinated the latter as part of the Millennium celebrations in London (Weller 2002: 138; Braybrooke 2007: 8). In Australia, the Springvale City Council was the first local government organisation to form an interfaith network (now the Interfaith Network of the Greater City of Dandenong) in Victoria during the 1990s (Baldock 1997: 198).

In addition, The Interfaith Center of New York (ICNY) shifted the emphasis of their programs away from theology 'to serve basic community needs' during this period, focusing on health care, domestic violence, immigration and navigating the court system. The ICNY was a pioneer in developing partnerships between state actors and religious actors to work together to solve common problems (Weiner 2006 quoted in Bharat and Bharat 2007: 239–240). The ICNY also arguably led the way in transforming multifaith engagement in the USA away from dialogue and global action towards a more grassroots, service-oriented model.

Many participants in this study confirmed the above observations. Participants cited the WFDD as evidence of new partnerships forming between religious communities and global institutions <Braybrooke 2007, UK; Marshall 2007, USA>.

According to Braybrooke <2007, UK>, initiatives such as the WFDD acknowledge faith communities as 'agents for change' and that religion can make a positive contribution to society. In addition, several participants mentioned the programs of the ICNY, which continues to bring religious actors and state actors including police, judges and social workers together on common issues, as a successful example of multi-actor peacebuilding networks begun in the 1990s <Breyer 2007, USA; Margaryan 2007, USA; Marshall 2007, USA>.

The Religion and Peacemaking Program, established at the United States Institute of Peace in Washington in 2000, was also described as one of the innovative initiatives to have brought religious and state actors together on issues of common security <Smock 2007, USA>. Brian Pearce <2007, UK>, Director of the Inter Faith Network for the UK (INUK), also confirmed that an increase in state involvement in multifaith activity occurred in the UK in the 1990s, particularly in response to the tensions surrounding the *Satanic Verses* controversy and also the preparations for the Millennium Celebrations. He explained how the INUK began to engage with the Local Government Association during this period, encouraging the development of local interfaith initiatives. In Australia, Maureen Postma <2008, AUS>, General Secretary of the Victorian Council of Churches, Melbourne, Australia also recalled how the Victorian Government began to take more of an interest in issues of faith in the late 1990s.

Despite long-held suspicions and resistance, participants described how these developments reflected a growing recognition among state actors, IGOs and NGOs of the need to partner with religious communities, at both the local and the global level <Braybrooke 2007, UK; Seiple 2007, USA>. Seiple <2007, USA> recounted that due to religions' ambivalent role in both perpetuating and ameliorating ultramodern crises, it became critical for state actors and global institutions to form partnerships with religious actors and to develop greater understanding of religion during this period:

> … all these issues we face here are global and they have two characteristics. One is [that] no single entity can solve them in and of themselves, state or non-state. The second is, it's not a question of if, but when you partner. Here are all the players, NGOs are the new player on the stage since the 90s and … religions are the new player that nobody knows how to talk to, they have always been there, but these guys, government, military, UN have been uncomfortable dealing with them … [But] [y]ou gotta understand religion … <Seiple 2007, US>

Academia also displayed a heightened interest in religion in the 1990s. The Pluralism Project, which continues to document the changing face of the religious landscape throughout America, was established at Harvard University in Boston (Eck 2001: 17, 12, 20), while multifaith centres were established at the University of Derby in the UK (Bharat and Bharat 2007: 68–69), and Monash University and Griffith University in Australia. Monash University also conducted several multifaith research and community engagement projects in the 1990s (Baldock 1997: 198).

These actor perspectives describe the rise of multi-actor peacebuilding networks at the end of the twenty-first century in which religious leaders and organisations have partnered with state, NGO, IGO and UN actors in response to global risks and injustices. These collaborative networks therefore provide further evidence of new possibilities for cosmopolitan governance at the local and global level, in which religions are playing an increasingly prominent role. The benefits and challenges of this growing proximity among religious, state, NGO, IGO and UN actors will be discussed in more detail in subsequent chapters.

Muslim Communities and Crisis Events

As Muslim communities were frequently at the centre of crisis events in the late 1980s and 1990s, such as the '*The Satanic Verses* Controversy' in the UK and the First Gulf War, a rise of Islamophobia, fermented by divisive discourses emanating from state actors and the media, spread throughout Western societies (Weller 2008: 155, 163–167, 194–195; Eck 2001: 2, 8, 296–300, 303, 306). As a result, Muslim communities became proactive in countering negative stereotypes, often through multifaith activities, and new multifaith alliances were formed especially among Christians, Muslims and Jews (Eck 2001: 341–347, 374; Bharat and Bharat 2007: 236).

In the UK, *The Satanic Verses* Controversy, also known as 'the Salman Rushdie affair', brought rising tensions about the privileges granted to Christianity over and above other religions in the UK to the fore. *The Satanic Verses* Controversy highlighted the fact that Islam and other religions were not included in the blasphemy laws and Muslims consequently campaigned for their extension. Following *The Satanic Verses* Controversy, multiculturalism and its policies became the subject of frequent attack and debate in the UK and internationally. In addition, a rise of discrimination against and harassment of Muslims was recorded in the UK during the 1990s. Hindus, Sikhs, Pagans and members of New Religious Movements also frequently reported incidents of discrimination and hostility towards them (Weller 2008: 155, 163–167, 186–187, 194–195). In Australia, a backlash against multiculturalism and a rise of xenophobia also unfolded in the 1990s, as evidenced by the rise of Pauline Hanson's One Nation Party and John Howard's narrow nationalism (Jayaraman 2000: 151).[1]

Similar developments occurred in the USA. A lack of awareness about and a resistance to an increasingly plural religious America contributed to the growth of fundamentalist Christian groups such as the Moral Majority and Christian Coalition, who invoked the exclusive language of a 'Christian America' in the public sphere (Eck 2001: 2). Many Americans were threatened by pluralism as evident in the publication of books such as Peter Brimelow's *Alien Nation* and Arthur Schlesinger Jnr's *The Disuniting of America* (Eck 2001: 29). As Eck (2001: 46) describes, a 'deep-seated contradiction' arose in American minds between 'the coexistence of a commitment to religious liberty' and the 'deep structures of Christian entitlement and ideological Christian exclusivism'. During the 1990s there were a significant

[1] These Australian developments are discussed in more detail in Chap. 8.

number of attacks against Muslims and mosques and also against other religious communities such as Sikhs, Hindus and Buddhists throughout the USA as religious minorities became the most easily identifiable subjects of peoples' fears and prejudices, and thus objects of hostility. These fears were exacerbated by a steady stream of negative media images, full of denigrating stereotypes such as 'Sikh militant' or 'Islamic fundamentalist'. In addition, subsequent to the 1995 Oklahoma City bombings, for which the media initially falsely blamed Muslims, Islamic centres and Muslim women, men, youth and children were targeted in a spate of backlash attacks against Muslim communities. The Oklahoma City events have been described as a turning point for Muslim communities in America as they became conscious of their increasing vulnerability (Eck 2001: 8, 296–300, 303, 306).

As a result of these events, diverse faith communities joined together with Muslim communities to show solidarity and joint outrage in response to these hate crimes. Solidarity among faith communities was also shown following attacks on Jewish, Hindu and Sikh communities in the USA in the 1990s (Eck 2001: 341–347). Eck (2001: 373) described how post-crisis multifaith initiatives, such as the interreligious service held by Washington's InterFaith Conference after the 1994 Hebron massacre, 'proved the importance of these networks of trust', as '[w]ithout a fifteen-year history of interfaith cooperation, this would have been unthinkable'. '[H]aving such bridges of trust in place is essential', according to Eck (2001: 373), 'for when the water rises it is often too late to create them'. Eck (2001: 343) also argued that '[t]he chasms opened by hate crimes can become the sites of new bridge building'. The direct impact of global crisis events on multifaith relations was also evident in new alliances of Jews, Christians and Muslims formed in response to the Persian Gulf War (Eck 2001: 374). The Three Faiths Forum (TFF), promoting understanding and respect among Islam, Christianity and Judaism, was also established in London in 1997 (Bharat and Bharat 2007: 236).

Several participants in this study confirmed these observations, describing how increased tensions between Islam and the West led to a rise of Muslim involvement in multifaith activities. Abu-Nimer <2008, USA> explained how growing tensions between Islamic societies in the Middle East and the USA were becoming apparent in the 1990s, particularly around the time of the First Gulf War. This placed great strain on Islamic–USA relations, yet at the same time created new possibilities for religious and multifaith peacebuilding initiatives:

> … by the early 90s, at the end of the Cold War, the US as a hegemonic power in the international arena established … a supreme role in the international stage, and … by the early 90s with the war in Iran/Iraq ending and then the First Gulf War, it was a clear indicator … that Islam and US relations … [were] going to be more tense and more conflictual and … the role of religion and peace at that time also began emerging as more possible than [in] the 80s or the 70s. <Abu-Nimer 2008, USA>

Sherene Hassan <2008, AUS>, Interfaith Officer of the Islamic Council of Victoria (ICV), similarly described how, while there was a rise of anti-Muslim sentiments in Australia in the 1980s and 1990s, around the time of the First Gulf War and the Salman Rushdie fatwa, 'there were a number of [Muslim] people who took it upon themselves to actually try and start this whole process of interreligious understanding' in response to 'international issues, as well as just wanting to make the current climate a bit more peaceful'. Mehmet Ozalp <2008, AUS>, Chief Executive Officer of the Affinity Intercultural Foundation (AIF), also stated that 'there was a need to get out there and speak, especially in the post–1991 Gulf War era, [as] it became clear that people didn't know about Islam, Muslims and that made them hostile, fearful'. In addition, he explained how, after the end of the Cold War, Islam replaced Communism as the new enemy of the West:

> The other thing is … the fall of Communism coinciding with the New World Order, from the Muslim world perspective it appears that Islam has been replaced as the so-called 'other'. Instead of Communism we now have Islam to deal with … the contradiction between [the] Gulf War and the Bosnia issue where Western powers, the whole world was prepared to go in and free Kuwait but they didn't do anything to free Bosnia, and all these things, the world events and the changes in global politics coinciding with globalisation, gave Muslims the impression that well they have to do something about this, they have to respond to this new circumstances that are developing beyond themselves. And this made Muslims move more open[ly] into interreligious dialogue … [To] see that we do need to improve the relationships between the religions … in order to have a peaceful world. <Ozalp 2008, AUS>

Ficca <2007, USA> also confirmed that the Oklahoma City bombing was a pivotal event that led to Muslim communities becoming more proactive in multifaith engagement:

> … the Oklahoma City bombing … totally caught the United States off guard and the first 18 hours of that or 36 hours, everybody was convinced it was an Islamic terrorist attack, so that kind of discourse was all over the media and in everybody's mind and then we found out it was homegrown terrorism. But I will say that that experience also led religious communities to begin getting to know each other. <Ficca 2007, USA>

Many participants described how, as a result of this series of events, Muslim communities became more active in dialogues with Christians and Jews in the 1990s <Braybrooke 2007, UK; Dupuche 2008, AUS; Jones 2008, AUS; Postma 2008, AUS; Shashoua 2008, UK>. Similarities between the three Abrahamic faiths were said to aid this process, yet histories of conflict also intensified the need for bridge building among these communities <Dupuche 2008, AUS>. It is important to note that many of these activities were conducted as bilateral interfaith dialogues between Jews and Muslims or Muslims and Christians rather than multifaith initiatives. For example, throughout the 1990s and in 2000 and early 2001, discussions took place between the National Council of Churches (NCC) and the Australian Federation of Islamic Councils (AFIC) <Jones 2008, AUS>. Similarly, the Victorian Council of Churches began a dialogue with the Islamic Council of Victoria in the 1990s <Postma 2008, AUS>. However, the Three Faiths Forum focused on developing a trialogue among the Abrahamic traditions <Braybrooke 2007, UK; Shashoua 2008, UK>. In addition, Muslim communities in Australia began to be more active in initiating Mosque Open Days in 2001 in response to these events, before the September 11 terrorist attacks <Ozalp 2008, AUS>. Finally, while dialogue among the Abrahamic faiths was part of vital conflict resolution and peacebuilding strategies, dialogue between Hindus and Buddhists and Christians, Jews and Muslims was described as lacking the same urgency at the end of the twentieth century, while remaining equally valuable <Dupuche 2008, AUS>.

The participants' comments demonstrate that as tensions were building in the 1990s between Islam and the West, Muslim peacebuilders became more proactive in countering negative stereotypes. In turn, religious organisations already involved in multifaith initiatives reached out to support Muslim communities in times of crisis. While anti-cosmopolitan actors grew increasingly hostile toward immigrants, and Muslims in particular, cosmopolitan actors such as multifaith peacebuilders found ways to turn crisis events into opportunities to build bridges between diverse communities by uniting in response to common concerns.

Conclusions

The end of the Cold War and increasing tensions between Muslims and the West led to a rise of public and state interest in religion. Consequently, a dramatic increase in multifaith initiatives and multi-actor peacebuilding networks occurred during the 1990s with the aim of countering global risks and advancing common security in Western societies. While both religious extremist and multifaith movements rose up to critique inequitable market forces, the multifaith movement was committed to addressing injustices non-violently. Not only did multifaith actors challenge cultures of violence, both direct and structural, promoted by capitalist globalisation, they also challenged cultures of violence within their own traditions such as exclusivity, terrorism and gender inequality. Religious and multifaith peacebuilders recognised that, as religion has played a role in promoting cultures of violence, it was their responsibility to promote cultures of peace in their stead. As a result, the imperatives to address global risks and injustices and to challenge exclusivity became increasingly prominent within the multifaith movement at the turn of the twenty-first century.

During the 1990s, Muslim communities were increasingly at the centre of crisis events and consequently experienced rising discrimination in Western societies. As a result, the focus of multifaith activities began to shift away from East–west dialogue of the 1970s and 1980s to the Abrahamic traditions, as Jewish and Christian actors extended support to Muslim communities and Muslim peacebuilders began to take a more proactive role in multifaith initiatives throughout the twentieth century. As crises have occurred in different locations, each new event has led to tensions and fears developing between different communities. '"Othering" shifts'[2] as negative stereotypes and misperceptions abound immediately following a crisis event and shift from community to community, aimed at those who are perpetuating

[2] The author first described this phenomenon when speaking on an untitled panel at the Centre for Strategic and International Studies (CSIS), Transatlantic Dialogue on Terrorism in Melbourne, October 19–20, 2007.

or fleeing the crisis. This phenomenon has been documented in Australia, as religious and/or racial vilification has shifted from Catholic, to Italian and Greek, followed by Vietnamese, Russian, Muslim and more recently to African immigrants. Newly arriving communities, often those who are fleeing a crisis in their country of origin, become the target of the host community's fears. However, over time, as communities come to understand one another, and as the focus of international crises shifts, the ethnic group under pressure becomes gradually accepted by the host society, and fears and prejudices are transferred to another newly arriving group of immigrants (Lentini et al. 2009: 28, 37). Due to this process, the focus of multifaith engagement has also shifted accordingly: from Hindu/Buddhist communities at the turn of the twentieth century, to Jewish communities after the Holocaust, back to Buddhist communities in the 1970s when nuclear and peace issues rose to the fore, to Indigenous communities in the 1990s with a focus on environmental crises, to Muslim communities in the late 1990s and early 2000s, and back to Indigenous communities in the late 2000s with the renewed focus on climate change.

The multifaith movement, by shifting its focus to different groups in response to crisis events, has challenged exclusivist attitudes and countered fears and stereotypes by developing understanding between groups who are experiencing these kinds of tensions and/or who have particular wisdom to impart as to how to solve such crises, be they social or environmental. As described above, during the 1990s this focus shifted to Muslim communities and stayed there until the global risk of climate change eclipsed the risk of terrorism in the mid-2000s. These developments will be discussed in more detail in the next chapter.

As a result of this rising prejudice against Muslim communities, rising critiques of multiculturalism and a corresponding increase in narrow nationalism in Western societies in the late 1980s and 1990s, there was a need for vigilance to maintain a commitment to pluralism in the face of growing anti-cosmopolitan and assimilationist attitudes that were prevalent at this time (Braybrooke 1992: 315). In the face of exclusivist challenges, multifaith engagement continued to be implemented as a strategy to combat rising prejudice in increasingly diverse Western societies throughout the 1990s. Consequently, the multifaith movement's aim of normalising pluralism became even more important at the turn of the twenty-first century.

While religious resurgence in the form of religious extremist movements has been well documented by sociologists and political scientists, these actor perspectives demonstrate that religions have played a constructive cosmopolitan peacebuilding role in ultramodern societies. The 1990s-rise of multifaith initiatives and multi-actor peacebuilding networks, in which religious actors increasingly featured, indicate that religions' capacity for peacebuilding began to be taken more seriously in the field of international relations and among global institutions such as the World Bank. As a result, these actor perspectives provide evidence to back up Sampson's (1997: 304) assertion that by the end of the twentieth century, religious peacebuilding initiatives including multifaith movements had certainly become 'increasingly intentional and systematic' and Brodeur's (2005: 43) observation that the multifaith movement was being noticed by 'traditional centres of power'. They also demonstrate that many of the features that characterise post–September 11 multifaith peacebuilding strategies have long been present within the multifaith movement, and that by the end of the 1990s the multifaith movement was well poised to lead the way in formulating a cosmopolitan peacebuilding response to this global crisis event.

References

Abu-Nimer, Mohammed. 2001. Conflict resolution, culture, and religion: Toward a training model of interreligious peacebuilding. *Journal of Peace Research* 38(6): 685–703.

Appleby, R.Scott. 2003. Retrieving the missing dimension of statecraft: Religious faith in the service of peacebuilding. In *Faith-based diplomacy: Trumping realpolitik*, ed. Douglas Johnston, 231–258. Oxford: Oxford University Press.

Baldock, John. 1997. Responses to religious plurality in Australia. In *Many religions, all Australian: Religious settlement, identity and cultural diversity*, ed. Gary D. Bouma, 193–204. Melbourne: The Christian Research Association.

Beck, Ulrich. 2006. *The cosmopolitan vision*. Cambridge: Polity Press.

Beckford, James A. 1990. The sociology of religion and social problems. *Sociological Analysis* 51(1): 1–14.

Beckford, James A. 2003. *Social theory and religion*. Cambridge: Cambridge University Press.

Bharat, Sandy, and Jael Bharat. 2007. *A global guide to interfaith: Reflections from around the world*. Winchester: O Books.

Braybrooke, Marcus. 1992. *Pilgrimage of hope: One hundred years of global interfaith dialogue*. London: SCM Press Ltd.

Braybrooke, Marcus. 2007. *Interfaith witness in a changing world: The world congress of faiths, 1996–2006*. Abingdon: Braybrooke Press.

Brodeur, Patrice. 2005. From the margins to the centers of power: The increasing relevance of the global interfaith movement. *Cross Currents* 55(1): 42–53.

Brodeur, Patrice, and Eboo Patel. 2006. Introduction: Building the interfaith youth movement. In *Building the interfaith youth movement: Beyond dialogue to action*, ed. Patel Eboo and Brodeur Patrice, 1–14. Oxford: Rowman and Littlefield Publishers, Inc.

Casanova, José. 1994. *Public religions in the modern world*. Chicago: University of Chicago Press.

Eck, Diana L. 2001. *A new religious America: How a "Christian Country" has become the world's most religiously diverse nation*. New York: HarperOne.

Habermas, Jürgen. 1981. New social movements. *Telos* 49: 33–37.

Habermas, Jürgen. 1987. *The theory of communicative action: Vol. 2 Lifeworld and system: A critique of functionalist reason*. Cambridge: Polity Press.

Halafoff, Anna, and Conley Tyler Melissa. 2005. Rethinking religion: Transforming cultures of violence to cultures of peace. In *UNESCO Paris and International Outlook Conference, Religion in Peace and Conflict: Responding to Militancy and Fundamentalism*. UNESCO, Paris, 12–14 April 2005, pp. 365–371.

Hegedus, Zsuzsa. 1989. Social movements and social change in self-creative society: New civil initiatives in the international arena. *International Sociology* 4(1): 19–36.

Hick, John. 1985. *Problems of religious pluralism*. Basingstoke/London: Macmillan.

Hick, John. 2001. *Dialogues in the philosophy of religion*. Basingstoke/New York: Palgrave.

Jayaraman, Raja. 2000. Inclusion and exclusion: An analysis of the Australian immigration history and ethnic relations. *Journal of Popular Culture* Summer: 135–155.

Johnston, Douglas. 1994a. Introduction: Beyond power politics. In *Religion, the missing dimension of statecraft*, ed. Douglas Johnston and Cynthia Sampson, 3–7. Oxford: Oxford University Press.

Johnston, Douglas. 1994b. Looking ahead: Toward a new paradigm. In *Religion, the missing dimension of statecraft*, ed. Douglas Johnston and Cynthia Sampson, 316–338. Oxford: Oxford University Press.

Johnston, Douglas (ed.). 2003. *Faith-based diplomacy: Trumping realpolitik*. Oxford: Oxford University Press.

Johnston, Douglas, and Cynthia Sampson (eds.). 1994. *Religion, the missing dimension of statecraft*. Oxford: Oxford University Press.

Juergensmeyer, Mark. 2003. *Terror in the mind of god: The global rise of religious violence*, 3rd ed. Berkeley: University of California Press.

Kaldor, Mary. 1999. *New & old wars: Organized violence in a global era*. Cambridge: Polity.

Kirkwood, Peter. 2007. *The quiet revolution: The emergence of interfaith consciousness*. Sydney: ABC Books.

Knitter, Paul F. 1995. *One earth many religions: Multifaith dialogue and global responsibility*. Maryknoll: Orbis Books.

Lentini, Pete, Halafoff Anna, and Ogru Ela. 2009. Perceptions of multiculturalism and security in Victoria: Report to the Department of Premier and Cabinet, State Government of Victoria. Global Terrorism Research Centre, Monash University, Melbourne.

Little, David, and Scott Appleby. 2004. A moment of opportunity? The promise of religious peacebuilding in an era of religious and ethnic conflict. In *Religion and peacebuilding*, ed. Harold Coward and Gordon S. Smith, 1–26. Albany: State University of New York Press.

Marshall, Katherine, and Lucy Keough. 2004. *Mind, heart, and soul in the fight against poverty*. Washington, DC: The World Bank.

Marty, Martin E., and R.Scott Appleby. 1992. *The glory and the power: The fundamentalist challenge to the modern world*. Boston: Beacon.

Patel, Eboo. 2007. *Acts of faith: The story of an American Muslim, the struggle for the soul of a generation*. Boston: Beacon.

Sampson, Cynthia. 1997. Religion and peacebuilding. In *Peacemaking in international conflict: Methods and techniques*, ed. I. William Zartman and J. Lewis Rasmussen, 273–318. Washington, DC: United States Institute of Peace Press.

Schmidt-Leukel, Perry. 2004. Part of the problem, part of the solution: An introduction. In *War and peace in world religions*, ed. Perry Schmidt-Leukel, 1–10. London: SCM Press.

Smock, David R. (ed.). 2002. *Interfaith dialogue and peacebuilding*. Washington, DC: United States Institute of Peace Press.

Smock, David R. (ed.). 2006. *Religious contributions to peacemaking: When religion brings peace, not war*. Washington, DC: United States Institute of Peace.

Weiner, Matthew. 2006. The real interfaith work: From Emerson's room to urban interfaith on the ground. *Harvard Divinity Today*, May 2006.

Weller, Paul. 2002. What we might think and how we might act – Diplomacy, challenge and exploration in multi-faith Britain. In *Multi-faith Britain: An experiment in worship*, ed. David A. Hart, 127–139. Alresford: O Books.

Weller, Paul. 2008. *Religious diversity in the UK: Contours and issues*. London: Continuum.

Wolfensohn, James D. 2004. Foreword. In *Mind, heart, and soul in the fight against poverty*, ed. Marshall Katherine and Keough Lucy, xi–xiii. Washington, DC: The World Bank.

World Conference of Religions for Peace (WCRP). 1989. *Melbourne declaration*. Geneva: WCRP.

Chapter 5
21st Century Multifaith Initiatives

Chapter 4 demonstrated how the multifaith movement has always been responsive to risks, and how the focus of multifaith activities has changed accordingly. This chapter describes how following September 11, the focus on environmental issues within the multifaith movement was eclipsed by the threat of terror, and examines the impact that this tragic event had on Muslim communities in particular. It also explains how a dramatic increase in multifaith engagement occurred in the USA, the UK and Australia in response to the September 11 and July 2005 London bombings, as multifaith initiatives were implemented as peacebuilding and countering violent extremism strategies. This included a rise in multi-actor peacebuilding networks and also academic and state interest in multifaith initiatives. Finally, it explores how following the release of Al Gore's *An Inconvenient Truth* in 2006, the global risk of climate change re-emerged as its primary focus of the multifaith movement and broadened multifaith engagement beyond the Abrahamic faiths to again include Indigenous, Hindu and Buddhist communities.

Multifaith Responses to September 11

The multifaith movement has been described as a 'quiet revolution' (Gopin 2000: 4; Kirkwood 2007) of 'mostly unrecognised efforts' (McCarthy 2007: 2) by diverse religious communities to create a more peaceful world. However, the events of September 11 'put religion front and centre on the world stage', transforming multifaith engagement from 'merely an academic exercise, or a spiritual luxury' into 'a global imperative, and a global necessity' (Kirkwood 2007: v–vi). Three days after September 11 then President George Bush called for a national day of mourning, which was marked throughout the USA by a plethora of multifaith ceremonies. At this moment, 'the interfaith movement moved from periphery to centre' in the American public mind (Brodeur and Patel 2006: 4). In addition, subsequent to

A. Halafoff, *The Multifaith Movement: Global Risks and Cosmopolitan Solutions*,
DOI 10.1007/978-94-007-5210-8_5,

September 11, multifaith engagement was identified as a potential solution to counter religious extremism, which suddenly propelled it to 'the centre stage of world attention' (Brodeur 2005: 42; Braybrooke quoted in Bharat and Bharat 2007: 225). As a result the need for management (Bouma 1995, 1999), and/or governance of religious diversity (Bader 2007), suddenly rose to the top of policy agendas in Western societies (Eck 2001: xiii). Although September 11 and the need to counter religiously motivated terrorism created 'a new sense of urgency' for multifaith engagement, it is critical to recognise that this momentum was building in the multifaith movement well before 2001, and particularly during the 1990s, as described in the previous chapter (Niebuhr 2008: xxii; Smock 2002: 3).

From Tragedy to Opportunity: Mainstreaming the Multifaith Movement

While there was a rise of discrimination aimed largely at Muslim, Sikh and South Asian immigrants following the events of September 11 in multifaith societies such as the USA and Australia, there was a corresponding increase in multifaith initiatives and educational programs that reached across religious boundaries at the local and national level (Eck 2001: xiii–xix; Bouma et al. 2007: 61–66, 106; Kirkwood 2007: v–vi; Niebuhr 2008: 5–7, 10–11). In 1980 there were 24 multifaith councils in the USA. By 2006 the number had grown to 500 (National Council of Churches 1980, Pluralism Project 2006 cited in McCarthy 2007: 85). As a result, McCarthy (2007: 85) described multifaith engagement as becoming an 'increasingly mainstream phenomenon'.

The impact of September 11 was felt far beyond the borders of the USA. While multifaith engagement 'was often considered "suspect"' within the Church of England, after September 11 '[d]ialogue developed teeth' and suddenly became 'legitimate' in the UK. More recently, and particularly following the 7 July London bombings of 2005, it has become '"de rigueur"—being even more mainstreamed and integrated in the life of society' (Capie quoted in Bharat and Bharat 2007: 233–234). There were 27 local interfaith organisations in the UK in 1987, while in 2007 the number had grown to 200 (Pearce quoted in Bharat and Bharat 2007: 245–246). A significant growth of multifaith engagement after September 11 and the Bali and London bombings was also reported in Australia (Cahill et al. 2004: 86–88; Bouma et al. 2007: 6, 55, 57–59).

Many participants in this study affirmed these observations. According to Breyer <2007, USA>, the events of September 11 put the multifaith movement 'on a map in a mainstream way that it hadn't been before'. Before September 11, Simon Keyes <2007, UK>, Director of the St. Ethelburga's Centre for Reconciliation and Peace, noted that 'it wasn't a sort of public phenomenon in the way we see interfaith dialogue now', and Postma <2008, AUS> recalled how public displays of solidarity among faith leaders condemning violence immediately following September 11 increased the visibility of the movement. The events of September 11 were also described as lending more urgency to multifaith engagement <Smock 2007, USA; Dellal 2008, AUS> and as intensifying the need for understanding among diverse communities <Lacey 2008, AUS>. Consequently, the multifaith movement gathered strength <Braybrooke 2007, UK> and a greater awareness of the importance of cooperation and understanding across faith communities emerged at both the local and global level. Indeed, Sr. Joan Kirby <2007, USA>, the Temple of Understanding's United Nations Representative, exclaimed how after September 11, 'it's as if the wave is cresting. There's such enormous interest in interfaith dialogue and cooperation' from the grassroots all the way to the United Nations. Shashoua <2008, UK> similarly stated that 'interfaith and religion is coming more to the fore, that everybody is talking about [it] … it's becoming in the public consciousness … it's being unwrapped and demystified'.

Several participants in this study described September 11 as a terrible tragedy, but also paradoxically as an 'unprecedented opportunity' to consolidate the prior efforts of religious peacebuilders <Ramey 2007, USA> by bringing diverse religious communities closer together to condemn acts of violence, to renew hope and promote non-violent responses to terrorism <Gibbs 2007, USA; Landau 2008, AUS>. These developments are well illustrated by the comments of both Ibrahim Abdil-Mu'id Ramey <2007, USA>, Director of the Human and Civil Rights Division at the Muslim American Society Freedom (MAS Freedom), and Melanie Landau <2008, AUS>, a Lecturer in Jewish Studies at Monash University, below:

> … it was a devastating, literally world changing and world stopping event that has impacted [on] virtually everything in the interfaith community and particularly the Islamic community in the United States since then. There have been numerous ways of characterising it. I tend to see it as both a tragedy, obviously in terms of the impact of the unlawful killing of civilians and the damage done to the US and effectively to the world economy because of the militarisation of the US economy and the militarised response, but also … an unprecedented opportunity for people to both look at the global dimensions of violence and warfare and terrorism on one hand and also … looking at ways in which non-violent response[s] to terrorism and to violence might be part of an evolving new interfaith agenda. So for those of us that do interfaith work it was an opportunity to really consolidate the efforts of peace-builders in different faith traditions … <Ramey 2007, US>

> … after these kinds of tragedies maybe there's a sense of wanting to sort of re-use it to bring people closer together and to reinstate a sense of hope. Maybe use it, instead of to create further division, but to use it to come back to a sense of shared humanity. I feel like I am going to cry. <Landau 2008, AUS>

These actor perspectives demonstrate that while there had already been a substantial rise of multifaith engagement in the late twentieth century, the events of September 11 led to a further dramatic increase in multifaith initiatives, at local and global levels. September 11 also lent more urgency and visibility to the multifaith movement and to the positive peacebuilding role of religions. As described in the previous chapters, once again, a devastating tragedy provided the impetus for multifaith engagement.

Cosmopolitan and Anti-cosmopolitan Responses to September 11

Following September 11, and building on the literature of the 1990s described in the previous chapter, many scholars have focused on the ambivalent role religions play in perpetuating both cultures of violence and cultures of peace (Appleby 2000, 2003; Juergensmeyer 2003; Huntington 2003; Schmidt-Leukel 2004; Halafoff and Conley Tyler 2005). However, while religion's role in contributing to conflict at the turn of the twenty-first century has been extensively documented, the role of religious and multifaith peacebuilding remains largely ignored (Smock 2006: 4). In addition, the ever-increasing body of counter-terrorism literature seldom explores the role of religious communities or community leaders in combating terrorism (Halafoff and Wright-Neville 2009). This study aims to address these omissions.

Several participants described how the events of September 11, and the ensuing 'War on Terror', brought the ambivalent nature of religion to the fore. Religion's role in conflict was made public, in both Islamic and Christian discourses that justify violence, and religious peacebuilders were mobilised into action, challenging these cultures of violence and advancing cultures of peace in their place. According to Knitter <2007, USA>:

> … [September 11] made it very clear that religion can be just as great, if not greater a source of conflict and violence, or a means to justify conflict and violence, as it can be a source for peacemaking. This has always been the case … First of all, in the case of Islam … but also … that Christianity has been and can be, and is being used also as a means to bring God's blessing upon the war in Iraq, or the invasion into Afghanistan … Anytime you declare people you are opposed to as evil-doers, that means God's on your side and something else is on their side, and so it's a question of you fighting God's cause, and that language [was] being used as much by George W. Bush, although he's modified it somewhat recently, as by Osama bin Laden … it's that realisation: "Oh my God what religion is capable of", and that, strangely, paradoxically, the awareness of this horrible misappropriation or exploitation of religion has alerted so many, call it responsible religious people … and in a sense been a clarion call that we need to do something about this … we're going to have to work with people in our traditions. So the misuse of religion has become, paradoxically, an occasion for a greater dialogue of religions. <Knitter 2007, USA>

Religious peacebuilders such as Ficca <2007, USA> condemned the September 11 attacks, and also the violent responses of the Bush Government and its allies. Both Ficca <2007, USA> and Rev. Charles Gibbs <2007, USA>, Executive Director of the United Religions Initiative, acknowledged the attempts of religious peacebuilders such as Rev. Jim Wallis who, alongside fellow religious leaders, proposed an alternative non-violent response to the events of September 11 by the USA and UK governments, which was unfortunately ignored by state actors.

In addition, Patel <2007, USA> posited that the way people reacted to September 11 depended largely upon how it was framed conceptually and on the orientation of the viewer:

> … the question about 9/11 right now is, what does it mean and how is it framed? So for some people it means a dramatic increase in defence budgets and war and for others it

means how do you create a global architecture of positive relationships with different people from different backgrounds? So again you always have multiple responses to single events because people look at that and they take multiple meanings from it. <Patel 2007, USA>

Voll <2007, USA> similarly explained how the reaction to September 11 could roughly be divided into two responses—a fear-based exclusivist response and a peacebuilding, pluralist one:

> … 9/11 had two consequences, because there were two general religious responses to 9/11 … Now, you had a very small proportion of the people who felt challenged and threatened going out and harassing Muslims or attacking mosques and things like that, but that sort of belligerent violent response to Muslims was very limited, but it was a reflection of the fact that there was a significant proportion in the society who had … a relatively self-contained exclusivist religious identity who felt that this was an attack, and that in fact they believed Osama bin Laden, that the attack was part of the great Islamic jihad against unbelievers … these kind of people tended to … give support, then, to intensification of homeland security kinds of things. And these are then the people nowadays that if they hear somebody talking, speaking Arabic on an airplane, they go and tell the pilot and they say, "you've got to turn around. We've got potential, they make me nervous", and things like that. On the other hand, the people coming out of this globalised pluralism, religious resurgence, recognising pluralism, essentially had been aware "oh, sure, there are Muslims in America", but they hadn't been aware that there were Muslims down the street from them, and in that context, the other response was to say, "I've got to know more about Muslims in general, and I've got to know more about my neighbours who are Muslims", and so that my experience has been that there has been a qualitatively different number, a real increase in Christian communities in the United States and Jewish communities who want to interact with their Muslim neighbours, and Muslims have similarly felt that this is an important thing, so that 9/11 had the paradoxical, if you will, response of making people feel that they have to do more to establish a pluralist interfaith identity. <Voll 2007, USA>

Following a similar argument, Aly <2008, AUS> described how for those who already had developed an 'interreligious framework', multifaith engagement provided a logical platform from which to mitigate the negative impacts of September 11:

> … the aftermath of events like [9/11] lends itself to societal fracture and they want to take some kind of step to militate against that. I think it's as simple as that. Now for religious people, and for religious groups, whether they be church groups or other groups, I think the easiest way for them to do it, the way they can understand best, is through that interreligious framework. They belong to religious communities … they naturally look for other religious groups to speak to, because there's something common to talk about … they both value religion. So I think it was probably motivated more by social concerns than anything theological. I don't get the impression that there were a lot of churches out there who suddenly decided they had a theological fascination with what we might call Oriental religions or anything … it was a social imperative that drove them to it and … [I]nterreligious dialogue … was the most logical vehicle for them, or the most readily comprehensible vehicle for them to engage in that process … And so for those churches that were interested in building social bridges, and have probably been interested in that forever, I think it's just the obvious thing to do. <Aly 2008, AUS>

These actor accounts demonstrate that religious peacebuilders who were involved in multifaith initiatives in the 1990s reacted to the events of September 11 in a vastly different way to actors who did not already have a commitment to pluralism and non-violent principles. Where a cosmopolitan ethic of valuing diversity was prevalent people wanted to extend a hand to their neighbours, and many Christian and Jewish groups already engaged in multifaith activities reached out to Muslim communities during this time of need. Conversely, those with exclusivist, anti-cosmopolitan agendas, such as terrorist movements and the Bush and Howard Governments, seized on the events of September 11 as a way to further their self-centred interests by promoting a culture and politics of fear. As people felt increasingly threatened, it appeared as though cosmopolitans were losing ground to anti-cosmopolitans. However, the multifaith movement chose to respond non-violently to the events of September 11 and this consequently provides evidence of a cosmopolitan approach to countering terrorism founded on a *politics of understanding* rather than fear. This assertion will be further explored in the concluding chapter.

The Impact of September 11 on Muslim Communities

As described in Chap. 4, a series of crisis events in the 1990s led to an increase in Muslim community involvement in multifaith peacebuilding initiatives at the end of the twentieth century that well preceded September 11 (Eck 2001: 341–347, 374; Bharat and Bharat 2007: 236); <Braybrooke 2007, UK; Ficca 2007, USA; Abu-Nimer 2008, USA; Dupuche 2008, AUS; Hassan 2008, AUS; Jones 2008, AUS; Ozalp 2008, AUS; Postma 2008, AUS; Shashoua 2008, UK>. However, as stated above, these multifaith initiatives did not occupy a significant place in the public mind until September 11, when religion and principally Islam became the focus of media attention (Shelar 2001 cited in Eck 2001: xvii, Eck 2001: xvi). According to Eck (2001: xx), the 'iconography of inclusion took a quantum leap forward' after these events, evident in images of then President Bush standing with Muslim leaders at the Massachusetts Avenue Mosque in Washington and meeting with Sikh leaders in the White House (Eck 2001: xvii–xviii). The sudden interest in religion, especially Islam, subsequent to the events of September 11 also resulted in a rise of Muslim voices in the media and of interest in radio programs that provided opportunities for in-depth conversations about religion such as *Speaking of Faith* in the USA (Bouma et al. 2007: 59–60; Lentini 2007: 56; Tippett 2007: 135–152). Conversely, other scholars have stated that while stories of violence abounded in the media following the September 11 attacks, the positive stories of multifaith engagement received little media attention (Aly 2007: 250; Bharat and Bharat 2007: 170; Tippett 2007: xi, 2–3; Niebuhr 2008: 5, xxxv).

Many participants in this study confirmed the fact that Muslim communities suddenly became 'visible' after September 11, thereby heightening awareness of Islam and of Muslims in Western societies <Ramey 2007, USA; Harper 2008, USA; Shashoua 2008, UK>. According to Ramey <2007, USA>:

> … 9/11 was the incident that didn't so much define the Muslim community in the United States as make the Muslim community visible for the first time to millions of people who were not even thinking about Muslims or only had very peripheral and incidental contact with Muslims. So people literally discovered that there is a community of 8–9 million people of various racial and ethnic and national backgrounds living in the United States who are Muslim, so, to the extent 9/11 was kind of a discovery moment for the majority

> community in the US, it was an opportunity for Muslims to become visible. It also became a catalyst for the examination on the part of non-Muslims of the actual text and historical reality of Islam … there probably were more Qur'ans purchased and exchanged and read by non-Muslims in the two or three months following 9/11 than probably in any other period in American history or at least modern American history. <Ramey 2007, USA>

Several participants also recalled how, after September 11, a new imperative to include Muslim communities in multifaith activities arose within the multifaith movement <Pearce 2007, UK; Kearns 2008, USA; Postma 2008, AUS>. Many participants described how the false identification of Islam in public discourse 'as an enemy of the West' during this time led to a rise of religious peacebuilding activities aimed at addressing this misnomer <Abu-Nimer 2008, US; Toh 2008, AUS>. Faith communities reached out to support Muslim communities and also to develop greater understanding between their religious traditions, and of Islam in particular <Amatullah 2007, USA; Kearns 2008, USA; Harper 2008, USA; Toh 2008, AUS>.

Participants also recounted how multifaith initiatives provided a platform for Muslim communities to differentiate themselves from terrorists, to dispel negative stereotypes of Muslims and to affirm their commitment to non-violent principles <Mogra 2007, UK; Toh 2008, AUS>. Muslim organisations were inundated with an unprecedented number of requests for information about Islam and Muslim communities <Hassan 2008, AUS>. Whereas prior to September 11, Christian communities reported difficulty in engaging Muslim communities in multifaith activities, following September 11 Muslim communities were more willing to take part in multifaith initiatives <Blundell 2008, AUS>. September 11 was thereby seen as a notable turning point for Muslim multifaith engagement in that Muslim communities became more proactive in initiating dialogue and educational activities to dispel misconceptions and to promote the peacebuilding aspects of Islam <Braybrooke 2007, UK; Gibbs 2007, USA; Smock 2007, US; Hassan 2008, AUS; Woodlock 2008, AUS>. These developments are well illustrated by the following quotations:

> … Muslims began to intentionally, both organisationally and individually, attempt to redefine the way in which Islam was being perceived in the United States. Sometimes that was reactive because people would come to us and ask us for radio and TV interviews, or ask us to participate in dialogue sessions in community centres or in university fora, but often it was also because these Muslim communities began to recognise the importance of a more proactive kind of self-definition and outreach, not only in terms of explaining who we are and that we are categorically against the killing of innocent people but also to become more active in civic engagement. <Ramey 2007, USA>

> So for the first time I feel that Muslims … actually took the initiative. In the past I feel at least, my experience has been, even my own experience I did not make a conscious decision to join interfaith. I was actually brought in by others, by other friends, particularly Christians … and of course there must be some Muslims who initiated it but very few in comparison … <Mogra 2007, UK>

> I think there was a lot of interfaith work happening prior to September 11, in the 90s and even beforehand, but one key difference was that Muslims were not active participants. They were sometimes invited and they were reactive, they reacted to invitations or sometimes were simply not interested. For the first time we are seeing probably in modern history that Muslims are really getting into it, and I think that made a big difference … and we have seen many events, initiatives, programs, projects being initiated. <Ozalp 2008, AUS>

> … we can see what the Muslim community has had to endure over this, but in some of the Muslim communities [they] have also developed strength out of some of this as well and it's then an opportunity … to have more dialogue with other communities and explain Islam to other communities … there's been a lot of questions there and people haven't had the courage to ask or have not known how to ask or who to ask … now there is a lot more information for other people out there and resources where other people can go to … it's increased that as well so people don't … have to necessarily live in ignorance, and fear. <Dellal 2008, AUS>

Rachel Woodlock <2008, AUS>, a researcher at the Centre for Islam and the Modern World at Monash University, also explained how increased participation in multifaith events began to raise the legitimacy of multifaith engagement within Muslim communities, thus replacing initial fears and scepticism:

> … and then of course once people started to do it they weren't scared by it as much and once one mosque had an open day, other mosques had open days, and they could see that there were genuine fruits to come out of this exchange and that kind of led as well … [to a realisation that] we need to do this for our own PR. I think there was a sense that that was a watershed moment and allowed us to then spread, those of us who think that it's important activity, we sort of had some proof against the nay-sayers, saying oh you need to do this, this is important. <Woodlock 2008, AUS>

In addition, Ramey <2007, USA> described how, subsequent to September 11, Muslims increasingly used the media to counter negative perceptions and to have their voices heard on numerous social issues:

> So, you can see for example, in the increasing number of op-eds written by Muslims, and the increasing visibility of Muslims in major dialogue in US media and in presentations to editorial boards and so on, that Muslims in this particular period following 9/11 became much more engaged in the sense of recognising that we are a part of a broader social community that has interests … <Ramey 2007, USA>

In Australia, through his public role in the media as a Muslim community leader, Aly <2008, AUS> reported that he has received numerous invitations to be involved in multifaith events. In this way his prominent media profile has facilitated the spread of 'interfaith messages' in the broader community. *Salam Café*, an Australian Muslim comedy/talk show on which Aly is a panellist, was also cited as a positive example of using the media to challenge negative stereotypes and to 'normalise Muslims' on Australian TV <Aly 2008, AUS; Hassan 2008, AUS>.

Finally, several participants explained how, while the focus within multifaith engagement was on 'Islam at the moment' <Pascoe 2008, AUS>, there were some parallels between Christian–Jewish relations in the 1950s and 1960s and Christian–Muslim relations in the early 2000s, as crisis events provided the incentive for the first stage of developing greater understanding between these communities <Braybrooke 2007, USA>.

As described in the previous chapter, Muslim communities were frequently at the centre of crisis events in the 1990s and, as a result, were becoming more involved in multifaith initiatives by the end of the twentieth century as a way of dispelling negative stereotypes and enhancing understanding about their communities. The events of September 11 made Muslims and Islam more visible, which in turn led to increased participation in multifaith events among Muslims and Muslim communities.

These actor perspectives also reveal that the rise of multifaith engagement following September 11 happened primarily in response to a crisis. Moreover, they offer further evidence to support the assertion that the process of 'othering' shifts from community to community in response to crisis events, as does the focus of multifaith engagement. Participant observations also demonstrate that the first three aims of multifaith engagement, described in Chap. 2—namely developing understanding of diverse faiths, challenging exclusivity and normalising pluralism and responding to crises, addressing global risks and injustices—were all accentuated in post–September 11 multifaith responses and that consequently multifaith initiatives played a central role in peacebuilding and post-conflict reconstruction strategies in the aftermath of these tragic events.

The London and Bali Bombings

Building upon the growing interest in multifaith engagement after September 11, an increase in multifaith initiatives occurred in the UK and Australia following the 7 July and 21 July 2005 London bombings (Bouma et al. 2007: 6, 55, 57–59; Braybrooke 2007: 1, 13; Pearce quoted in Bharat and Bharat 2007: 245–246; Bouma 2008: 13). Many participants in this study confirmed these assertions <Mogra 2007, UK; Pearce 2007, UK; Cass 2008, UK; Hassan 2008, AUS; Murdoch 2008, UK>. Indeed, Mogra <2007, UK> described how Muslim communities and imams became far more proactive and open to multifaith activities after the 7 July London bombings. While there had been a new focus on interfaith dialogue between Christians and Muslims and also between Jews and Muslims in the 1990s, and while the Three Faiths Forum had already been formed in the UK in 1997, several participants explained how a new emphasis on trialogue among Jewish, Christian and Muslim communities emerged in the USA, the UK and Australia subsequent to the events of September 11 and the London bombings <Keyes 2007, UK; Voll 2007, USA; Jones 2008, AUS>. In addition, participants stated that the 'homegrown' nature of the terrorists involved in the London bombings at once increased fears and prejudices and also provided greater impetus for multifaith engagement in both the UK and Australia:

> … 7/7 brought to a head, because of the origin of where the bombers came from and the fact that it was completely homegrown … I do feel that there was a real desire post 7/7 for communities to come together and that as you say the impetus was this shared risk that society faced. <Cass 2008, UK>

> … people realised they needed to find out more about their Muslim neighbours, particularly of course when the 7/7 bombers were shown to be people who were just British citizens and … part of mainstream society, so it's kind of logical isn't it, thinking people then want to understand more, how could this happen, how could someone think about it. <Murdoch 2008, UK>

> … the London bombing … probably had the most adverse effects because these were homegrown terrorists. And in the minds of many, it was "oh, hang on, terrorism isn't something to be feared; it isn't some unknown foreign element. It actually could be amongst us", and [so] there was a great amount of tension in the wider community after the London bombing … <Hassan 2008, AUS>

While Hassan <2008, UK> reported some setbacks to multifaith engagement in Australia among Muslim communities after the London bombings, Pearce <2007, UK> and Gibbs <2007, USA> both confirmed how in the UK and USA multifaith networks that were well established after September 11 enabled quicker and more effective responses to these crisis events:

> I think it would be fair to say by July 2005, one of the noticeable aspects of that was that there were local interfaith structures already in place, so that in many parts of the country, for example, key faith leaders met together and issued joint declarations and statements in that context. <Pearce 2007, UK>

> I remember when the bombings in the London subway took place, within minutes after I heard about it I had a call from a friend … who was the President of the Islamic Society in San Francisco. He said that Muslim organisations in the Bay Area are having a press conference tomorrow, would you please come and join us, that you have the relationships and the more you abide with each other the more those relationships are there … <Gibbs 2007, USA>

Australian participants also stated that the 12 October 2002 Bali bombings had a negative effect on communities and that multifaith initiatives played a significant role in remedying the effects of this crisis, as reflected in both Hassan's <2008, AUS> and Patricia Blundell's <2008, AUS>, Coordinator of Chaplaincy at Griffith University, comments below:

> … the Bali bombing had a huge impact on interreligious discussion and dialogue because Australians felt that they were being targeted, and a lot of our friends in the wider community were really concerned that Muslims were going to suffer negative impact[s] and be discriminated against and harassed, so they also tried to initiate a lot more interfaith dialogue in that regard. <Hassan 2008, AUS>

> We did get a bit of reaction after the Bali bombing so we had more involvement with the Balinese and Hindu groups after that, so … the movement responds to what's happening at the time and people's needs, and we did put on a memorial service here at the [Griffith] Multifaith Centre after the Bali bombings … but I didn't realise how the Balinese, a whole group travelled up the coast and a lot came from around the Brisbane neighbourhood. They really needed to speak to people and say they were sorry because they felt a responsibility because they should have been able to take care of guests in their own country, so … sometimes we don't realise just what's happening in some of the groups and they need some way of dealing with what's happening. <Blundell 2008, AUS>

Increased State Involvement in Multifaith Activities

Following the UK 'Summer of Violence' in 2001 and the events of September 11, 2001 a shift in emphasis occurred away from multiculturalism toward 'social cohesion' in national and local government policy. This intensified after the London and the Bali bombings, indicating growing popularity for a more assimilationist approach to managing religious diversity in the UK and in Australia. Concurrently, these governments increasingly promoted multifaith engagement, at the local and national level, as a strategy to tackle religious extremism and promote community and social cohesion (Cahill et al. 2004: 86–88; Braybrooke 2007: 1, 13; Pearce quoted in

Bharat and Bharat 2007: 245–246; Bouma et al. 2007: 6, 22–26, 55, 57–60; Bouma 2008: 13; Weller 2008: 198–199). Several participants in this study confirmed these observations. Pearce <2007, UK> described how the UK Summer of Violence 2001 was a significant crisis event that created a new focus on the need for community cohesion among diverse cultural and religious groups in the UK and on the role that faith communities could play in this process. In this regard, Pearce <2007, UK> cited the Summer of Violence, September 11 and the London bombings of 7 and 21 July 2005 as events that substantially increased multifaith engagement in the UK:

> Of course the year 2001 was also significant for us here because of the disturbances in the north of England in Bradford … and Burnley, and that had also led to increased emphasis on moves for community cohesion, as it had become known … the events of 9/11, as it were, came shortly after that and of course we've since had the events of the 7th of July in 2005 … So there had been a significant increase in the amount of local interfaith activity and obviously national interfaith organisations responded as well … to those events. And if you look at a chart showing the growth of local interfaith organisations in this country, you can see a significant upswing post-summer and autumn of 2001. Now of course in part that was in response to the kind of events in the north of England and in part to 9/11 and then a further increase after July 2005. <Pearce 2007, UK>

Following the events of September 11 and the London bombings in particular, in addition to social cohesion strategies, the UK Government developed a parallel strand of initiatives aimed at preventing violent extremism <Pearce 2007, UK>. Participants described how this led to increased state engagement with religious communities and to a rise in capacity-building funding for multifaith initiatives <Braybrooke 2007, UK>, particularly after the London bombings <Keyes 2007, UK>. According to Catriona Laing <2007, UK>, Project Manager of the Cambridge Inter-Faith Programme at the University of Cambridge, this growth in state support of multifaith engagement resulted in a plethora of new multifaith organisations 'cropping up all over the place'.

In addition, many state-supported multifaith initiatives in the UK have focused on Muslim communities with concurrent aims of preventing extremism and assisting Muslim communities to counter prejudices and misunderstandings in the broader community <Braybrooke 2007, UK; Pearce 2007, UK>. Braybrooke <2007, UK> explained how 'the government is very aware [of issues facing Muslim communities] but I don't think it really knows what to do, there's only so much you can do from outside', and how, as a result, 'Muslim leaders are now taking far more initiative' and a new awareness has developed among state actors of the need to work together with faith communities in response to, and specifically to prevent, crises. In addition, Mogra <2007, UK> also recounted how in recent years there was a heightened presence of Muslim leaders on local councils, including women and youth, and also in Parliament, including 'four parliamentarians in the Lower House … [and] a handful of Lords and Baronesses in the Upper House'.

According to Australian participants, the Australian Government similarly increased funding for multifaith initiatives under its *Living in Harmony* community relations grants scheme during this period <Toh 2008, AUS> as a strategy designed to promote social cohesion <Summers 2008, AUS> and to counter extremism

<Ozalp 2008, AUS>. Jones <2008, AUS> described how the Federal Government allocated a large portion of its *Living in Harmony* grants to initiatives focused on Muslim communities, and established a Muslim Advisory Board subsequent to September 11. The Australian Government also established the annual Asia-Pacific Regional Interfaith Dialogue conferences in 2005, thus far held in Indonesia, the Philippines, New Zealand, Cambodia and Australia, to promote positive multifaith relations in the region <Jones 2008, AUS; Toh 2008, AUS>.

Many participants also recalled how State Governments in Australia, especially in Victoria, Queensland and New South Wales, assumed a stronger interest in religion and the role of multifaith initiatives in promoting community harmony after September 11 <Aly 2008, AUS; Blundell 2008, AUS; Camilleri 2008, AUS; Dellal 2008, AUS; Dupuche 2008, AUS; Hirst 2008, AUS; Lacey 2008, AUS; Pascoe 2008, AUS; Postma 2008, AUS; Ozalp 2008, AUS; Toh 2008, AUS>. Victoria was cited as a leader among Australian states in promoting multifaith relations as part of a broader social inclusion strategy <Pascoe 2008, AUS>, and Victoria Police were praised for prioritising engagement and cooperation with Muslim <Hassan 2008, AUS; Ozalp 2008, AUS> and Jewish communities <Hirst 2008, AUS>. These developments are described in more detail in Chap. 8. In addition, Queensland Police were also commended for initiating and supporting multifaith engagement <Blundell 2008, AUS>, as were the New South Wales Police for working collaboratively together with Muslim communities <Ozalp 2008, AUS>.

In the USA, following the events of September 11, Muslim communities became more active in political processes, advising state actors on community issues and uniting with other religious actors to campaign for common concerns <Ramey 2007, USA>. According to Ramey <2007, USA>, Muslim communities and organisations in the US increasingly 'became much more engaged in dialogue with law enforcement, [and] with government agencies' after September 11. They also became more involved in political processes, collaborating with issues-based organisations to protest against the wars in Afghanistan and Iraq and campaigning alongside Christian groups against nuclear weapons. Ramey <2007, USA> explained how these common actions constitute examples of how 'cooperation between religions can become part of not only interreligious dialogue but also part of a growing consensus for changing the policies of nation-states towards things that are more peaceful and more just'.

While Chap. 4 presented a brief discussion of how there had been an emerging focus on multifaith youth engagement in the 1990s (Brodeur and Patel 2006: 4; Bharat and Bharat 2007: 190; Patel 2007), many participants in this study explained how, subsequent to September 11, the Bali bombings and especially the London bombings, a new emphasis on multifaith youth initiatives emerged in the USA, UK and Australia with a focus on countering extremism and homegrown terrorism <Epstein 2007, USA; Mogra 2007, UK; Cass 2008, AUS; Dellal 2008, AUS; Shashoua 2008, UK; Young 2008, AUS>.

Cass <2008, UK> described how, as a multifaith youth worker, he became 'a conduit between the grassroots and the state players', including governments and police, who were very supportive of local multifaith youth initiatives. In Australia, after the London bombings and the 12 December 2005 Cronulla riots in Sydney, the Victorian Multicultural Commission (VMC) formed a Multifaith Multicultural Youth Network (MMYN). Elizabeth Young <2008, AUS>, a student and multifaith youth organiser at Flinders University, described how state actors became concerned about young people from more marginal communities 'not fitting in' or feeling that they were being discriminated against. Consequently, Young <2008, AUS> explained that increased state involvement in youth multifaith initiatives 'definitely relates to the security thing, that they're worried about if one group does feel discriminated against or does feel isolated, then it's more likely to produce tensions and conflicts'. As Shashoua <2008, UK> remarked:

> … the focus on youth and why, community cohesion, was it going this way—yes it was … [but] would it have reached the level it had gotten to without a few different factors namely someone saying 'hey this is possibly a good thing for anti-terrorism'—no it wouldn't have gone to this extent unfortunately … <Shashoua 2008, UK>

Participants in this study also echoed Kathryn Lohre's (2007: 11) research findings from the USA that there was a significant rise of women's multifaith initiatives subsequent to the events of September 11 as women's interfaith networks were also formed in Australia and the UK after September 11 and the Bali and London bombings <Lacey 2008, AUS; Murdoch 2008, UK>.

As the events of September 11 shifted much of the emphasis of multifaith engagement onto countering risks and promoting social cohesion, the theological and philosophical underpinnings of multifaith initiatives were somewhat marginalised in the early twenty-first century (Braybrooke 2007: 25). Braybrooke (2007: 25) suggests that this shifting focus has been detrimental as it ignores the fact that building positive relations among religious communities needs to be rooted in shared theological and philosophical principles such as interdependence. However, the growth of interest in Scriptural Reasoning in recent years offers some contrary evidence to this claim. David Ford (2006: 345, 347–348) describes how Scriptural Reasoning can provide a means of wisdom-seeking engagement among diverse religious traditions that fosters the common good. Scriptural Reasoning emerged in the early 1990s in the USA within a long tradition of Jewish–Christian dialogue. Initially it occurred within universities in the USA and UK and at the American Academy of Religions' annual meeting. By the late 1990s it had expanded to include Jews, Christians and Muslims and has attracted increasing interest since September 11 (Ford 2006). While East–West, Hindu/Buddhist–Jewish/Christian, relations were frequently the focus of multifaith engagement for much of the late twentieth century, the rise of religious extremism in the 1990s and particularly the events of September 11 shifted the focus of the multifaith movement to Jewish–Christian–Muslim relations, broadening the conversation to include more Muslim communities, yet narrowing the focus on Abrahamic faiths (D'Arcy May quoted in Bharat Lohre Bharat 2007: 122).

Finally, Abu-Nimer <2008, USA> offered a pertinent reminder that funding comes in cycles, shifting from issue to issue, and that while multifaith networks have recently received an increase in state-funded support in response to risks such as terrorism, this is likely to change over time:

> … [in] the US, also on the state level, civil society, at the grassroots, you'll find [with] interfaith dialogue … sometimes like in many other programs, the funding drives the project and the funding drives the interest, and some do believe that these things go in cycles, so you definitely can say that we are on the rise in the cycle and the peak of the cycle of religious peacebuilding funding, and it's a matter of time probably when this also will be reduced or re-reviewed by foundations and by states as well. <Abu-Nimer 2008, USA>

These actor perspectives provide evidence not only of a rise of multifaith engagement and Muslim involvement in multifaith initiatives but also of a growth in partnerships between religious and state actors in the UK, Australia and the USA subsequent to the events of September 11, the Bali and London bombings. Especially in Australia and the UK state actors have supported and initiated multifaith activities as part of social cohesion and counter-terrorism strategies. Many of these initiatives have been focused on youth. There has also been a rise of women's multifaith networks as a result of these events. In the USA, faith communities have become more active in political processes yet have not received the same level of government support as have initiatives in the UK and Australia. The benefits and challenges that this increased proximity between religion and state actors are described in more detail in the next chapter. Concerns have also been raised that the increased focus on security and the Abrahamic traditions have lessened the focus on theological and philosophical underpinnings and excluded Hindu, Buddhist and Indigenous communities. This will also be discussed in more detail in Chap. 6.

Global Multi-actor Peacebuilding Initiatives

Chapters 3 and 4 described how, since the 1980s and especially in the 1990s, several global institutions began to recognise the need to work in partnership with religious organisations. A rise of multi-actor peacebuilding networks among religious communities, political actors and NGOs also occurred following the events of September 11, evident in the formation of organisations such as: Globalization for the Common Good (GCG): An Inter-faith Perspective, in Oxford in 2002 (Bharat and Bharat 2007: 243); the Interreligious and International Peace Council (IIPC), first held in New York in 2003; and the Tripartite Forum on Interfaith Cooperation for Peace (Tripartite Forum), which includes UN and NGO faith-based actors (Petrovsky 2003: 49; Williams in Bharat and Bharat 2007: 281).

Several participants in this study mentioned the Tripartite Forum as evidence of a new interest in issues pertaining to religion and peacebuilding within the United Nations <Kirby 2007, USA; Knitter 2007, USA; Ramey 2007, USA>. Camilleri <2008, AUS> also cited the 2001 UN year of 'Dialogue Among Civilizations', instigated by Mohammad Khatami former President of Iran, as a recent UN initiative advocating collaboration with faith leaders in order to address the most pressing risks of our times. In addition, both Braybrooke <2007, UK> and Marshall <2007,

USA> mentioned the World Economic Forum's (WEF) Council of 100 Leaders (C-100), founded in 2004 and focused on 'West–Islamic issues', as drawing on expert opinion from multiple, including religious, sectors. Marshall <2007, USA> also listed the meeting of religious leaders that took place in Russia prior to the G8 meeting in 2006/2007 as a sign of increased interest in religion in the global public sphere. According to Braybrooke <2007, UK>:

> … a lot of this is happening not just because of the bombs [of September 11 2001 and London 2005] … in the 90s [there] were a growing number of people in different disciplines not necessarily specifically religious … [recognising] that there is a moral dimension to life, it's interesting how this has happened in the business, economic world, you know about the World Economic Forum, but they in the last five years have begun to include religious leaders and now there is a group of 100 who go and the last three years they now come as full members rather than as an attached group, and so there's quite a lot going on, business ethics and so on, and growing conversations with the World Bank, there is … the World Faiths [Development] Dialogue and a recognition that faith communities are the ones who can be agents for change in a community, so religion is being seen as having a positive contribution … <Braybrooke 2007, UK>

Subsequent to the events of September 11, Religions for Peace acknowledged this new emphasis on cooperation across multiple sectors by coining the phrase 'shared security', as Vendley <2007, USA> described below:

> … the big issue there was shared, a deep sense of reciprocity that has both moral and practical dimensions to it. The moral dimension is that each of the traditions has some bearing to the golden rule, I'm responsible for you, I'm diminished if you are diminished, your plight, your suffering, your difficulties, are in some profound way linked to my own wellbeing. So that's expressed at the moral level and religions are remarkable in their consistency in terms of that observation. But today that's reinforced by a state of peril in which people broadly recognise … on a practical level, you simply can't build walls high enough against other people's insecurity to protect your own. So there's an odd moment of congruence between moral imperative and practical exigency. Practically we need to work together, morally we've always known we have to … <Vendley 2007, USA>

While there were several notable examples of global multi-actor peacebuilding networks established during the 1980s and 1990s, these actor perspectives demonstrate that there was a significant increase in such networks after September 11. In particular, a heightened interest in religion, and partnering with religious actors, emerged within the United Nations during this period. The benefits and challenges of this increased engagement between religious groups and global institutions will be discussed in Chap. 6.

Researching Religion: The Academy, Foundations and Institutes

Following the September 11 attacks, the number of academic programs in religious studies in American universities also enlarged dramatically (Niebuhr 2008: 105). Actor perspectives gathered in this study confirm this observation, as many participants described how research regarding religion's role in conflict and peacebuilding took on a new importance as a result of this crisis event <Amatullah 2007, USA; Glasman 2007, UK; Laing 2007, UK; Smock 2007, USA; von Hippel 2007, USA; Abu-Nimer 2008, USA; Dellal 2008, AUS; Dupuche 2008, AUS> due to the prevalence of religious issues in the media and a rise of public and state interest in issues of faith <Laing 2007, UK>. In the USA, this increased interest was evident in academic institutions, research institutes and foundations <Amatullah 2007, USA; Smock 2007, USA; von Hippel 2007, USA; Abu-Nimer 2008, USA>, as illustrated by the description offered by Smock <2007, USA>, of how the Religion and Peacebuilding program at the USIP suddenly leapt to prominence after September 11:

> … the program Religion and Peacemaking was fairly marginal to the [United States] Institute [for Peace] and its general mandate and its visibility until 9/11, and then all of a sudden, the President of the Institute and the Board realised … here we have a program, we haven't been paying much attention to it but it's critically important in this new day where religion is so salient, and I think that's true in many cases even though a lot of our work has nothing to do with 9/11, or Islamophobia or even Muslim extremism, it just has lifted up the importance of religion and religious peacemaking and the role of faith-based organisations generally. <Smock 2007, USA>

US participants described how the Henry Luce Foundation, Ford Foundation and the Carnegie Corporation increased funding for research initiatives focused on religion following September 11. In addition, the Fulbright Program, Georgetown University, Boston University, the Social Science Research Council in New York and the Centre for Strategic and International Studies (CSIS) in Washington all began to prioritise research regarding religion <von Hippel 2007, USA; Abu-Nimer 2008, USA>. As Karin von Hippel <2007, US>, Director of the Post-Conflict Reconstruction Project at the Centre for Strategic and International Studies, noted following the events of September 11 religion suddenly became 'a new issue in the States'.

Similarly, Australian participants described how an increase in academic research and also in educational programs for school students around religion occurred in Australia after September 11 and the London bombings <Dellal 2008, AUS; Dupuche 2008, AUS>. Several new centres were established in Australian universities including the UNESCO Chair in Intercultural and Interreligious Relations–Asia-Pacific at Monash University in 2004, the Asia-Pacific Centre for Inter-religious Dialogue at the Australian Catholic University and the Centre for Dialogue at La Trobe University in 2006 <Dupuche 2008, AUS>. A post–September 11 scholarly interest in religion was also evident in the UK <Braybrooke 2007, UK; Glasman 2007, UK>, despite initial scepticism, as described by Glasman <2007, UK> below:

> … there has been a very big change within the universities, certainly, and when I started doing this work, maybe five or six years ago … looking at faith as a means of engaging with politics … looking at how you can live together, the hostility from my colleagues and from management was, you could say ferocious … Now what's happened in the last five or six years is that it's gone from that degree of hostility to me receiving really very strong support from the management of the university for what I was doing … <Glasman 2007, UK>

These actor perspectives reveal that not only was there a rise of multifaith engagement following September 11, but there was also a growth of interest in issues pertaining to religion more generally. In particular, there was an increase in research and teaching in the field of religion. Consequently, scholars, alongside funders of research, played a critical role in multi-actor peacebuilding networks established during this period, often acting as a conduit between religious communities and state actors, informing policy through evidence-based research.

A Renewed Focus on Climate Change

A renewed focus on environmental issues emerged within the multifaith movement subsequent to the commercial release of *An Inconvenient Truth* in 2006. While environmental issues began to occupy a prominent place in the public sphere during the 1990s (Rockefeller 1992: 167), by the end of the twentieth century, as neoliberal economics converged with conservative religion, the environmental movement encountered a great deal of opposition (Kearns and Keller 2007: xii). Indeed, the so-called War on Terror, combined with a widespread apathy and denial of climate change across various sectors including conservative religious groups, marginalised the issue of climate change from the public mind (Tucker 2007: 496).

However, faith-based environmental organisations maintained their proactive commitment to addressing the issue of climate change throughout this regressive period. In 2006, the National Religious Partnership for the Environment (NRPE) organised screenings of *The Great Warming* and *An Inconvenient Truth* for faith communities throughout the USA (Kearns 2007: 102). These documentaries heightened awareness of the risk of climate change and environmental issues have consequently resurfaced to the top of community, policy, academic and multifaith agendas, especially since the commercial release of *An Inconvenient Truth*. Mary Evelyn Tucker (2007: 500, 495–496) describes the need to place environmental issues at the centre of the emerging dialogue among civilisations to create 'a multiform planetary civilization inclusive of both cultural and biological diversity'. Laurel Kearns and Catherine Keller (2007: xi) also describe a '*green shift*' in which the humble beginnings of the environmental movement, through a '"butterfly effect" of change', have created 'a tipping *counter*point', resulting in 'an avalanche of responsible action'. Keller and Kearns (2007: 12) refer to this shift as 'a greener cosmopolitanism'. In addition, since the release of *An Inconvenient Truth* and a global rise of interest in environmental issues, as multifaith engagement is becoming increasingly refocused on climate change, it is gradually returning to Indigenous and Hindu and Buddhist perspectives as guiding principles on how to cooperatively counter global crises. This was particularly evident in the 2009 Melbourne Parliament of the World's Religions at which both Indigenous actors and environmental issues played a prominent role (PWR 2009).

Participants in this study confirmed and expanded upon many of these observations. While environmental issues have re-entered the public mind in the mid-2000s,

Shaw <2007, AUS> expressed a sense of sadness that calls from Indigenous communities and the multifaith movement in the latter part of the twentieth century to deal with the looming environmental crisis had been largely ignored until recently:

> … Western culture decided 'thank you very much for coming—we're going to turn the other direction' … humanity had a choice at that time, and was given that choice in many different ways by the Indigenous ancient cultures, and so those things just lay and bubbled along and the world went the way it did, until somebody like Al Gore, and he said, 'I've known about this since 1959. My teacher started to document the CO2 levels way back then', and … suddenly the media were full of it … <Shaw 2007, AUS>

Kearns <2008, USA> also described how the focus on environmental issues in the 1990s was sidelined by the War on Terror:

> … for us in the United States the increased funding of the military has sort of paralleled the decreased funding on environmental issues, and there's a broader ideological rave behind that that's not just an issue of where the money goes but sort of in the interest of national security. We might say that global climate change is a very big national security issue, and certainly environmentalists have tried to say that, but it was hard to get people to think about a longer-term threat when they were so busily being convinced of this immediate threat. So … it really struck a hard blow of efforts to try and get in this country responses on global warming for instance. <Kearns 2008, USA>

However, Kearns <2008, USA> and Harper <2008, USA> also explained how green faith-based groups spread awareness of climate change by widely screening *An Inconvenient Truth* and *The Great Warming* throughout the USA and promoting educative initiatives and practical action to address this crisis:

> … the Al Gore film has made a tremendous difference. I wouldn't pin it all on the Al Gore film because our headlines have been just filled with, that the ice caps are melting faster, that scientists are more and more convinced and so … it's been a combination of certainly here in the United States, I'm sure people told you about the Renewal Project and the Interfaith Power and Light that worked with groups like GreenFaith and others to show that film in 4,000 different religious congregations. So, that was a major effort to get it into the religious community, along with a study guide and then there's a couple of other films, one called *The Great Warming*, that was even more specifically oriented toward religious communities … then of course, Hurricane Katrina or that series of hurricanes, which aren't directly attributable but made people really start listening to the scenario of extreme weather events, drought and all that … those kind of more empirical realities have made people pay attention. <Kearns 2008, USA>

> In relationship to climate change … we are still in the early stages of seeing religious responses to that issue. What I've seen have been the use of the film by the Vice-President Gore in several thousand religious institutions around the country and other educational films about climate change as part of an explicitly educational initiative … on the part of the faith community that has been followed up in a number of places … to advocate for stronger global warming legislations, and that have also taken steps to encourage their members to conserve energy and to make use of renewable energy in their own homes, religious institutions and places of work. <Harper 2008, USA>

Participants also recounted how the issue of climate change has broadened the multifaith movement to include more mainstream religious communities <Harper 2008, USA; Toh 2008, AUS>. For example, in Australia major religious and faith organisations joined together in 2006 to make a *Common Belief* statement on climate change <Toh 2008, AUS>. Landau <2008, AUS> and Shashoua <2008, UK> also explained how growing global environmental concerns have highlighted the interdependent nature of life and the need for collaborative responses aimed at countering risks:

> … [there's] a recognition, even if it's not overt, that we can't do it alone … environmental [risks] for example, there's just this realisation of maybe a common destiny … <Landau 2008, AUS>

> … when I was a kid I remember having a conversation with my father, and we had discussed what will bring world peace and he said an external threat, and so a UFO coming down putting us all in harm's way and we have to band together for our survival, now the external threat is now the environment, and so it's an internal threat because it depends on us as well. Is this the only way? <Shashoua 2008, UK>

Finally, Harper <2008, USA> and Kearns <2008, USA> described how multifaith organisations with an environmental focus have also received increased state support in the form of funding following the release of *An Inconvenient Truth*:

> … I have been surprised by … the relatively significant extent to which a number of State Governments here in the US, and to some degree the Federal Government, have been involved in funding religious responses to climate change … GreenFaith … has received both State and Federal funds for our work … obviously that support has been very important materially and has allowed GreenFaith and other religious environmental groups in the US to grow and it's had a good impact. <Harper 2008, USA>

> … here in New Jersey, certainly GreenFaith has gotten funding but it's not so much to fund it as the interfaith work but to have it be a conduit to get folks interested in government programs. So that money certainly helps GreenFaith exist and so … there might be those kind of programs in other places, for instance California, New Jersey's been quite a leader on the work on climate change and on renewable energy, so it's a question of they're giving grants for something that they're wanting to have happen in other communities also of which the religious community is one. <Kearns 2008, USA>

These actor perspectives indicate that by the mid-2000s the global risk of climate change began to eclipse the global risk of terrorism in the public mind, as the most prominent perceived threat to public security. Consequently, the multifaith movement shifted its focus toward environmental issues. It is also critical to note that as environmental risks had been at the forefront of public consciousness and of the multifaith movement in the 1980s and 1990s, many multifaith organisations maintained a focus on environmental issues even when they were largely sidelined by state actors' responses to the global risk of terrorism. Indeed, these actor perspectives provide evidence that multifaith organisations, especially in the USA, played a significant role in publicising climate change, thereby re-introducing the issue to the public sphere. They also confirm that the contemporary focus on climate change has a powerful potential to unite communities in common action in the same way that environmental concerns elicited a cosmopolitan response from diverse actors in the 1980s and 1990s. While precious time was lost during the anti-cosmopolitan Bush and Howard eras, the recent mainstreaming of environmental awareness offers hope that cosmopolitan peacebuilding strategies, which holistically address human and environmental security, are finally gaining the kind of popular acceptance that multifaith actors envisaged some time ago.

Conclusions

These actor perspectives demonstrate that religion came to occupy a prominent place in the public mind in the early 2000s, largely as a result of the September 11 terrorist attacks and subsequent Bali and London bombings. Multifaith initiatives also suddenly became more visible as they were increasingly implemented as peacebuilding and counter-terrorism strategies in Western multifaith societies, to counter the negative impact of these crisis events. While multifaith initiatives have no doubt received more public recognition since September 11, networks of trust across faith communities were already well established by the multifaith movement and by the trailblazers of multi-actor peacebuilding networks such as the Interfaith Centre of New York (ICNY) and the World Faiths Development Dialogue (WFDD) in the 1990s.

The tragedy of September 11, similar to previous crisis events such as WWII and the Cold War, served as a stimulus for a plethora of peacebuilding activities in the USA, the UK and Australia. Existing multifaith networks, many of which were founded in the 1990s, were well poised to respond to this event. These cosmopolitan, multifaith responses to September 11, particularly evident at the grassroots, community-based level, challenged direct and structural violence within religious traditions and in broader society. Consequently, religious peacebuilders from diverse faith traditions joined together to condemn acts of violence; to call for more equitable distribution of power, resources and privileges; to affirm the positive aspects of religions; and to counter negative stereotypes of religious communities—thereby propelling multifaith initiatives into the public sphere.

At the grassroots level, numerous initiatives occurred spontaneously and independently as communities reached out to one another for support and to develop greater understanding. There is no doubt that the events of September 11 made Islam and Muslim communities more visible in Western multifaith societies. Initially the focus was negative and fear and prejudice abounded. However, many Muslim communities, supported by other faith communities, countered negative stereotypes and condemned violent extremism through the platform of multifaith initiatives, which also provided opportunities to develop understanding and relationships among adherents of diverse religious traditions. The London bombings, due to their 'homegrown' nature, placed even greater importance on the need to better understand and build bridges across divided communities, especially among youth who were viewed as principally at risk of radicalisation. Multifaith initiatives for youth became increasingly viewed as countering violent extremism strategies, and multifaith engagement in general, including women's interfaith networks, was promoted as part of community and social cohesion strategies in Western multifaith societies such as the UK and Australia.

In addition, in response to crisis events such as September 11, the Summer of Violence in the UK, and the Bali and London bombings, collaboration between state and religious actors increased in order to combat local and global risks and to advance common security. The emphasis on social cohesion and countering extremism in Australia and the UK, especially after the London bombings, lifted the profile of multifaith initiatives and gave new legitimacy to the multifaith movement. Consequently, multifaith initiatives received funding support from states and foundations as part of counter-terrorism strategies and increasingly included conservative as well as liberal actors. It was primarily for this reason that the multifaith movement continued to grow during this period when other social movements, such as the environmental and women's movements, were largely marginalised.

Following these crisis events, academics and universities also played an important role not only as facilitators of multifaith initiatives, but also as conduits of religious communities' views, gathered in research aimed at informing policy. While an increase of state funding for religious and multifaith initiatives occurred in the UK and Australia as a result of September 11, the Bali and London bombings, a substantial amount of funding has also come from foundations and institutes that are independent of government, especially in the USA. Following the pioneering example of the World Bank's WFDD in the 1990s, a rise of multi-actor peacebuilding networks also emerged at the global level after September 11, as evidenced by initiatives implemented by the UN and the WEF. These multi-actor peacebuilding networks constitute further evidence of an emerging cosmopolitan condition in ultramodernity with increased collaboration between religious and non-religious actors from diverse sectors in response to poverty, terrorism and climate change, the most pressing crisis events of our time.

Indeed, while much of the focus of multifaith initiatives since September 11 has been on countering extremism and on Christian–Jewish–Muslim relations, a renewed concern has recently emerged around the global risk of climate change, and the multifaith movement is shifting its attention towards this new crisis. As the multifaith movement has long maintained a focus on environmental issues and states have realised the capacity of religious organisations to mobilise their communities in times of crisis, multifaith organisations in the USA have also received some state funding to combat environmental risks.

Therefore, the actor perspectives documented in this chapter further substantiate the theory that the multifaith movement has been highly responsive to global risks, and also that the focus of crises, and consequently of peacebuilding initiatives, has shifted over time. The participants' accounts also provide further evidence that the impact of global risks and corresponding 'othering' has shifted from community to community, as has the need to provide support to communities at risk or under pressure during times of crisis. It follows that the impetus to address global risks and injustices, to counter extremism and normalise pluralism and to develop understanding of diverse faiths has strengthened following September 11. However, concerns have also been raised that the increased focus on security has lessened the theological and philosophical focus on developing understanding of the nature of reality within the multifaith movement in the twenty-first century, and that Indigenous, Hindu, Buddhist communities came to be largely excluded from multifaith initiatives in the early 2000s.

While the multifaith movement has shifted its focus away from the risk of terrorism towards climate change, it appears that multifaith initiatives may have reached their peak in terms of the funding cycle. However, as state actors in Western societies have increasingly recognised the peacebuilding capacity of religions, particularly after September 11, they are now more likely to continue to collaborate with religious actors in response to current risks such as environmental and economic crises. The recent establishment of the Tony Blair Faith Foundation in the UK and the Centre for Faith Based and Community Initiatives in the USA offers some evidence to support this assertion.

While there is no doubt that there has been a steady rise of multifaith engagement in ultramodernity, there is little empirical evidence regarding its benefits and challenges, and very little understanding of precisely how multifaith initiatives contribute to addressing global risks. As discussed in previous chapters, concerns have also been raised regarding the growing proximity of religious and state actors in promoting multifaith initiatives as strategies to counter terrorism and build social cohesion at the turn of the twenty-first century. The following chapters will address these issues in detail.

References

Aly, Waleed. 2007. *People like us: How arrogance is dividing Islam and the West*. Sydney: Picador.

Appleby, R.Scott. 2000. *The ambivalence of the sacred: Religion, violence, and reconciliation*. Maryland: Rowman and Littlefield Publishers, Inc.

Appleby, R.Scott. 2003. Retrieving the missing dimension of statecraft: Religious faith in the service of peacebuilding. In *Faith-based diplomacy: Trumping realpolitik*, ed. Douglas Johnston, 231–258. Oxford: Oxford University Press.

Bader, Veit. 2007. *Secularism or democracy? Associational governance of religious diversity*. Amsterdam: Amsterdam University Press.

Bharat, Sandy, and Jael Bharat. 2007. *A global guide to interfaith: Reflections from around the world*. Winchester: O Books.

Bouma, Gary D. 1995. The emergence of religious plurality in Australia: A multicultural society. *Sociology of Religion* 56(4): 285–302.

Bouma, Gary D. (ed.). 1997. *Many religions, all Australian: Religious settlement, identity and cultural diversity*. Melbourne: The Christian Research Association.

Bouma, Gary D. 1999. From hegemony to pluralism: Managing religious diversity in modernity and post-modernity. In *Managing religious diversity: From threat to promise*, ed. Gary D. Bouma, 7–27. Melbourne: Australian Association for the Study of Religions.

Bouma, Gary D. 2008. The challenge of religious revitalization and religious diversity to social cohesion in secular societies. In *Religious diversity and civil society: A comparative analysis*, ed. Brian S. Turner, 13–25. Oxford: The Bardwell Press.

Bouma, Gary D., Sharon Pickering, Anna Halafoff, and Hass Dellal. 2007. *Managing the impact of global crisis events on community relations in multicultural Australia*. Brisbane: Multicultural Affairs Queensland.

Braybrooke, Marcus. 2007. *Interfaith witness in a changing world: The world congress of faiths, 1996–2006*. Abingdon: Braybrooke Press.

Brodeur, Patrice. 2005. From the margins to the centers of power: The increasing relevance of the global interfaith movement. *Cross Currents* 55(1): 42–53.

Brodeur, Patrice, and Eboo Patel. 2006. Introduction: Building the interfaith youth movement. In *Building the interfaith youth movement: Beyond dialogue to action*, ed. Patel Eboo and Brodeur Patrice, 1–14. Oxford: Rowman and Littlefield Publishers, Inc.

Cahill, Desmond, Gary D. Bouma, Dellal Hass, and Michael Leahy. 2004. *Religion, cultural diversity and safeguarding Australia*. Canberra: Department of Immigration, Multicultural and Indigenous Affairs.

Eck, Diana L. 2001. *A new religious America: How a "Christian Country" has become the world's most religiously diverse nation*. New York: HarperOne.

Ford, David F. 2006. An interfaith wisdom: Scriptural reasoning between Jews, Christians and Muslims. *Modern Theology* 22(3): 345–366.

Gopin, Marc. 2000. *Between Eden and Armageddon: The future of world religions, violence, and peacemaking*. Oxford: Oxford University Press.

Halafoff, Anna, and Conley Tyler Melissa. 2005. Rethinking religion: Transforming cultures of violence to cultures of peace. In *UNESCO Paris and International Outlook Conference, Religion in Peace and Conflict: Responding to Militancy and Fundamentalism*. UNESCO, Paris, 12–14 April 2005, pp. 365–371.

Halafoff, Anna, and David Wright-Neville. 2009. A missing peace? The role of religious actors in countering terrorism. *Studies of Conflict and Terrorism* 32(11): 921–932.

Huntington, Samuel P. 2003. *The clash of civilizations and the remaking of the world order*. London: Simon & Schuster.

Juergensmeyer, Mark. 2003. *Terror in the mind of god: The global rise of religious violence*, 3rd ed. Berkeley: University of California Press.

Kearns, Laurel. 2007. Cooking the truth: Faith, science, the market, and global warming. In *Ecospirit: Religions and philosophies for the earth*, ed. Laurel Kearns and Catherine Keller, 97–124. New York: Fordham University Press.

Kearns, Laurel, and Catherine Keller. 2007. Preface. In *Ecospirit: Religions and philosophies for the earth*, ed. Laurel Kearns and Catherine Keller, xi–xvi. New York: Fordham University Press.

Keller, Catherine, and Laurel Kearns. 2007. Introduction: Grounding theory – Earth in religion and philosophy. In *Ecospirit: Religions and philosophies for the earth*, ed. Laurel Kearns and Catherine Keller, 1–20. New York: Fordham University Press.

Kirkwood, Peter. 2007. *The quiet revolution: The emergence of interfaith consciousness*. Sydney: ABC Books.

Lentini, Pete. 2007. Countering terrorism as if Muslims matter: Cultural citizenship and civic pre-emption in anti-terrorism. In *Terrorism, organised crime and corruption: Networks and linkages*, ed. Leslie Holmes, 42–59. Cheltenham: Edward Elgar.

Lohre, Kathryn. 2007. Women's interfaith initiatives in the United States Post 9/11. *Interreligious Insight* 5(2): 11–23.

McCarthy, Kate. 2007. *Interfaith encounters in America*. Piscataway: Rutgers University Press.

National Council of Churches, Committee on Regional and Local Ecumenism. 1980. Survey of interfaith/inter-religious councils in the United States. [Online] Available at: http://www.nain.org/library/councils.htm.

Niebuhr, Gustav. 2008. *Beyond tolerance: Searching for interfaith understanding in America*. New York: Viking.

Parliament of World's Religions (PWR). 2009. Available at: http://www.parliamentofreligions.org/index.cfm?n=8&sn=5. Accessed 29 July 2011.

Patel, Eboo. 2007. *Acts of faith: The story of an American Muslim, the struggle for the soul of a generation*. Boston: Beacon.

Petrovsky, Vladimir. 2003. An interreligious council at the UN: UN charter possibilities and constraints. *International Journal on World Peace* XX(4): 49–57.

Pluralism Project. 2006. Resources by tradition: interfaith. The President and Fellows of Harvard College and Diana L. Eck, The Pluralism Project. [Online] Available at: http://www.pluralism.org/resources/tradition/index.php.

Rockefeller, Steven C. 1992. Faith and community in an ecological age. In *An interfaith dialogue, spirit and nature: Why the environment is a religious issue*, ed. Steven C. Rockefeller and John C. Elder, 139–172. Boston: Beacon.

Schmidt-Leukel, Perry. 2004. Part of the problem, part of the solution: An introduction. In *War and peace in world religions*, ed. Perry Schmidt-Leukel, 1–10. London: SCM Press.

Sheler, Jeff. 2001. US News and World Report. Panel participant, a new religious America: American Academy of Religion Annual Meeting, 23 November 2001.

Smock, David R. 2002. Introduction. In *Interfaith dialogue and peacebuilding*, ed. David R. Smock, 3–12. Washington, DC: United States Institute of Peace Press.

Smock, David R. 2006. Mediating between Christians and Muslims in Plateau State, Nigeria. In *Religious contributions to peacemaking: When religion brings peace, not war*, ed. David R. Smock, 17–20. Washington, DC: United States Institute of Peace.

Tippett, Krista. 2007. *Speaking of faith: Why religion matters – And how to talk about it.* New York: Penguin.

Tucker, Mary Evelyn. 2007. Ethics and ecology: A primary challenge of the dialogue of civilizations. In *Ecospirit: Religions and philosophies for the earth*, ed. Laurel Kearns and Catherine Keller, 495–503. New York: Fordham University Press.

Weller, Paul. 2008. *Religious diversity in the UK: Contours and issues*. London: Continuum.

Chapter 6
Benefits and Challenges of Multifaith Engagement

While the events of September 11 led to an increase in the number and activities of multifaith initiatives and multi-actor peacebuilding networks, there has been relatively little research regarding their effectiveness and their benefits for religious groups and broader society (Garfinkel 2004: 2; Tyndale quoted in Bharat and Bharat 2007: 275). Chapters 6 and 7 investigate the benefits and challenges of multifaith engagement by drawing on the small amount of previously published material and largely upon actor perspectives gathered specifically for this study. Following a cosmopolitan methodology, participants were encouraged to comment on these positive and difficult aspects with the aim of enhancing understanding of multifaith initiatives and also assisting state and non-state actors in the ongoing refinement of multifaith practices and policies, at local and global levels.

This chapter outlines the benefits of and the challenges faced by the multifaith movement as it engages in three of its principle aims: developing understanding of diverse faiths and of the nature of reality; challenging exclusivity and normalising pluralism; and creating multi-actor peacebuilding networks. The benefits and challenges faced when addressing global risks and injustices are discussed in more detail in Chap. 7.

Developing Understanding of Diverse Faiths and of the Nature of Reality

Many participants in this study described how multifaith initiatives increase opportunities for contact and communication among people of diverse faiths, thereby contributing to greater levels of understanding across faith communities <Saffour 2007, UK; Aly 2008, AUS; Cass 2008, UK; Dellal 2008, AUS; Pascoe 2008, AUS>. Ozalp <2008, AUS> explained how multifaith engagement enables a more authentic

A. Halafoff, *The Multifaith Movement: Global Risks and Cosmopolitan Solutions*,

DOI 10.1007/978-94-007-5210-8_6,

level of understanding to develop between faith traditions as representatives of religious communities share knowledge about themselves and their religions directly:

> … [in the past] we tended to explain other's faith[s] from our own frame of reference, this is a big problem. For example, Orientalists have been writing about Islam, now … they are outside observers sometimes very hostile, at the same time Muslims would view other religions very superficially as well, so one of the key initiatives that we [now] have is to find out about each other's faith … from the followers of that faith, how do they understand it …. Similarly I expect … that I should be given the chance to explain my own faith and we do get a lot of chances from schools, church groups, and so this is a very important aspect of interreligious dialogue, that we should see each other in their own frame of reference, and momentarily even get into that frame of reference in order to understand it, even if we disagree, even if we come out of it, and this is very important, in appreciation of the other. <Ozalp 2008, AUS>

These observations demonstrate that multifaith initiatives provide opportunities for people of diverse faiths to meet, to get to know one another and to learn about each other's religious traditions directly from representatives of religious communities themselves. In this way, multifaith initiatives can counter ignorance by developing understanding as described in more detail below. They also confirm that developing understanding of diverse faith traditions is a principle aim of the multifaith movement.

The Role of the Media

One of the greatest challenges that the multifaith movement faces is dealing with the media. The role of media in providing information to the general public places it in a powerful position to either promote or destroy positive relations between faith communities and broader society more generally <Aly 2008, AUS>. For example, the post–September 11 rise of fear and prejudice in Australia was attributed to the mainstream media's propagation of conservative political views during the Bush and Howard eras <Shaw 2007, AUS>. Nurah Amatullah <2007, USA>, Executive Director of the Muslim Women's Institute for Research and Development, described how the media in the USA undermined a sense of 'shared security' and the positive effects of multifaith and multi-actor peacebuilding networks by spreading a culture of fear:

> I think "shared security" is a good way to describe it; however … there's also a place of disconnect or disjuncture … in our human daily lives, in the places where we live, our neighbourhoods, our communities, this sense of shared security is real and there are efforts and projects and people who are engaged in operationalising this sense of shared security. And then you have this other place where the media and the global politicians, we can call them players on the international level, are involved in this perception shaping, which does not really give a sense of shared security, and is still very much operating on a kind of winner take all, I have the biggest bomb, I have the bigger state, so I will bludgeon you into agreement, and that gets operationalised or activated with fear. So even when I wake up and turn on the television … you live in this constant state of anxiety, with really no sense of security, because we all know in our hearts, bombing some place doesn't make me anymore secure. But then you are bombarded with all of these images and all of these messages and it's just

> so very contradictory to the very local efforts of community and co-existence and helping people regroup, recover from natural disasters and the trauma[tic impact] that they have on us, but then we are constantly traumatised by the media and the images that we see and the messages that are out there, and it is not easy to try to reconcile. <Amatullah 2007, USA>

According to Aly <2008, AUS>, ideally speaking, the media's role 'should be to facilitate the flow of clear, accurate information'. However, due to the largely irreligious orientation of journalists, especially in Australia, that is seldom the case pertaining to issues of religion, which generally receive poor coverage. In this way, Aly <2008, AUS> concurs with Amatullah <2007, USA> in asserting that the media has undermined the effectiveness of multifaith engagement:

> … mass media generally doesn't do religion very well. Journalists are … disproportionately atheistic or irreligious, more so than the general public, so they tend to treat religion with more scorn than perhaps their readers and viewers might generally and with far less understanding … [this] creates enormous difficulties for the interfaith worker … religious reporting is generally pretty bad, it occurs obviously in a political context, and in a grossly oversimplified context. And faith generally is treated as something that is not the domain of rational people … So from that perspective, I would say the media has been negative on interfaith relations … but as a forum, it's potentially very useful. <Aly 2008, AUS>

Krista Tippett <2007, USA>, broadcaster and author of *Speaking of Faith* at American Public Media, expressed similar views. While she had no doubt that multifaith and multi-actor peacebuilding activities are positive, she viewed the media's scepticism and tendency to produce largely superficial coverage and to concentrate on the negative and controversial aspects of religion as inhibiting its ability to accurately report on these initiatives. In her program *Speaking of Faith*, Tippett <2007, US> seeks to address this omission and, given the extra time she devotes to these issues, she is able to promote the benefits of multifaith and multi-actor networks to her audience as illustrated by her comments below:

> I just don't think there's any doubt that when people are coming together across distance and on the basis of their deepest values, the sources of truth and meaning in their lives, that is really powerful … that power is real, is felt in families and communities, and in academic disciplines, in fields of endeavour, it's felt in places of education and medicine and public health. I still think that there's an irony that those kinds of very positive, constructive options on the part of religious people are not going to make the news in the same way people who drop bombs make the news … the stereotype that's been on the rise in sceptical minds is that this is a kind of Pollyanna-ish stuff, off to the side of the real work, which is always hard and gritty and about conflict, so how do you change imaginations about the relevance of this kind of work? Because I have no doubt that the work is relevant but it's going to be able to be more influential the more it's recognised as such, and that's part of what I try to do is to bring out those voices and … the trouble is that in kind of sound-bite media and sound-bite culture there's not much space for anybody to express big important ideas with any kind of adequacy, so where I have the chance to do these in-depth interviews, that's a step in the right direction and convening conversations … that outward communication is … really important … to this kind of work having the effect that it should. <Tippett 2007, US>

Aly <2008, AUS> also described several benefits of working with the media, and of using the media as an 'extremely important' forum for countering fears and ignorance, as 'it gives you a much bigger platform' and has 'a much bigger impact' than do localised multifaith activities.

Local and global media are powerful modes of communication that have the ability to further both cosmopolitan and anti-cosmopolitan principles. The media can be used to spread fear and division and to promote the self-centred interests of anti-cosmopolitan movements, brutish states and market forces. Conversely, according to a cosmopolitan framework, the media, alongside intellectuals and religious leaders, can play a positive role in fostering understanding among diverse faiths and also by critiquing states and markets, thus contributing to common security. This is evidenced by the work of media actors such as Tippett and Aly. Unfortunately their calibre of journalism is a rare commodity in ultramodern times. These participants' views thus affirm the observations of scholars, community actors and participants (Bouma et al. 2007: 59–60; Lentini 2007: 56; Tippett 2007: 135–152); <Aly 2008, AUS; Hassan 2008, AUS> described in Chap. 5 which indicate that, while the media has been largely responsible for the propagation of fears and negative stereotypes pertaining to religious groups around the turn of the twenty-first century, it can also be used as a powerful peacebuilding tool by religious communities and public intellectuals to counter the negative impacts of crisis events.

Dispelling Misconceptions and Promoting the Peacebuilding Role of Religions

Participants described how, subsequent to the events of September 11, Muslim communities initiated or participated in multifaith initiatives as peacebuilding strategies to dispel misconceptions and fears about Muslims and Islam in Western societies <Woodlock 2008, AUS>, fears that had been largely created by the media <Hassan 2008, AUS>. Consequently, multifaith initiatives were implemented to break down barriers <Marshall 2007, USA; Aly 2008, AUS> and to build bridges between communities in their stead <Voll 2007, USA; Dellal 2008, AUS>. As stated in Chap. 2, according to a Habermasian (2007: 15–16, 18) framework, disruptions in communication can lead to mutual mistrust and communication breakdowns. It follows that multifaith initiatives, which established relationships between Muslims and other religious and non-religious groups, created the possibility for 'mutual understanding' to begin to be developed between previously divided communities in the wake of this crisis event.

Participants recounted how Muslim leaders utilised multifaith initiatives as platforms to separate themselves from terrorists <Mogra 2007, UK> and to affirm their commitment to principles of non-violence <Ramey 2007, USA>. According to Amal Saffour <2007, UK>, a Muslim youth worker at King's College London, multifaith initiatives were implemented to 'dispel the myths that surround Islam' and Muslims in the wake of September 11 and also the London bombings. In this way, Ozalp <2008, AUS> explained how multifaith engagement provided an opportunity to prevent 'generalisations … for the Western world [that] all Muslims are potential terrorists, [and] in the Muslim world [that] the whole Western world is out to get them … generalisations that really do not serve anything for peace'. As Hassan <2008, AUS> stated, 'people only fear the unknown', and multifaith engagement provided an effective strategy for 'normalising Muslims' in the broader community, which had previously had little contact with Muslims:

> Most of the people that I'm presenting to have never met a Muslim before, the only Muslims they have met or the only Muslims they are familiar with are those on the television, the most extreme examples. So it's just a matter of normalising Muslims, of people being able to see Muslims in a normal light, that they meet me, I'm a teacher, my husband's a doctor, I talk about just everyday experiences and not just about my religion—I talk about the football team that I barrack for … it's about dispelling misconceptions and myths … [it's] about normalising Muslims … <Hassan 2008, AUS>

Ficca <2007, USA> similarly described how, through increased contact, multifaith engagement provides 'positive experience of difference' and thereby humanises 'the other' <Ficca 2007, US>. In this regard, Ozalp <2008, AUS> stated that 'we tend to dehumanise issues and matters, and … when we meet at interfaith dialogue we realise our humanity above all, so we are all human beings, we are not just this scary monster that is sometimes portrayed'.

In addition, Mogra <2007, UK> and Woodlock <2008, AUS> explained how public affirmations of friendship and collaboration between religious communities could assist in diminishing negative stereotypes pertaining to religion, instead affirming its peacebuilding role in the wider community:

> … non-religious society always felt that the problems of the world are because these religions can't get along, they don't see eye to eye and they are always fighting and causing these wars. What the religious communities can now demonstrate is, look, we are friends, we can live together, we agree to disagree and we can do things together … so that's another benefit where wider society can begin to regard religion as an asset rather than a liability, where they see the positive contributions of religious communities to society as a whole and I think it will make life for religious people easier and better, because we become part and parcel, an accepted component of society. <Mogra 2007, UK>

> … when you are told that religion is the cause of problems in the world … it gives you a sense of satisfaction that you're doing something different, that this isn't true for you and your experiences, that your religious practice is not about violence it's about peacebuilding and about connecting with other human beings … <Woodlock 2008, AUS>

These actor perspectives reveal that multifaith initiatives can dispel misconceptions and fears, and act as peacebuilding strategies following crisis events by assisting in normalising and humanising the so-called 'other'. As described in Chaps. 4 and 5, during the 1990s and especially in the wake of September 11, as 'othering' shifted to Muslim communities, multifaith initiatives provided opportunities not only to develop a greater understanding of Islam and Muslims but also to show that the majority of Muslims condemned these violent attacks. The multifaith movement proved that different religions were capable of uniting for peace, thereby challenging the prevalent view propagated in the popular media at that time that religions, and Islam in particular, were exclusively sources of violence. Consequently, the multifaith movement enabled a greater understanding of the peacebuilding potential of religion in the ultramodern public sphere.

Networks of Trust

Participants also described how connections forged through multifaith engagement enable relationships to deepen, building genuine foundations for understanding and future collaboration <Mogra 2007, UK>. According to Ozalp <2008, AUS>:

> … as … we get in touch and talk to people on a sustained basis, we see that certain relationships build, develop, and people tend to accept and tolerate each other more, people say that tolerance is not a good word, but … we do need tolerance to begin with, religious dialogue starts with tolerance, then it moves on to the relationship phase and from then you move on to the cooperation phase, so the benefits are that people can deal with problems in a much more constructive way. <Ozalp 2008, AUS>

Many participants recounted how networks of trust established among communities through multifaith engagement after September 11 assisted in times of subsequent crises <Gibbs 2007, USA; Mogra 2007, UK; Pearce 2007, UK; Cass 2008, UK; Ozalp 2008, AUS>. Mogra <2007, UK> recalled how this was particularly evident following the London bombings:

> … in Leicester … immediately after the July bombings, within a few days we had a rally, a peace rally in one of the large parks which was attended by all the faith communities … everyone was standing shoulder to shoulder and each speaker, one after another, acknowledged that Muslims, the vast majority of Muslims in this country, are peace-loving, law-abiding citizens. I don't think that could have happened if we did not have this interfaith engagement, that because we've had this engagement people know us, they know our track record, they were able to say it without any hesitation because they knew it for a fact. If they didn't know it, they would have been hesitant, so it has proven to be a very, very beneficial thing. <Mogra 2007, UK>

In addition, Marshall <2007, USA> explained how the success of these established networks in responding quickly to new crisis events provides evidence of the value of multifaith engagement:

> Personally, I'm very convinced that [multifaith engagement is] important, because what you're doing is establishing relationships among improbable groups, and particularly when you know there are tensions, it's very clear that later, when the time comes, it's much easier to call somebody whose email you have and whose telephone you have and that you know who they are, and that you can reach out to them. <Marshall 2007, USA>

These actor perspectives demonstrate that multifaith initiatives create networks among people of faith that foster trust and understanding between them. They also provide further evidence of the effectiveness of such networks of trust that are well poised to respond to crisis events and to provide support for faith communities in times of crisis (Eck 2001: 373), in this case after September 11 and the London bombings.

According to these actor accounts, the multifaith movement and multi-actor peacebuilding networks develop understanding of diverse faiths and the nature of reality through communicative and dialogical processes. By developing 'mutual understanding' through 'multiple perspective taking' (Habermas 2007: 18) multi-faith initiatives provide opportunities to dispel negative stereotypes and misconceptions about diverse faith traditions Moreover, multifaith initiatives provide opportunities for understanding the struggles of one's dialogue partners by seeing them through their eyes (Benhabib 2002b: 44 citing Benhabib 2002a). This awareness can thereby lead to addressing the underlying causes of conflicts thereby countering them more effectively (Habermas 2007: 18). The need to develop greater understanding—of diverse faiths, of the underlying causes of conflicts and of the nature of reality—is a central tenet of both the multifaith movement and ultramodern cosmopolitan theories as they strive to create genuinely peaceful societies.

Challenging Exclusivity and Normalising Pluralism

Many participants explained how normalising religious pluralism through multifaith engagement can assist in countering alienation and radicalisation in ultramodern societies. Chapters 1 and 5 described how, subsequent to the events of September 11 and the London bombings, multifaith initiatives began to be implemented in the form of countering violent extremism strategies in Western societies. However, despite the dramatic increase in state funding for multifaith engagement there remains very little understanding of precisely how multifaith initiatives contribute to countering alienation and radicalisation (Halafoff and Wright-Neville 2009). Several participants in this study outlined ways in which multifaith engagement assists in addressing the global risk of terrorism. Firstly, public multifaith peacebuilding alliances can raise the profile of non-violent religious leaders thereby potentially reducing the influence of religious leaders who promote violent ideologies <Toh 2008, AUS>. Following a similar argument, Patel <2007, USA> explained how normalising religious pluralism contributes to marginalising extremist agendas, with particular reference to September 11:

> … one very clear thing that 9/11 did was to say, if you're not building religious pluralism then you forfeit the world to the people who are dealing with religion and a lot of them are religious extremists … the landscape is shifting so if you're not putting your idea in the culture, you just forfeit that space to other people … when you expand it, when you create a pattern, a normal pattern of positive interfaith relations, then you dramatically marginalise other ideas. Here's the problem right now, that the landscape of religious relations is undefined so it is not ok for black people and white people to hate each other. It's not ok, that's defined, right. It's not ok for French and Germans to hate each other, so if you're a French person that hates Germans, you're a misfit. Because there is a defined good, and there's a pattern of that. Right now the best that we do as people from different religions on earth is that we ignore each other and if there's a vacuum, if there is no defined good, then don't be surprised if someone comes around and injects a definition which is bad. So part of what we're trying to do is be proactive and intentional about what is good between people from different religions that's the vision, then you have to give people activities and language with which to do that and then you have to move that into something that can become a pattern … <Patel 2007, USA>

According to Ficca <2007, USA> multifaith engagement provides opportunities for contact and for greater understanding to develop across diverse faith communities, thereby reducing feelings of alienation:

> … in that the conditions that might lead people to resort to terrorism are conditions … of alienation, or that their plight in oppression, a sense of poverty they might feel, is a result of the rest of the world not knowing them, to the degree that the interreligious movement can reach out, can make contact, might lessen the conditions. <Ficca 2007, USA>

Several participants also described how multifaith initiatives provide a forum that allows people from diverse communities to voice their concerns <Hassan 2008; AUS>, to ask and answer questions <Dellal 2008, AUS> and to air their grievances in a non-violent way <Hassan 2008, AUS; Ozalp 2008, AUS>. Ozalp <2008, AUS> explained how such forums can thus assist in countering processes of violent radicalisation:

> … it allows people a platform to be listened to, hence the feeling of being understood, even if people disagree with what you have to say, you get the feeling that I did have an opportunity to talk about my views … this is very important, the feeling of being understood and being acknowledged sometimes … for instance, Muslim communities feel under scrutiny in Australia, from politicians, media and the public through talkback radio, if they have no outlet, this [is] what gives way to radicalism and eventually violence, so interfaith dialogue provides that outlet… <Ozalp 2008, AUS>

These actor perspectives offer much-needed evidence of how multifaith initiatives have contributed to countering the risk of terrorism. By normalising religious pluralism, they have contributed to creating an inclusive society, in which all groups are respected and their religious needs recognised, thereby minimising the risk of alienation. By enabling deliberative democratic processes, they have encouraged religious actors to express their concerns and to play a non-violent critical role in the public sphere. Finally, by highlighting the capacity of faith traditions to cooperate in response to common crises, they have challenged cultures of violence and exclusivity within their own traditions and raised the public profile of religious peacebuilders, thus reducing the influence of religious extremists. The nexus between multifaith initiatives and countering radicalisation is further explained in the final chapter.

Multifaith Youth Engagement

The multifaith movement has been criticised for lacking participation by women and youth (Bharat and Bharat 2007: 7, 287; Tyndale quoted in Bharat and Bharat 2007: 276). However, as described in the previous chapter, since the events of September 11, and in particular the London bombings, there has been a dramatic increase in multifaith youth initiatives in the USA, the UK and Australia (Brodeur and Patel 2006: 4; Bharat and Bharat 2007: 190; Patel 2007); <Epstein 2007, US; Mogra 2007, UK; Dellal 2008, AUS> and in women's multifaith networks (Lohre 2007: 11); <Lacey 2008, AUS; Murdoch 2008, UK>.

According to Penn <2007, USA>, young people can play a prominent role as 'change makers' in ultramodern societies as they have a lot of energy and enthusiasm to bring to multifaith initiatives. Young <2008, AUS> also explained how, as her generation have grown up with an understanding of global interdependence and responsibility, they are well placed to collaboratively address common issues with older generations:

> Growing up in this day and age you're bombarded with that straight away, we are one world, it's a small world, so right from the start we knew that everyone was connected … we're all one, we're all one family, all part of the earth, we're all elements of creation …

> growing up in the last few decades, you just have a completely different perspective on life because you grow up through school with an awareness of the whole world, not just an awareness of your own little town or even just your own country … <Young 2008, AUS>

Young <2008, AUS> added that youth are innovators and need to be given ownership over projects and the ability to grow the movement in ways they think are important and not have initiatives imposed upon them by others:

> … we've got to allow that we can work with [older people] and they can work with us and also especially when its youth-led things that come from our ideas rather than someone saying here's a plan, we'll have young people fill it. If it's something that we've come up with … we'll own it a lot more. <Young 2008, AUS>

The importance of providing young people in a networked age with skills to set up their own multifaith initiatives was also affirmed by Patel <2007, USA> below:

> Did anybody ever say from the podium [at the 2007 Interfaith Youth Core Conference] "you have to join this"? No, right, did anybody ever say "you have to start an Interfaith Youth Core chapter", "you have to organise your work like this"? No, right, what we are trying to do is to harness a Google-based world, which is a world that is based on networks and activities. So what we do at the Interfaith Youth Core is we provide … usually you'll hear people say … "thank you for the language", ok. And we say … storytelling is important, so you know what, tell your story. Everything that we do is meant to encourage your participation. Interfaith service projects are important, so run an interfaith service project and we'll hold it up, you see what I'm saying? … What do they do? They are part of activities. Well how do you move them along? Well you say instead of being a part of an activity, you organise an activity. You see what I'm saying? … You also have to have a model where you are resourcing people with language, with a vision, with activities that they can do on their own and then you are making them feel like part of something bigger. That's the work, that's the model that we do, and … this is part of the architecture of 21st century civil society… <Patel 2007, USA>

As Freeman Trebilcock <2008, AUS>, Secretary of Loving Kindness, Peaceful Youth (LKPY), explained, youth involved in multifaith initiatives have a vital role to play in normalising pluralism, in prioritising global responsibility and in affirming the need to draw on religious and spiritual wisdom to create more harmonious and sustainable societies:

> … the role of young people is really, really vital because, as Eboo Patel says, we're changing the normal ideas, what's normal, and we're changing the attitude, it's a movement of ideas … if there's going to be a radical change, in a short period of time … it has to come from the young people … <Trebilcock 2008, AUS>

In addition, Trebilcock <2008, AUS> described how the multifaith movement, by promoting a positive peacebuilding image of religion, 'represents a little bit of hope' to young people who see religious violence as hypocritical and have thereby lost trust in religious institutions.

Multifaith projects, focused on common action for the common good, many of which have an environmental focus, were also viewed as highly effective in developing connections and friendships, especially among young people of diverse faith communities <Cass 2008, UK>. According to Woodlock <2008, AUS>:

> … an environmental project might help young Muslims, Jews, Christians, Buddhists … get together and have an interfaith connection in a non-threatening environment, because if

> you're doing something like trying to plant trees or clean up a river system or whatever you are not there with your faith on your sleeve. You're there as a responsible Jew or a responsible Muslim trying to make the world better for everyone, and then if you are doing that alongside fellow Jews and Christians and Muslims and you're making friendships, and you are building connections … <Woodlock 2008, AUS>

These actor accounts reveal that young people are playing an increasingly prominent role in the multifaith movement and that these initiatives are most effective when they are led and implemented by young people themselves. Having grown up in multifaith societies in a globalised world, young people are in an ideal position to play an important role in normalising pluralism and in spreading an awareness of interdependence and global responsibility in ultramodern societies. Multifaith engagement among young people provides opportunities for increased contact and to form friendships, thereby building mutual understanding among previously divided communities. Youth-led multifaith initiatives focused on both local and global concerns have the added benefit of empowering young people to have a critical voice and to take non-violent action to effect social change. In this way they can provide alternatives to extremist movements that advocate violent processes and feed off feelings of alienation. Finally, by countering alienation through social inclusion and encouraging young people from diverse faith traditions to play a non-violent critical role in deliberative forms of governance, multifaith youth initiatives contribute to building genuinely peaceful societies. It is encouraging to note that youth played a prominent role at the 2009 Melbourne Parliament of the World's Religions (PWR 2009), and that with the assistance of the Interfaith Youth Core (IFYC), Australia now has a multifaith youth movement embodied in a new grass-roots, multifaith youth organisation InterAction (2009).

The Need to be More Inclusive

While the multifaith movement has been criticised for being predominantly led by Westerners, Christians and men (Bharat and Bharat 2007: 7, 287; Tyndale quoted in Bharat and Bharat 2007: 276) and for excluding New Religious Movements and Pagan traditions (Bharat and Bharat 2007: 47, 50), participants in this study did not raise many of these issues. Participants were more concerned that Hindu, Buddhist and Indigenous religions and spiritualities, which had previously played a major role in multifaith engagement in the 1980s and 1990s, had been sidelined by the events of September 11 <Kirby 2007, USA; Woodlock 2008, AUS>. These concerns echoed the views of John D'Arcy May (quoted in Bharat and Bharat 2007: 122), who has noted the exclusion of Hindu and Buddhist communities from twenty-first century multifaith initiatives in particular. Several participants explained how, after September 11, the emphasis of multifaith engagement had narrowed to be primarily focused on the Abrahamic faiths, and on Jewish, Christian and Muslim relations. Woodlock <2008, AUS> mentioned that while it was encouraging to see Muslim communities take a prominent role in multifaith initiatives alongside Christian and

Jewish traditions, there was a need to broaden the engagement to include Hindu and Buddhist religions, Indigenous spiritualities and New Religious Movements. Kirby <2007, USA> echoed these sentiments below:

> … with all of this emphasis on Christian, Muslim and Jewish understanding, among the Abrahamic traditions, I think we risk losing the richness of the Asian traditions, we risk ignoring the very peacemaking basis of Ahimsa, and of what the Asian traditions have to offer us … And the Indigenous religions … unity is at the heart of the Asian traditions … that's the risk of where we are now, focusing on security. <Kirby 2007, USA>

However, Shashoua <2008, UK> remarked that while multifaith engagement since September 11 'hasn't been on an even footing', more recently it was 'coming more to a level playing field' by becoming more inclusive of multiple faith traditions. Furthermore, as the multifaith movement was originally focused on bringing together religious groups, it did not set out to include humanists, atheists and agnostics. However, several participants described how recently there have been calls for the multifaith community to 'consciously … reach out' to non-religious people and communities <Epstein 2007, USA> and to include them in multifaith initiatives <Dubensky 2007, USA; Shaw 2007, AUS>.

These actor perspectives demonstrate that, following the events of September 11, 2001, multifaith engagement focused largely on Jewish–Christian–Muslim relations at the exclusion of Indigenous, Hindu and Buddhist traditions which had previously played a central role in multifaith initiatives. The participants' accounts also indicate that, according to cosmopolitan principles, multifaith engagement should strive to be inclusive of all diverse faiths and spiritualities, including Indigenous, Pagan, Hindu, Buddhist, Sikh, Jewish, Christian, Muslim and New Religious Movements (NRMs). In addition, non-religious communities should also be encouraged to participate in multifaith activities, particularly as very few multifaith initiatives have previously included these communities (Lentini et al. 2009: 7).

The Melbourne PWR welcomed people of all faiths and no faith, including the so-called major religious traditions, Pagans, Indigenous spiritualities, NRMs, humanists and atheists. This indicates that in recent years, especially as the global risk of climate change has eclipsed that of terrorism, the post–September 11 focus on Abrahamic traditions in multifaith initiatives has shifted to a more genuinely inclusive spirit of multifaith engagement, drawing upon the wisdom of all faith and humanist traditions to address common environmental crises.

Creating Multi-actor Networks for Common Security

While many participants in this study described the benefits of multifaith engagement and multi-actor peacebuilding networks, several scholars and multifaith practitioners have raised concerns over whether faith-based actors have been able to retain their independence in partnerships with state actors and over disparities in power relations between faith-based and non-faith-based actors in the twenty-first century. The implications of this new proximity between governments and faith communities, and also between faith communities and global organisations, need to be further analysed (Bharat and Bharat 2007: 8, 40–42; Pearce quoted in Bharat and Bharat 2007: 245–246; Muzaffar quoted in Bharat and Bharat 2007: 274). Anti-religious secularists have also protested against the increased influence of religion in the ultramodern public sphere (Pearce quoted in Bharat and Bharat 2007: 245–246). A rise in attacks against religions by secularists and atheists at the turn of the twenty-first century also poses new challenges for the multifaith movement (Braybrooke 2007: 1).

Participants expressed a wide range of responses regarding the increased engagement between religious and state actors, following September 11 and the London bombings. In Australia, where multifaith initiatives have been implemented as part of preventive counter-radicalisation strategies, several participants praised the rise of state interest and support of multifaith engagement, as illustrated by Ozalp's <2008, AUS> and Woodlock's <2008, AUS> comments below:

> I really think that if the Australian Government sees radicalism as a potential security problem, they do need to invest in initiatives, preventive initiatives rather than just legal and policing. I am aware that billions of dollars are being spent on this in terms of upgrading of police force, army and so on, and if a certain amount of money is spent on promoting interfaith activities that's welcome. <Ozalp 2008, AUS>

> … I am quite keen for these partnerships to be explored, because it also gives religious people a sense that they're being listened to, that they can contribute, and I do believe that where religious communities are marginalised that's where you get vulnerability to radicalisation and extremism, because they feel like they are not being listened to, they feel like they've got no place in the society, so I am really quite keen for that to happen. <Woodlock 2008, AUS>

An increase in state involvement in and support of multifaith initiatives as peace-building strategies was viewed as a positive development <Toh 2008, AUS>. These actor perspectives provide evidence that as multifaith initiatives in Australia are perceived as positive strategies to counter extremism and promote common security, state support of these initiatives has been largely welcomed.

In addition, many participants in Australia and the UK felt that the primary role of partnerships between religious and state actors was for religious representatives to act as advisors on issues that were of concern to their communities. However, while collaboration between state and religious actors in Australia and the UK has no doubt increased in recent years, participants questioned just how deliberative the role played by religious actors has been in the public sphere. Participants raised concerns regarding the preparedness of state actors to engage with communities that did not agree with them <Braybrooke 2007, UK>, and questioned whether governments are willing to listen to challenging opinions <Dupuche 2008, AUS>. While one participant in Australia was in favour of multifaith councils acting as advisory bodies to governments <Jones 2008, AUS>, another was suspicious of government-appointed, and thereby government-controlled, multifaith advisory bodies <Lacey 2008, AUS>. UK participants also stated that ideally religious communities should play a role in advising government, especially as religion is increasingly playing a role in people's lives and in politics <Shashoua 2008, UK>, citing the Faith

Communities Consultative Council at the national level as an example of how religious communities have recently fulfilled this role in the UK <Pearce 2007, UK>. Mogra <2007, UK> believed that, as a result of increased consultation between state bodies and religious communities, these communities felt that their needs were being heard and met, which in turn gave more credibility to the state in the eyes of religious persons:

> We are asked, we are engaged with, they want to know what the religious rulings are and then accordingly they will produce the policies and then introduce the law … This is brilliant, it gives confidence to the religious communities, it gives the government more credibility that this is a government that listens, so it benefits all sides. <Mogra 2007, UK>

Moreover, alliances among faith communities on issues of common concern had produced changes in government policy:

> … for example, the requirement for non-stunned halal meat, we get a lot of support from the Jewish community, with circumcision services the Muslims and Jews join hands, early burial, the need for non-intrusive post-mortems and autopsies we support one another, the need for faith schools, Christians, Muslims, we all support each other. Recently I supported the establishment of a Sikh school in the Midlands, so this is the mutual benefit that we all get from these interfaith activities and we are very quick to lend support to any of the projects or activities of the other groups. <Mogra 2007, UK>

These comments positively describe the results of collaboration between religious actors on state policies. However, they also raise some disturbing concerns regarding the potential of multifaith alliances to join forces on controversial issues that can be perceived as contravening rights, in this case circumcision of children and non-stunned killings of animals, for the sake of maintaining religious traditions. Scholars have recently raised similar concerns over the rise of conservative religious groups seeking to reshape policies according to religious beliefs, especially regarding abortion and homosexuality (Bouma 2006: 197; McCarthy 2007: 57). Indeed, Shashoua <2008, UK> stated, 'I don't want … the government to bend down to every whim that religious groups say' as it is necessary to 'keep a certain structure' for 'the sake of the entirety' that 'might upset some people' but maintains a common good. Landau <2008, AUS> similarly remarked that there should be a place for religious voices in the democratic process, but that the state has a responsibility to act as an ethical mediator to moderate exclusive religious discourses and practices that contravene the rights of others:

> … if the religious interests are representative of communities, real people, then it seems kind of even pragmatic for them to have real involvement so that they're not marginalised … but I also think that it's good that … it comes from an overriding policy perspective beyond just the perspectives of the communities that meet their own will … So … first I started off by saying that it's democratic to actually have the religious voices but then maybe the other side of it is … the state [needs] to … mediate … [the] way that … religious knowledge is practised … <Landau 2008, AUS>

Participants from the USA exhibited a much higher level of mistrust of increased state involvement in multifaith engagement than did participants from the UK and Australia <Breyer 2007, USA; Voll 2007, USA>. According to Breyer <2007, USA>, religions must preserve their traditional role as critic of the state. She raised concerns that by relying on or even accepting government funding religious communities are at risk of being co-opted by states and in danger of losing their autonomy:

> … there is a slight danger … as [the multifaith movement] becomes more mainstream, as there is more government funding there's the risk of being co-opted, obviously and becoming a, religious leaders being a mouthpiece for a political agenda … the prophetic stance and one that challenges a lot of the powers that be, is perhaps where we're most true to the initial visioning of the [USA's] founders as it were. So preserving that tension is a really important one, and you saw the early, in Jewish and Christian traditions that was really the role of the early prophets was to critique the kings and in a democratic society it works a little differently but I think we're, religious traditions are really important in preserving that. <Breyer 2007, USA>

Participants in Australia and the USA also voiced concerns that increased governmental support of multifaith initiatives could lead to competition, rather than a culture of cooperation in response to common issues among religious and multifaith groups <Breyer 2007, USA; Aly 2008, AUS>. As Breyer <2007, USA> explained below:

> … religions start to fight with each other if they're competing for government resources, well you can see that would also, could happen between interfaith organisations as well, that any time you have large amounts of money thrown at something, particularly with, if they come from the US Government, you then have competing political agendas to get that money, and that's always the risk that comes with it. <Breyer 2007, USA>

A new emphasis on social cohesion and countering extremism has lifted the profile of and given new legitimacy to the multifaith movement, however these actor perspectives demonstrate that while there is an appreciation of increased state support, especially in Australia and the UK, there are also mounting concerns emerging from the USA and Australia that by accepting state funding and support religious actors risk compromising their critical voice in the public sphere. The participants' observations also provide evidence that while religious organisations and multifaith advisory councils offer advice to states that, according to cosmopolitan principles, can assist in developing and refining policies, in as much as it is important for religions to maintain their critical role in the public sphere, they too need to be made accountable to common laws and to respecting the rights of others. While several states grant exemptions to religious groups, in the name of freedom of religion, the findings of this study align with cosmopolitan principles that stipulate that religious individuals and communities have a right to exert their influence in the deliberative public sphere alongside other citizens and groups, conditional on the principle that they respect the rights and freedoms of others (Habermas 2005: 27–28). Thus, religions should not be allowed to gain too much influence at the expense of others' rights, while at the same time the critical voices of religions should not be silenced in order to appease state interests. Participants' accounts demonstrate that deliberative forms of democracy that encourage multifaith voices to have input into devising and revising policies, while respecting the common good that these laws and rights intend to protect, can thus enable both the state and religious organisations to participate in collaborative mutually beneficial processes.

In addition, in the UK the main concern regarding increased state involvement in multifaith activities was that an emphasis on community cohesion and countering extremism risked overriding the original spiritual imperatives behind multifaith engagement <Braybrooke 2007, UK; Pearce 2007, UK>. According to Braybrooke <2007, UK>:

> … my worry is that the sort of interfaith dialogue which is concerned with theology and questions of true spiritual meeting is slightly being downplayed … sometimes what I think we are now into is trying to build up good inter-community relations … I suppose my own real commitment to the dialogue is that I believe by sharing our understandings we actually grow in our understanding of the divine, so it is a spiritual connection … the money has gone into naturally what governments, [think will] … produce some fairly immediate benefits … <Braybrooke 2007, UK>

Similarly, Pearce <2007, UK> stated that communities have long engaged in multifaith initiatives for their own benefit, not as instruments of social policy, and while 'obviously interfaith work may be of relevance and may contribute towards the preventing violent extremist agenda' it was important to remember that this was 'only a strand within a much broader [multifaith] agenda':

> … it's very important not to lose sight of the significance of interfaith work for faith communities themselves. In other words, it's not simply an activity being carried out in order to fulfil some government agenda because of course interfaith engagement goes back a long way before government took any interest in it from a community cohesion perspective … in that context, particularly in the monastic encounter, and … it's very important that we don't get into a situation where interfaith work is seen as being purely kind of instrumental in terms of social policy issues. <Pearce 2007, UK>

Dupuche <2008, AUS> also stated that, in Australia, encountering different religious viewpoints through multifaith engagement remains an inherently interesting and valuable exercise for personal spiritual development, regardless of any crisis event.

Finally, Laing <2007, UK> described how, since September 11 and the London bombings, multifaith engagement has 'become a craze, it's fashionable', and argued that while there are benefits of partnerships between religious and state actors there was also a danger that as a result of these 'knee-jerk responses', multifaith engagement was being somewhat 'dumbed down':

> … there are so many people looking for quick-fix solutions, they get government funding for a year to deliver a program on interfaith, you can't teach stuff about interfaith in a year because it takes a long time, it's a relational subject that needs really long, careful relationship building. <Laing 2007, UK>

According to these actor perspectives the post–September 11 shift in focus towards countering the risk of terrorism—as evidenced by increased interest in and support of multifaith initiatives by state actors—has overlooked the original imperative of multifaith initiatives, namely to deepen understanding of diverse faiths and of the nature of reality. Following this argument, the real value of multifaith engagement is in danger of being subsumed by the security agenda of state actors, many of whom are unaware of the long history of the movement and the central role that theological and philosophical principles play in informing action for common security.

Local and Global Engagement: Maintaining Connection with the Grassroots

Many participants confirmed Brodeur's (2005: 43) assertion that the multifaith movement is 'glocal in nature', that is, focused at once on local and global issues. They also raised some concerns regarding the bifocal nature of multifaith engagement. Several participants noted that while it is important for multifaith and multi-actor peacebuilding networks to prioritise global issues, it is crucial to simultaneously maintain a local focus and not to lose sight of their commitment to working at the grassroots level <Jafari 2007, USA; Ficca 2007, USA; Gibbs 2007, USA; Saffour 2007, UK>. Sheherazade Jafari <2007, USA>, Assistant Program Director of Religion and Conflict Resolution at the Tanenbaum Centre for Interreligious Understanding, stressed that ideally religious peacebuilders working at the grassroots level should also be the religious actors at 'global governance, diplomacy tables'. Ficca <2007, USA> similarly stated that it was vital that religious peacebuilders who are heading up high-level dialogues, initiatives or organisations have spent significant amounts of time working at the grassroots level and that they maintain this commitment, regardless of the context in which they find themselves working. For example, working at the grassroots level in Australia is not the same as working at the grassroots level in Indonesia; therefore, grassroots experience in one context does not necessarily easily translate to another, so there is always the need to develop local expertise and understanding in multifaith engagement. In addition, Gibbs <2007, USA> cautioned against the building of 'high-level structures' which have the capacity to 'recapitulate … domination systems' and inflate the egos of religious leaders. He suggested that effective multifaith and multi-actor peacebuilding networks must instead prioritise time and resources toward building relationships at the grassroots level.

Vendley <2007, USA> and Cass <2008, UK> also spoke of the importance of working across the local, national and global levels concurrently:

> … the opportunity to work simultaneously at local, national, regional and global levels, that's terribly useful for two reasons. One because so many problems are simultaneously local, through national, regional and global in dimension and scope, and secondly, and perhaps more foundationally, religions are present locally, nationally, regionally and globally and so they need mechanisms to collaborate at precisely those same levels. <Vendley 2007, USA>

> [What is needed is] a recognition from global players, national players, that the key interactions are the local interactions, that global geopolitical events [and] trends have an impact on local communities but that … communities are local and the problems, the solutions to problems that local communities face are within those communities, so it's joining up all those levels … <Cass 2008, UK>

As described in previous chapters, the multifaith movement is made up of many diverse components that act in different ways at different levels. These components include: religious organisations headed by religious leaders; faith-based service organisations; faith-based women's organisations; faith-based youth organisations;

local and global multifaith organisations; state-appointed multifaith councils and committees; and multi-actor peacebuilding organisations and networks. While some participants stressed the need for religious peacebuilders to maintain connection to the grassroots level and that religious community leaders with extensive grassroots experience could often provide greater insight than could heads of faith traditions, others affirmed the importance of working simultaneously at all levels. This multi-levelled model aligns with ultramodern cosmopolitan principles that no longer pit grassroots actors against state actors, but rather stress the benefits of collaboration across diverse sectors.

Lack of Resources, Evaluation and Evidence of Efficacy

A common difficulty facing multifaith organisations is that they are often poorly resourced (Wuthnow 2005: 301). Many participants described how, after September 11, multifaith and religious organisations experienced increasing demands for engagement which exceeded their capacity <Dubensky 2007, USA; Ficca 2007, US; Blundell 2008, AUS; Cass 2008, UK>. This was especially evident within Muslim communities, which had suddenly become the focus of multifaith engagement and were often largely dependent on volunteers <Hassan 2008, USA; Kearns 2008, USA>. In addition, several participants stated that multifaith youth initiatives in particular required additional support in the form of resources and encouragement <Mogra 2007, UK; Saffour 2007, UK; Cass 2008, UK>. According to Cass <2008, UK>:

> … it's just a slog … a drop in the ocean … though we can talk about ripple effects and changing attitudes within their own peer groups … We did some research on the value of the interactions that we were putting these young people through and undoubtedly there was an effect during the course of the program, whether it sustained over a period of time, we'll have to go back and do some follow-up research, but … even if it does make a difference it's still only 20 people a go and I'm a bit of a cynic in that for an interaction to be meaningful it needs to be more than just a woman's group from the local church going to visit the Hindu [temple] … there needs to be a connection at some kind of level, an emotional engagement with one another, and that requires time and it requires money and it requires confidence, a lot of which is missing. <Cass 2008, UK>

Several participants also explained that because multifaith initiatives do not necessarily produce immediate benefits <Marshall 2007, USA; Ramey 2007, USA; Ozalp 2008, AUS> it can be difficult to measure their efficacy and thereby justify increased funding <Marshall 2007, USA>. These actor perspectives affirm Wuthnow's (2005: 301) claim that a lack of resources is one of the most significant challenges facing the ultramodern multifaith movement. These comments also indicate that multifaith initiatives require additional capacity-building support and that more research into the efficacy of multifaith initiatives is required, particularly in the form of longitudinal studies.

Conclusions

These participant accounts demonstrate how, since the events of September 11, by providing opportunities for greater contact and communication, multifaith networks have contributed to developing understanding and trust between previously divided and in some cases isolated communities, across faith traditions and sectarian lines. As a result, they have proved effective in dispelling common misperceptions and fears, and countering ignorance through educative and communicative processes. In this way underlying causes of conflicts can be addressed, preventing conflicts from reoccurring in the future. The need to develop greater understanding—of diverse faiths and of the underlying causes of conflicts—is a central tenet of both the multifaith movement and ultramodern cosmopolitan theories, particularly Habermas's (1984, 1987, 2006) *Theory of Communicative Action* and Benhabib's (1992b, 2004, 2007: 455) 'discourse ethic'.

In addition, by normalising and promoting pluralism, multifaith engagement sends a valuable message to society that all religious traditions are welcome in multifaith societies, provided that they abide by the law, thereby concurrently affirming cosmopolitan principles and countering processes of alienation. Peacebuilding alliances, through which religious leaders publicly denounce violence committed in the name of religion and affirm the peacebuilding principles of their religious traditions, can also assist in lessening the stronghold of extremist ideologies and leaders. In so doing, extremist agendas are marginalised and thereby lose traction in societies that genuinely respect diversity and the rights of all people. Youth-led multifaith initiatives have played an increasingly important role in advancing these peacebuilding processes in the twenty-first century. Therefore, multifaith initiatives have played a significant role in preventive countering violent extremism strategies and in advancing common security following the events of September 11. Moreover, established multifaith networks of trust have been well poised to respond to subsequent crisis events such as the 2005 London bombings, thereby lessening their negative impacts.

These actor perspectives also confirm that, in response to crisis events such as September 11 and the London bombings, there has been a rise of interest in religion in the public sphere, largely due to increased media attention. The media, while acknowledged as playing a negative role in spreading fear and division through uninformed and sensationalist reporting, has also provided powerful platforms from which religious peacebuilders have been able to counter negative prejudices and build greater understanding about and across diverse religious communities. This heightened interest in religion in the public sphere has also contributed to a rise of multi-actor peacebuilding networks that include religious communities, state actors, and global institutions. These networks have enabled mutual understanding to develop across diverse sectors and for religious communities to play a greater role in local and global cosmopolitan governance. By encouraging deliberative processes that have provided opportunities for diverse communities to non-violently air their concerns, to feel understood and acknowledged and to make recommendations on policies, these networks are providing the foundations for genuinely peaceful societies. As Beck (2006: 3–4, 23, 35–36, 89) asserts, global risks provide new opportunities for collaboration among diverse sectors including state and non-state actors. This 'cosmopolitan competence' depends on 'the art of translation and bridge-building', in this case modelled by the multifaith movement.

A new emphasis on social cohesion and countering extremism in Australia and the UK has also lifted the profile of multifaith initiatives and given new legitimacy to the multifaith movement. As multifaith and multi-actor peacebuilding networks have played a positive role in developing strategies to counter radicalisation, state support of these initiatives has increased and been largely welcomed by religious communities, in Australia and the UK. However, concerns were raised among USA participants that increased state involvement in multifaith initiatives risks impeding the critical role of religious actors in the public sphere. These issues are further explored in Chap. 7.

On the international level, participants stated that global multifaith institutions should maintain a connection to the grassroots, community-based level and affirm the importance of working simultaneously at local, national and global levels. In addition, as much of the focus of multifaith engagement has centred on Jewish, Christian and Muslim faiths subsequent to September 11, multifaith engagement needs to be more inclusive of all communities, of faith and no-faith, of immigrant and host communities, including Hindu, Buddhist and Sikh religions, Indigenous faiths, NRMs and also humanists, agnostics and atheists. Finally, among the main challenges faced by multifaith actors is a lack of resources—as the scope of the movement expands—and the need for further research into the efficacy and long-term benefits of multifaith initiatives.

References

Beck, Ulrich. 2006. *The cosmopolitan vision*. Cambridge: Polity Press.

Benhabib, Seyla. 1992a. Models of public space: Hannah Arendt, the liberal tradition and Jürgen Habermas. In *Habermas and the public sphere*, ed. Craig Calhoun. Cambridge: MIT Press.

Benhabib, Seyla. 1992b. *Situating the self gender, community and postmodernism in contemporary ethics*. New York/London: Routledge/Kegan and Paul.

Benhabib, Seyla. 2002a. *The claims of culture: Equality and diversity*. Princeton: Princeton University Press.

Benhabib, Seyla. 2002b. Unholy wars. *Constellations* 9(1): 34–45.

Benhabib, Seyla. 2004. *The rights of others: Aliens, citizens and residents*, The John Robert Seeley Memorial Lectures. Cambridge: Cambridge University Press.

Benhabib, Seyla. 2007. Democratic exclusions and democratic iterations: Dilemmas of "just membership" and prospects of cosmopolitan federalism. *European Journal of Political Theory* 6(4): 445–462.

Bharat, Sandy, and Jael Bharat. 2007. *A global guide to interfaith: Reflections from around the world*. Winchester: O Books.

Bouma, Gary D. 2006. *Australian soul: Religion and spirituality in the twenty-first century*. Cambridge: Cambridge University Press.

Bouma, Gary D., Sharon Pickering, Anna Halafoff, and Hass Dellal. 2007. *Managing the impact of global crisis events on community relations in multicultural Australia*. Brisbane: Multicultural Affairs Queensland.

Braybrooke, Marcus. 2007. *Interfaith witness in a changing world: The world congress of faiths, 1996–2006*. Abingdon: Braybrooke Press.

Brodeur, Patrice. 2005. From the margins to the centers of power: The increasing relevance of the global interfaith movement. *Cross Currents* 55(1): 42–53.

Brodeur, Patrice, and Eboo Patel. 2006. Introduction: Building the interfaith youth movement. In *Building the interfaith youth movement: Beyond dialogue to action*, ed. Patel Eboo and Brodeur Patrice, 1–14. Oxford: Rowman and Littlefield Publishers, Inc.

Eck, Diana L. 2001. *A new religious America: How a "Christian Country" has become the world's most religiously diverse nation*. New York: HarperOne.

Garfinkel, Renee. 2004. *What works? Evaluating interfaith dialogue programs*. USIP Special Report 123. Washington, DC: United States Institute of Peace.

Habermas, Jürgen. 1984. *The theory of communicative action: Vol. 1 Reason and the rationalization of society*. Cambridge: Polity Press.

Habermas, Jürgen. 1987. *The theory of communicative action: Vol. 2 Lifeworld and system: A critique of functionalist reason*. Cambridge: Polity Press.

Habermas, Jürgen. 2005. Equal treatment of cultures and the limits of postmodern liberalism. *The Journal of Political Philosophy* 13(1): 1–28.

Habermas, Jürgen. 2006. Religion in the public sphere. *European Journal of Philosophy* 14(1): 1–25.

Habermas, Jürgen. 2007. *The divided west,* ed. and Trans. Ciaran Cronin. Cambridge: Polity Press.

Halafoff, Anna, and David Wright-Neville. 2009. A missing peace? The role of religious actors in countering terrorism. *Studies of Conflict and Terrorism* 32(11): 921–932.

InterAction. 2009. Available at: http://www.interaction.org.au/. Accessed 29 July 2011.

Lentini, Pete. 2007. Countering terrorism as if Muslims matter: Cultural citizenship and civic pre-emption in anti-terrorism. In *Terrorism, organised crime and corruption: Networks and linkages*, ed. Leslie Holmes, 42–59. Cheltenham: Edward Elgar.

Lentini, Pete, Halafoff Anna, and Ogru Ela. 2009. *Perceptions of multiculturalism and security in Victoria: Report to the Department of Premier and Cabinet, State Government of Victoria*. Global Terrorism Research Centre, Monash University, Melbourne.

Lohre, Kathryn. 2007. Women's interfaith initiatives in the United States post 9/11. *Interreligious Insight* 5(2): 11–23.

McCarthy, Kate. 2007. *Interfaith encounters in America*. Piscataway: Rutgers University Press.

Parliament of World's Religions (PWR). 2009. Available at: http://www.parliamentofreligions.org/index.cfm?n=8&sn=5. Accessed 29 July 2011.

Patel, Eboo. 2007. *Acts of faith: The story of an American Muslim, the struggle for the soul of a generation*. Boston: Beacon.

Tippett, Krista. 2007. *Speaking of faith: Why religion matters – And how to talk about it*. New York: Penguin.

Wuthnow, Robert. 2005. *America and the challenges of religious diversity*. Princeton/Oxford: Princeton University Press.

Chapter 7
'Expanding Cognitive Frames' from Exclusivity to Pluralism

This chapter continues to investigate the multifaith movement's benefits and the challenges it faces, as it addresses global risks and injustices in particular. It deals specifically with the notion of 'expanding cognitive frames' <Abd-Allah 2007, USA>, at the individual and collective levels, from exclusive anti-cosmopolitan mindsets to inclusive cosmopolitan paradigms. Many participants indicated that this was the key, not only to effective multifaith engagement but also to the future survival of the lifeworld and its citizens <Abd-Allah 2007, USA; Gibbs 2007, USA; Knitter 2007, USA; Seiple 2007, USA; Vendley 2007, USA; Voll 2007, USA>. Following this argument, participants explained how the wisdom inherent in theological and philosophical traditions is a critical component in advancing common security.

Affirming Common Values and Respect for Differences

Many participants described how multifaith initiatives concurrently affirm common values across faith traditions <Seiple 2007, USA; Tippett 2007, USA> and respect for diversity <Margaryan 2007, USA; Marshall 2007, USA; Seiple 2007, USA>. Participants recounted how multifaith initiatives provide opportunities to discover commonalities among diverse faiths, which in turn affirms the highest human qualities and values <Amatullah 2007, US; Margaryan 2007, USA; Ramey 2007, USA; Landau 2008, AUS; Woodlock 2008, AUS>. According to Ramey <2007, USA>, religion acts as a 'container of values' as religions provide 'universal understandings' of non-violence, justice and guidance on how best to conduct human relationships and economic transactions to avoid doing harm to others. Amatullah <2007, US> similarly described how religious traditions can affirm the highest of human ideals and also the 'sanctity and sacredness' of all life. Landau <2008, AUS> also explained how 'each faith is at its highest when it reticulates back to a sense of shared humanity … and planet'. As Ramey <2007, USA> argued, 'the best practices

A. Halafoff, *The Multifaith Movement: Global Risks and Cosmopolitan Solutions*,

DOI 10.1007/978-94-007-5210-8_7,

of religions certainly have a role to play in shaping human events and moving human events forward', by affirming common values, in particular respect for all life. These actor accounts thereby confirm scholars' views, outlined in Chaps. 3 and 4, that deepening personal understanding of religion and spirituality can assist in developing one's positive qualities and awakening a sense of altruism and thereby global responsibility (Knitter 1995: 71; Hick 1985: 29, 34, 2001: 16–17).

Participants explained how this self-reflexive process can lead to the questioning of societal norms, especially materialist values, and thereby provide the impetus to find more equitable and sustainable means of developing personal and collective happiness <Margaryan 2007, USA; Dupuche 2008, AUS>. They also confirmed the arguments of religious peacebuilders (Johnston 1994: 332; Vendley and Little 1994: 307–308, 312–313; Sampson 1997: 274; Abu-Nimer 2001: 686, 701; Appleby 2003: 240; Halafoff and Conley Tyler 2005) that religious actors question what is wrong with contemporary society, including their own traditions, and seek religious means to remedy these situations. Toh Swee-Hin <2008, AUS>, Director of the Multi-Faith Centre at Griffith University, clearly described how multifaith engagement, by reflexively challenging cultures of both direct and structural violence, can enable faith leaders to reform their respective traditions:

> … the eternal challenge … is that faith communities have to also engage in intrafaith dialogue, so when it comes to human rights … there may be doctrines or institutional practices over centuries that … are clear violations of human rights of particular groups, sectors, women, children, different sexual orientations, and that's a challenge for all faith communities but … we are seeing more openness in faith communities to do it … So interfaith dialogues will hopefully help us raise some of those difficult issues of internal transformation … <Toh 2008, AUS>

As Habermas (2007: 184, 15) stated, only 'self-critical dialogue between cultures' can address the root causes of risks such as terrorism and climate change. It is precisely this reflexive quality—of self-critical dialogue within and between religions and broader society—that enables multifaith peacebuilders to challenge cultures of violence within and beyond their own traditions and to advance cultures of peace in their stead.

In part due to the multifaith movement's emphasis on common values, a widely held fear about multifaith engagement is that it leads to syncretism (Wuthnow 2005: 301). However, several participants explained that multifaith engagement is not a conversion exercise <Hirst 2008, AUS; Landau 2008, AUS>, but rather affirms commonalities without leading to a blending of religious traditions <Marshall 2007, USA; Woodlock 2008, AUS> as it is based in 'an appreciation of difference' <Marshall 2007, USA>. Several participants noted that an appreciation of difference as well as commonalities leads to a greater understanding not only of others' faith but also of one's own. Jones <2008, AUS> claimed that you 'strengthen your own faith by interfaith dialogue, [as] you are forced to think about it'. Ozalp <2008, AUS> and Susan Pascoe <2008, AUS>, Chair of the Australian National Commission for UNESCO, expressed similar views that multifaith activity increases self-reflexivity and thereby heightened awareness of, and commitment to, one's own tradition:

> … people think that by engaging in interfaith dialogue you will somehow dilute your own faith and identity when in reality what happens is you enrich yourself, [and] your own faith and identity, because now you've got … different frames of reference, and your identity crystallises in a better way rather than developing on its own, and this has been a very counter-intuitive result … <Ozalp 2008, AUS>

> … interreligious dialogue isn't about finding common ground and determining your basis for engagement only in terms of commonality. It's about a confidence with your own faith tradition and your own ritual and liturgy and all that goes with it, and a sharing on the basis of that confidence. So you're not coming to enmesh yourselves … some people fear interreligious dialogue … because they think at the heart of it is a reductionist exercise to distil us all into one global entity, that is the bits that we all agree on … [however,] we continue to explore and renew and have confidence in our own faith traditions but we bring that to an engagement which ought to be on the basis of listening and respect of other traditions and then hopefully greater levels of understanding. <Pascoe 2008, AUS>

Moreover, Umar Faruq Abd-Allah <2007, USA>, Chairman of the Board and Scholar-in-Residence at the Nawawi Foundation, described the development of a new maturity that has occurred in multifaith relations, as a result of deepening knowledge of and respect for diverse faith traditions:

> … [during] my first involvement in interfaith … [in] 1977 … in Philadelphia … there was a lot of polemics and there was a lot of apologetics and I was not very impressed, and when I came back to the United States … to Chicago in 2000 … I saw that interfaith was different, it was not the same anymore … we talk a lot about commonalities and there are infinite commonalities. But there are also differences and there are differences in the way that we approach reality … our traditions are very different because they're like parallel universes … so that what I like about interfaith today … is that it does respect me as what I am and it says "be yourself" … <Abd-Allah 2007, USA>

As Pearce <2007, UK> wisely remarked, in plural, multifaith societies there is a need to emphasise 'unity within diversity … [to] hold both together, rather than saying diversity must be suppressed in the interest of unity or, on the other hand, diversity is all and there is no need for any common ground or coherence for a particular society'.

As described in Chaps. 3 and 4, religions have long offered methods for how to overcome self-centredness and how to cultivate more enlightened qualities such as compassion and altruism for personal and collective wellbeing. These actor perspectives demonstrate that multifaith engagement encourages a greater understanding of and respect for the differences across diverse traditions while concurrently affirming a commitment to the common good by drawing on theological and philosophical principles. Consequently, these participants' views validate the assertion that the multifaith movement can be described as having a 'mutual mission' (Hick 1985: 44) of: (1) developing understanding of diverse faiths and the nature of reality; and (2) addressing global risks and injustices through collaborative action, and that these two forces continually inform one another (Hick 1985: 44; Wuthnow 2005: 303; Bharat and Bharat 2007: 4, 116). Multifaith engagement can thus be described as offering evidence of processes of cosmopolitanisation in practice, as faith communities challenge direct and structural violence and promote cultures of peace and cooperation, both within their traditions and in broader society, through reflexive non-violent deliberative processes. The multifaith movement's emphasis on self-reflexivity also encourages the development of greater religious literacy and understanding not only of others' faiths but also of one's own faith traditions.

From Dialogue to Common Action

Many participants affirmed that following the atrocities committed during the Holocaust in Europe and the nuclear attacks in Japan the imperative to address global risks and injustices became the central theme of ultramodern multifaith initiatives. As a result of these crisis events a shift occurred away from theological/ philosophical dialogue towards common action within the multifaith movement <Breyer 2007, USA; Dubensky 2007, USA; Marshall 2007, USA; Camilleri 2008, AUS; Jones, 2008, AUS>. Religious peacebuilders from diverse faith communities can affirm common values, and mobilise their communities to act for common good through collective action such as public statements, declarations and religious services <Abu-Nimer 2008, USA>. Marshall <2007, USA> and Shashoua <2008, UK> explained the benefits of such initiatives:

> There's another approach … which is when groups don't seem to work together and don't know each other and don't have contacts, is rather than trying to meet and talk about theology or custom or religion, is to take a subject that's completely different and work on that … when very different groups come together and work on a specific problem, of which there are countless problems of development, that very often they get to know each other, and then when there is a crisis, they can diffuse it and they can also bring the communities together around objectives. <Marshall 2007, USA>

> … in … interfaith we can say that one is telling the other about themselves, but that is more the face to face, I would say the peacebuilding itself would be the side-to-side kind of championing the cause, same thing with the crisis situations, with the environment and others, it's not about faith, it is about the world, that standing shoulder to shoulder and using faith in certain kinds of ways to say well, this is our garden, look in all our books we must take care of it, but side to side I can't even say engagement, it's a standing shoulder to shoulder to engage together with the world and do a united front is something that has worked, is necessary … <Shashoua 2008, UK>

According to Laing <2007, UK>, multifaith engagement that concentrates on common action is far more effective than dialogue:

> … the key is to get away from the idea of interfaith dialogue and that's why people feel so disillusioned with this sort of work … because they see it as a talking shop and all of the seminars and conferences of religious people … they leave at the end of the day and they might know a little bit more, they probably won't … be doing anything. And what I've really come to believe is that the religious traditions and religious communities can really do stuff. They have the resources to really mobilise people and make things happen and this translates at a local level to getting religious communities to work together for a local issue, whether it's a planning application or local-level stuff like that, or also to an international

> level that the religions have resources to deal with HIV and AIDS… peacebuilding, climate change, global warming, these kinds of things are areas that interreligious work can really contribute to. So … the way forward is … to think about common action … to gather people and do something and then … one of the positive outcomes … is the interfaith encounter. <Laing 2007, UK>

However, Ramey <2007, USA> offered a pertinent reminder that religious peacebuilders have been inspired to work for social change by their theological and philosophical traditions, thereby echoing Braybrooke's (2007: 25) argument that the multifaith movement, although increasingly focused on action, should not lose its foundation in theological and philosophical principles:

> … our essential task in this coming era is to engage good Christians and Jews and Buddhists and Muslims and Taoists and Hindus and people of ethical traditions in an understanding that to be a good believer means that you work for global, environmental justice, that you work for a different way of distributing the resources in the world, that you work for demilitarisation and the abolition of war and a host of other things, that you work for the ending of the oppression of women either structurally or through cultural attitudes and certainly as a Muslim I believe that's a major challenge within Islam, in the 21st century. But … also … that the best practices that we have are practices that will enable us to really not just elevate ourselves spiritually but also engage in connecting with other people within and across these religious traditions that are also motivated, to try to work in some way to make the world better and safer and more loving for all of the human beings who live here. So it's really an ongoing challenge, I don't think it'll be won or lost in my lifetime or in the lifetime of my great grandchildren but I think it's one worth struggling for. <Ramey 2007, US>

This argument, that theological and philosophical principles inform religious peacebuilding practises, is further strengthened by the fact that the issue of climate change in particular has mobilised diverse faith communities to act collectively towards building more sustainable societies, inspired by a realisation—derived largely from faith traditions—of the interconnectedness and sacredness of all life. As Kearns <2008, USA> and Toh <2008, AUS> explained below:

> I think particularly on climate change, what it does finally bring about is this recognition that we really are all in it together and that there's far more to be gained in cooperation than in trying to outline our differences and have competition for adherents. So, in that sense almost every time I'm working on environmental issues that it creates a desire to work across faith traditions, it promotes a recognition of similarities among faith traditions about the sanctity of the world and a care for it … It creates a lot of situations where people are quite willing to go beyond their comfort zones and see how they can work together because this larger picture really does finally say we're all in the lifeboat together. <Kearns 2008, US>

> When faith leaders, communities are stepping forward to say we have to join this urgent mission to reverse climate change to live in harmony, that's another good news kind of story about faith, because if faiths can influence their own followers to lead more sustainable lifestyles, that will help, and if their own institutions are restructured or rebuilt, newly built in ways that are more green, then it becomes a role model as well. <Toh 2008, AUS>

In addition, many participants affirmed the view of scholars such as Sampson (1997: 275) and Little and Appleby (2004: 3) that there are several factors that predispose religions and religious leaders to peacebuilding and countering global risks.

According to Vendley <2007, US>, religious communities have 'unparalleled assets', which can be marshalled in response to crisis events such as climate change. Pascoe <2008, AUS> also described how religions provide the 'moral imperative' necessary to galvanise communities into action to confront and prevent such crises. By drawing on the mobilising power of religious organisations, Ficca <2007, US> similarly explained how the multifaith movement can 'tap … the long-sustained commitments', 'sacrifice and long-term vision' necessary to counter pressing global risks such as poverty and climate change, beyond short-term political and profit-driven agendas. Following a similar argument, Young <2008, AUS> stated that because people often feel powerless as individuals, 'the real power of religion' lies in its ability to bring people to collectively stand up against injustice and to work collaboratively towards social change.

Despite the overwhelmingly positive statements by participants regarding religion's mobilising ability in the face of crisis events, Landau <2008, AUS> noted that while 'religion's got a huge capacity to … inspire [people]… and to be able to harness that energy for collective good', 'it wouldn't hurt the religious leaders to just all speak out even more', because on environmental issues in particular there is still much work to be done. In addition, Knitter <2007, US>. spoke of the need for more 'genuine collaboration' and 'better networking' among multifaith organisations, echoing a commonly cited criticism among scholars in the field of multifaith relations that there is too much competition and not enough collaboration between the major multifaith organisations (Brodeur 2005: 51, 53; Bharat and Bharat 2007: 8–9; Tyndale quoted in Bharat and Bharat 2007: 275).

These actor perspectives reveal that as a result of rising concerns regarding global risks, such as terrorism and climate change, the multifaith movement has shifted its focus away from dialogue that fosters understanding and respect towards common action to address these crises. In doing this, religious and multifaith actors report that theological and philosophical imperatives continue to be a driving force in mobilising communities to act for the common good. This further confirms the argument developed throughout this study that developing understanding and countering risks are interwoven aims of the multifaith movement. While participants described how religions and multifaith organisations have inspired collective action on issues of common security, they also felt that there is a need for more collaboration and networking among existing organisations and also for more action in response to the pressing risk of climate change.

Beyond the '*Kum Ba Yah*' Factor and Preaching to the Converted

The most common criticism levelled at the multifaith movement is that it is 'preaching to the converted' and thereby reaching a limited liberal audience (Cox 1988: 732; Huff 2000: 94, 98; Bharat and Bharat 2007: iii, 244, 276; Kirkwood 2007: 262; Abdo 2008: 51–53). In addition, the multifaith movement continues to be mocked for its association with the peace movement and the so-called '*kum ba yah*' factor (Niebuhr 2008: xxxiv–xxxv). These perceptions were affirmed and expanded upon by some of the participants, while others disputed these claims, arguing that the multifaith movement is increasingly reaching a broader audience.

Several participants described how lavish international multifaith events and smaller-scale gatherings where 'it's all peace, love and mung beans' <Woodlock 2008, AUS> were viewed with scepticism, from both within and outside of the multifaith movement <Breyer 2007, US>. According to Marshall <2007, USA>:

> The biggest objection to interfaith … is … the *kum ba yah* factor … there are quite a few people who say they won't go to these meetings because … everybody's holding hands and singing and talking about love and peace and so on. So there's a certain amount of scepticism around that. <Marshall 2007, USA>

Breyer <2007, USA> also explained how these types of initiatives were seen as a waste of time and money and were also criticised for attracting 'the same sorts of people, ones from different traditions with a rather open-minded, and liberal, tolerant understanding of their respective traditions, which clearly does not include everyone'. Consequently, some participants stated that the multifaith movement has frequently been accused of 'preaching to the converted' <Marshall 2007, USA; Hassan 2008, AUS>. Aly <2008, AUS> similarly accused multifaith initiatives of 'singing to the choir', and raised concerns about whether they were reaching more conservative people and more marginalised individuals who were vulnerable to processes of radicalisation. Shashoua <2008, UK> also recounted the challenges of expanding multifaith engagement to reach mainstream society:

> … the big question that always surrounds interfaith … is whether or not it actually reaches people that it really needs to reach … it benefits the choir, but if you had scarce resources … If you really wanted to make a social difference, you would probably be targeting people who have more hostile dispositions … on these issues. And I'm not sure about how that works … <Aly 2008, AUS>

> … interfaith in a sense … creates islands … that communities will bring representatives to, and it's usually those believing in that process of interfaith but unfortunately there is a lot more water around than islands, so I don't think the process of island-making of interfaith is a good one. It has to be part and parcel of the whole society, it has to be in the water and so no longer should we bring interfaith to this space, but bring the space to society … <Shashoua 2008, UK>

However, Ficca <2007, USA> disputed these claims, arguing that multifaith engagement has long targeted diverse sectors of the community in different ways and is not as exclusive as its critics have claimed. Ficca <2007, USA> explained how the multifaith movement primarily engages with three societal groupings and described the benefits and difficulties of this engagement:

> There are those who see the interreligious movement as important, they have no problem as a religious person relating to people of other religions, they don't feel like they are compromising their traditions, so that's the choir. And sometimes we get criticised that that's basically who comes to our events. Well, to a large degree yes, it's self-selecting but lots of people from different communities who think alike still don't know each other so, we could just keep busy introducing those that know each other of every tradition, so there's that segment, they're already there.

> Then there's a segment, and I'm moving to the right here, instinctively left and right, there's another segment for whom this will never be a part of their religious life. It's too uncomfortable, it's too threatening and I think we have to be respectful of those communities, or basically it's a portion of any community, and we have to be respectful because sometimes the movement can kind of be self-righteous. I think if that group is going to impinge on the religious freedom or if they are going to be advocating against goals for peace, justice and sustainability, then there needs to be engagement and disagreement but they can't be castigated for who they want to be.
>
> For me the big, the frontier for me, the focus of the work is the centre that doesn't know yet what they think. A Christian who doesn't yet know a Muslim, who if you read the newspaper, the media or whether you pick up the subtle, broader and sometimes not-so-subtle messages, where you would be afraid perhaps, how can that person have a positive experience of difference and say, wait a minute, and tip more in the direction of openness … [there are] those who are just never going to be a part of it, but there's plenty of work to do in other places. <Ficca 2007, US>

Thus, Ficca <2007, US> describes how, even if it does not reach those on 'the right' of his typology, multifaith engagement is beneficial in that it has the capacity to facilitate more contact between groups that are willing to engage with one another and also to 'tip' those in the middle 'in the direction of openness', toward normalising pluralism and embracing the peacebuilding potential of religion.

Indeed, many participants described how conservative elements are present in all religious traditions and have often opposed multifaith engagement <Penn 2007, USA; Smock 2007, USA; Summers 2008, AUS>. As Di Hirsh <2008, AUS>, Interfaith and Intercultural Chair of the National Council of Jewish Women of Australia, remarked: 'The biggest obstacles I've faced are from people within my own community who say that we shouldn't be engaging … and I feel very strongly that we've got to fight that sort of opinion'. Pascoe <2008, AUS> similarly stated that a clash of 'competing theologies' between the more old-fashioned 'hard line' and modernising elements exists within the Catholic Church. Mogra <2007, UK> also recounted how similar tensions exist within Muslim communities, between those who support and those who condemn multifaith activities.

Building upon this argument, participants described how multifaith activities have the potential to cultivate *intra*faith understanding and respect, and thereby challenge the exclusive attitudes found within religious groups. As Mogra <2007, UK> stated: 'it has made me realise that I have to embrace the diverse Muslims as equals, as brothers and sisters, as I embrace others in humanity'. As so many conflicts have a sectarian component, this is a highly beneficial aspect of multifaith engagement. Indeed, participants argued that there is a need for more intrafaith peacebuilding initiatives to challenge exclusivity within religious traditions <Postma 2008, AUS; Summers 2008, AUS>.

Challenging these exclusive truth claims inherent in most religious traditions is a difficult yet crucial task that can be enabled by critical reflexive processes and by common action. According to Knitter <2007, US>:

> … Now, this notion of "one among many", of one voice, a very important voice, however, having to be integrated with and balanced by, and entering into a real dialogue with other religious voices, this is something that religions have not been very good at … [due to] the actuality that all religions have, in some way or another, made claims that they're the best,

> that they are superior over all others. Or, translated a little bit more explicitly, that theirs is the last word on issues. So this notion of "we're the best", or "God has chosen us", or "God has given us the final revelation", or "God has given us the only saviour", or "God has given us the final prophet". This is where it's going to take … some critical reappropriation and reinterpretation of some of these traditional religious teachings, if religion is going to be able to make its contribution in a truly dialogical, communal way. It's going to take more than just tolerating other religions: it's going to take genuine respect for other religions, and a respect built on recognition of the real validity of other religions … This is challenging news for a lot of religious people, but happily, more and more religious people, because they see the need to cooperate with others for the purposes of peace and security, that beginnings are being made, and this kind of opening up to the other. <Knitter 2007, US>

Exclusive attitudes can not only be an impediment to multifaith engagement, but they can also lead to extremism, thereby pointing to an even greater imperative to find new ways of engaging the more hard-line actors in multifaith initiatives. Toh <2008, AUS> stated that multifaith engagement that focuses on action is more effective than dialogue in achieving this aim because, regardless of how conservative or open actors are, there are certain issues that are of grave concern to everyone, and collaboration on a common cause can thus counter closed-mindedness and reduce alienation. Toh <2008, AUS> explained this process as follows:

> … whatever we believe in we [are] all confronting many common social, human problems … it affects everyone regardless of whether you are exclusive, extremist or inclusive … as human beings we need to … overcome ecological crisis … if we don't we all sink … if people can join hands in trying to resolve ecological crisis … across different faith divides, perhaps the very exclusive believer may [be] in contact with someone who is more inclusive, more plural and may, through getting together, through cooperating in common action … hopefully become a bit more open, at least to the point where … their exclusiveness will not lead them to be isolated from others … <Toh 2008, AUS>

While the task religious peacebuilders face in engaging extremists of any tradition in multifaith engagement is a particularly difficult one, in recent years the multifaith movement has attracted more conservative actors, as globalisation has brought diverse communities closer together and united them in response to common concerns <Glasman 2007, UK>. In ever more religiously plural societies, a new openness to multifaith engagement can be witnessed among more conservative actors, especially Evangelical Christians in the USA <Knitter 2007, USA>. As described in the previous chapter, multifaith alliances are increasingly being formed among progressive and conservative religious groups in order to seek state support for faith schools, burial rites, circumcision and the ritual killing of animals. As a result, and especially given the recent mainstreaming of multifaith initiatives, one can no longer assume that multifaith engagement is an entirely liberal endeavour.

Some participants in this study have raised valid concerns regarding whether multifaith initiatives are reaching beyond the progressive, cosmopolitan adherents of faith traditions. Yet these actor perspectives also indicate that as the scope of multifaith engagement has increased after September 11, more people 'in the middle' as well as conservative religious actors are participating in these initiatives. These observations thus reveal that more centrist and conservative religious actors and communities are joining or forming multifaith networks in response to common social, economic and environmental concerns, and that these activities may gradually assist them to become more open to respecting religious diversity and thereby soften their exclusivist attitudes. The findings of this study also suggest that, with time, participating in multifaith initiatives focused on common action could also assist diverse faith communities, both liberal and conservative, to develop more reflexive practices that challenge cultures of direct and structural violence within their traditions and in society more generally. It follows that the multifaith movement can thus be described as enabling processes of cosmopolitanisation within religious traditions.

Conversely, despite continuous calls for expanding multifaith initiatives beyond 'the usual suspects', the increased participation of conservative actors in multifaith networks carries with it certain risks. Due to the rise in number of conservative actors involved in multifaith initiatives, the multifaith movement is in danger of compromising its long held commitment to peacebuilding, especially to countering structural violence against women, homosexual people, children and animals, by offering a platform for conservative voices to gain strength within a movement that has been traditionally liberal. These issues require further investigation, beyond the scope of this study.

Finally, these actor perspectives—building upon the arguments put forward in the preceding chapters—demonstrate that the multifaith movement plays a primarily preventive role in countering processes of alienation and radicalisation by contributing to the creation of inclusive, pluralist societies. The multifaith movement also encourages faith actors and organisations to abide by the overarching framework of the law and human rights, while enabling non-violent, democratic, deliberative processes in which grievances can be aired and injustices can be addressed non-violently. Once individuals have already become radicalised they are unlikely to attend multifaith initiatives; however, multifaith youth networks that are focused on non-violent social change may offer alternatives to extremist violent social movements that target youth.

It follows that calls for the multifaith movement to engage with extremists are in many ways counter-productive and reflect a pronounced lack of understanding regarding the aims of multifaith engagement. As described above, including ultra-conservative voices in multifaith initiatives risks legitimising human rights abuses, and placing participants at risk of verbal abuse when exclusive views are aired, thus severely eroding the movement's principles. That is not to say that religious peacebuilders should not engage with extremist actors. Indeed, there is a moral imperative for highly skilled religious mediators and progressive leaders to engage in faith-based diplomacy in order to better understand and respond to the underlying grievances of actors within these extremist and conservative movements. However, this is very different from multifaith initiatives, which as described above play a more preventive, yet no less important, role in countering extremism. There are many forms of multifaith peacebuilding that are applicable in different contexts. Due to the dangers of religiously inspired violence it is crucial that they are skilfully applied. The precise role that multifaith initiatives can play in countering violent extremism processes are discussed in greater detail in the 'Conclusion'.

Finding a New Language for Difficult Conversations

Despite the benefits of multifaith initiatives that focus on developing understanding and common action, some participants expressed growing frustrations that multifaith activities still avoid dealing with the 'tough issues' <Penn 2007, USA; Hassan 2008, AUS>. Both Penn <2007, USA> and Keyes <2007, UK> highlighted the need to have more 'difficult conversations', despite strong resistance within the multifaith movement to such initiatives:

> I'm concerned about the direction of the movement … you have to engage in these tough issues, and I wasn't seeing that and I was feeling discouraged by that and discouraged that it seemed like we were fostering the kinds of programs that have limited engagement. You get together, you talk about shared values, you go off, you build a house, but that isn't going to sustain long-term change for an individual and what we've been moving toward more is to say, ok, you've got to fundamentally teach young people the skills that they need to engage in these difficult conversations. They need to have the difficult conversations … <Penn 2007, USA>

> For me there's a lot of questions about method, about the actual processes and agendas that underlie so-called interfaith dialogue, and it's one of the things we're trying to experiment with [at St. Ethelburga's], is trying to get some new ways … because so much of that industry is based on just trying to assert some rather broadly defined common values … there are huge real differences between the faith traditions, particularly around things like the role of women, about the fact we're dealing with hugely patriarchal institutions by and large … so for us the starting point here is to try and think how can we really understand difference in a way that genuinely leads to sharing of space with people who you fundamentally disagree with. And that's a different project to simply getting people to say, "well actually we must all collaborate for the greater good" … we've always said, at this Centre, [and] we never say one without the other, faith causes conflict, faith transforms conflict. Both those things are true in every situation. But I get a lot of dirty looks about the first one. <Keyes 2007, UK>

Following a similar argument, Knitter <2007, USA> called for the need for 'hard-nosed dialogue' to reflexively examine the role that religion, and theology in particular, plays in justifying violence, in order to best remedy or reinterpret traditional teachings according to peacebuilding principles:

> … there might be different ways in which religions can contribute to a greater sense of security … the primary way is … to help, to counteract the misuse of religion … to really address the way religion is being misappropriated, misused by certain political leaders or terrorists … you can offset the abuse of religion only by means of religion, to a great extent. It's not the only thing we have to do, but that is one of the primary things to do. And this is going to really require a very courageous and a very honest and forthright dialogue among the religions, because the exploitation of religions by politicians or movement leaders is rendered often times fairly easy because of certain teachings within the religion … to really address the problem of religious violence, it is not sufficient to say that these people like Osama bin Laden, or George Bush if you want to look at it that way, are exploiting Islam or exploiting Christianity. We have to look at what is part of the teachings of Islam and Christianity that make it so easy. And there is violence in our traditions, and the horrible misuse of religion is really calling us to be critical of our own traditions … and to address ways of remedying, of reinterpreting some of the traditional teachings about the just war theory, or about jihad … it's going to require a lot of courageous dialogue. Hard-nosed dialogue. <Knitter 2007, USA>

As described in the previous section, facilitating these difficult conversations around controversial issues requires particular skills. As Penn <2007, USA> explained below:

> … interfaith work is fundamentally about human beings making connections … but we don't take a lot of time thinking about how do I engage somebody … [to] really be able to hear them and so it seems to me that until we can learn to listen to each other and sit with our discomfort with different, with ideas that really push our buttons and make us angry and raise our fear levels … that that basic level of communication is imperative for any of this work … until we can sit with our discomfort but really hear the other point of view, I don't see any way out of where we are … <Penn 2007, USA>

Similarly, Seiple <2007, USA> remarked that the 'capacity to listen' forms the basis of developing respect and understanding. These actor perspectives demonstrate that assembling diverse religious leaders and communities is a task best facilitated by professionals who possess active listening and conflict resolution skills. These skills, modelled by the facilitator, can then be taught to participants in order for truly beneficial multifaith engagement to occur. This is particularly important in working with youth and when moderating difficult conversations. Without these skills, multifaith engagement risks being either superficial, thus avoiding difficult issues, or dangerous when led by those with insufficient experience. Once acquired, these skills can inform all kinds of communication. Indeed, Vendley <2007, USA> describes how the multifaith movement has created a 'linguistic revolution' in which religious communities have learnt to become bilingual, maintaining their primary religious discourse and developing a new 'public language' of mutual respect:

> … the truly stunning part of that is that the religious communities are now, in very large measure, accepting the prospect of collaboration, of multireligious collaboration, and there is a kind of silent revolution that is taking place, because to collaborate with others, other than your own religious community, there is a kind of linguistic revolution that takes place. Religious communities, in effect, become bilingual. They don't forfeit their own primary religious discourse within which they transact meanings, genetic and unfolding meanings of their traditions, but in fact they learn how to say or to mediate or transpose those meanings into a public idiom … you can go almost anywhere today in the world, and you will find that religious communities, different ones, can gather and are in the process of being able to discern areas of deeply held and widely shared moral concern as a platform for common action, and they're transacting that in a form of public language in which they can at least express moral ultimas, and … that's an extraordinary, that is a truly historic watershed in terms of the history of religion, and I don't see any signs of that stopping. Reactions against that are acute at times, painful or sensational, but are more epiphenomena compared to the large tidal wave of how religions are moving at this point in time. <Vendley 2007, USA>

Vendley's linguistic revolution aligns well with Habermas's (1984, 1987, 2007: 18) *Theory of Communicative Action*, whereby mutual understanding is reached through a process of 'multiple perspective taking', and Benhabib's (1992, 2004, 2007: 455) notion of a 'discourse ethic'. The multifaith movement has been developing a new public language of mutual respect, for both religious and non-religious voices to articulate and share their common concerns despite their differences, for well over a century. It follows that the multifaith movement needs to be acknowledged by sociologists as a pioneer of building these cosmopolitan mazeways based on communicative processes.

Embodied Multifaith Engagement

Several participants in this study explained that for multifaith engagement to be truly effective at the local and global level it needs to be embodied in role models, in personal stories and real relationships. Abd-Allah <2007, USA> illustrated the importance of personified multifaith experiences with reference to Martin Luther King Jr. and Eboo Patel:

> … the biggest revelation that came to me in working with interfaith people, Eboo Patel in particular … I'm a person who, by nature, loves ideas and books and history and all sorts of abstractions and what he emphasised and … it's very much the basis of what he does, is that human beings don't understand that well. What they do understand is other human beings and that for ideas to be meaningful, they must have human voices, they must have human faces and [for example] the Civil Rights Movement … that becomes meaningful when it's personified by Dr Martin Luther King, with his persona, his voice, his face, his courage, and so that is something that I got from interfaith. I got that from Eboo Patel … <Abd-Allah 2007, USA>

Similarly, Amatullah <2007, USA> and Knitter <2007, USA> described how real relationships between individuals from diverse traditions provide the best foundations for multifaith collaboration:

> … the state of it is evident in, the state of religion and the academy and its relationships with government and other actors has meaning and validity in relationships like ours. So, if not our faiths, our individual faiths, you [Anna Halafoff] being Buddhist, me being Muslim and the teachings of those traditions to respect each other, to hold human life sacred, to be courteous, to be hospitable. If individually we did not hold those values and practise them, and therefore cultivate a relationship in the practice of those teachings, we would not have a relationship, and we have a relationship that I value, so it is in these types of exchanges that the beauty of those things, of those teachings really become manifest and that is what counts. It's not a theological debate about texts … it's how we understand our traditions, how we practise them and how they inform our engagement of the other. <Amatullah 2007, USA>

> … the best way, maybe the only way, to break down some of our deeply rooted maybe prejudices or even our senses of superiority and exclusivity that we have inherited in our religious traditions … the best way to start questioning that is through friendships with people from other religions. When a human being enters into a relationship of genuinely caring for another human being and respecting another human being and then realising that that other being follows a totally different religious path, that is one of the most effective ways for self-reflection. And … we see the evils that can come out of religion in terms of violence, but that being the occasion for greater cooperation. [As a result of this] greater cooperation … friendships are developing. And once those friendships come, I think there's ever-greater hope that there can be real openness, genuine, genuine collaboration, genuine respect and affirmation of each other. <Knitter 2007, USA>

Respectful relationships cultivated through multifaith engagement are the most effective way to expand closed-minded, exclusive attitudes into open-minded awareness, thereby transforming ignorance and fear into mutual understanding and respect. As Abd-Allah <2007, USA> explained:

> … how do you expand a cognitive frame? I've thought about that a lot … What I discovered, and this is through interfaith, is that the ideas maybe are not that important. But what is important is a really effective relationship, a respectful relationship with another human being who, in my case, has a different orthodoxy but who likes me and I like them and who respects me and I respect them, so immediately the cognitive frame has opened and we didn't need a theology lesson and, in fact, the theology lesson might not have accomplished anything. It would have been interesting to me, but maybe it didn't accomplish anything and then there's another example here that, in Eboo [Patel]'s group this girl Cassie … when I came here to visit them, Eboo brought me here and we all got together and we had lunch together, and I found all these people amazing people, but her story really drove this home … I said "tell me about yourself". So we went around the table and we came to her and she said "I'm an Evangelical and I was at such and such Evangelical College and I was like a lot of Evangelicals very narrow and one day a Bangladeshi student came up to me and he was doing a report on exotic religions and he thought mine was, so he wanted to ask me questions. And I agreed. So we went to a place where we could talk and he asked me the questions and then, after we were finished, I said, 'now you give me the questions and I'm going to ask you'". And she said, "When he did that, I discovered him and one of the things that I discovered was that he prayed five times a day and for me that was impressive". So she said, "I remained an Evangelical, I wasn't converted, I didn't get married to him, we didn't even become boyfriend and girlfriend", but she said "that altered my experience", and to me that is the cognitive frame … and nothing affects people like stories. We're the great storytellers and we're the people who love to be told stories, but stories are human. So that would certainly be, for me, the great benefit that I've gotten from it so far. A very practical one at that … And … that's what enables us to do positive things. <Abd-Allah 2007, USA>

According to Abd-Allah <2007, USA>, the 'secret' to expanding 'cognitive frames' is to work at this personal level:

> … in reality, our only point of contact is that I can know you in a minute, you're Anna, and you can know me in a minute, I'm Omar, and I can never know you and you can never know me, and we can never know reality. But this we have, and … that kind of a personal, that's the whole secret of the thing as I see it, is the ability of the person to interact as a person and then we can work with things like cognitive frames … <Abd-Allah 2007, USA>

These actor perspectives demonstrate that multifaith engagement is most effective when it is embodied, whether in role models, in personal stories or in real relationships. It is at the personal level that cognitive frames can be expanded and that we can begin to learn and practise the new language of mutual understanding and respect. In fact, it is these real relationships that hold the multifaith movement together.

Expanding Cognitive Frames from Exclusivist to Pluralist Paradigms

Many participants commented on the importance of expanding cognitive frames from exclusivist to pluralist paradigms at the collective level, as well as the individual level. As Abd-Allah <2007, USA> remarked, 'the closing down of cognitive frames is the real destruction of democracy'. Voll <2007, USA> similarly described the clash *within* civilisations, between exclusivists and pluralists, as the 'struggle for the soul of humanity':

> … People will talk about the struggle for the soul of Islam, and what that reflects is that within Islam there is a great debate, or great debates in the plural, about what is the nature of the Islamic experience, and how does it fit into the 20th century world. And there … the contrasts are really the open, inclusive, pluralist approach to survival in the world … and the closed, exclusivist, protectionist kind of approach … [and] that is not a situation that is unique to the global Muslim community. In all of the great communities of the world, you get this kind of duality: … it's the struggle for the soul of humanity. Is humanity going to be open, pluralistic and recognise the absolute necessity for survival of pluralism if we're living in this world, or will we try and see it in terms of competitive, exclusivist units? <Voll 2007, USA>

As described in previous chapters, many participants affirmed the view of some scholars that the ambivalent nature of religion promotes both closed exclusivist and open pluralist paradigms. However, at their best religions can offer methods of transcending these narrow, self-centred perspectives to adopt altruistic and pluralist worldviews (Knitter 1995: 71; Hick 1985: 29, 34, 2001: 16–17); <Amatullah 2007, US; Margaryan 2007, USA; Ramey 2007, USA; Vendley 2007, USA; Voll 2007, US; Landau 2008, AUS; Woodlock 2008, AUS>. Following this argument, Voll <2007, USA> stated that 'the great religious traditions are still *the* strongest historic resource for humanity to get human beings outside of themselves and into a broader and open vision'. The great challenge, argued Vendley <2007, USA>, is how to reorient politics at the local and global level to be receptive to incorporating this religious wisdom from multiple faith traditions:

> … the first great challenge of multireligious cooperation is eminently practical—put out the fires, address, marshal the great assets of religion by cooperation to address the acute sufferings of the human family … The second great challenge is for each of the religions to learn how to mediate its own profound experiences of transcendence into public idioms … so that we might find together, at least, the openness to talk about the mystery of the human experience, that it is oriented beyond itself … Vaclav Havel, in recent writings, has very trenchant remarks to make that in fact there is the need … for an acknowledgement of the fact that the self, the very structure of the human self, is oriented beyond itself. That's the very capacity of grasping the other as the other … so there have been prophets of our own time that are pointing out that, in fact, without an acknowledgement of the fact of the openness of the human spirit … the fact that it is always out ahead of itself, it can't be contained, we are in a systematically distorting situation. Today the challenge is, since no one religion's understanding of transcendence can become the currency and capital for our public pluralistic orienting of ourselves in terms of political shape and order, how can multireligious cooperation begin to mediate public images of transcendence, which can be orienting a political discourse itself. Now that pragmatically shows up in early signs that political leaders of the UN want to talk with religious leaders, that is very valuable and very positive. It's as likely as not to be addressing that first area of practical work, whereas in fact it's the long-term area of … reorienting our political discourse itself, which is the second in companion challenge to the first. <Vendley 2007, USA>

While religions have always played a role in politics, the major challenge for religions in plural societies and in relation to cosmopolitan global governance is to learn how to share the public and political sphere with diverse actors and to collaborate across sectors to counter risks. According to Knitter <2007, USA>:

> … religions have always … been mixed with politics … in so far as all religions are trying to create a world in which human beings can live with each other in more peaceful, life-giving ways, they've got to be involved with people who are fashioning our society. I love Gandhi's statement, he said, "people who say that religion has nothing to do with politics don't really understand religion" …it is now … the responsibility of religions to develop ways, and this is going to take some effort and some practice and some help from outside of religion, on how to carry on a discourse with politicians in the presence of other religious traditions, in a way in which each religion will be able to make its contribution in a context in which each religion recognises that its contribution, as important as it may be, is one among many. <Knitter 2007, USA>

One such model is 'relational diplomacy', which Seiple <2007, USA> described as an ideal scenario of collaboration between state and religious actors, where a priori respect is given to the rule of law and human rights, recognising that the imperative contained in these so-called secular values is actually religious, and can be found in all faith traditions. According to Seiple <2007, USA>, cultivating 'an atmosphere of respect' for the best in all traditions, for the rule of law and human rights, and for multi-actor cooperation between 'governments top-down' and 'faith groups bottom-up' is at the heart of this 'relational diplomacy' model. In addition, Seiple <2007, USA> argues that the key to transforming the worst of any faith exists within the faith itself, but also in the ability of peacebuilders to work together, to defeat all forms of fundamentalism through the process of listening, understanding different perspectives and developing mutual respect.

As we live in ever more religiously and culturally diverse societies, there is a need for a new public language of mutual understanding and respect, which recognises that religion can play a constructive role in ultramodern governance. Ultramodern plural societies demand respect for all, enabling processes of deliberative democracy that provide a space for multiple, including religious, voices in the public sphere. As Habermas (2005: 27–28) described, religious individuals and communities have a right to exert their influence in the deliberative public sphere, alongside other citizens and groups, as long as they are respectful of the rights of others. Religious persons cannot separate their political views from their religious frameworks, in particular given that their concepts of justice are derived from their religious traditions (Habermas 2006: 8). Habermas (2006: 16, 20) thereby proposes a new multi-dimensional conceptualisation of reason, akin to 'relational diplomacy', that no longer excludes religion and whose success rests on the ability of both non-religious and religious citizens to behave self-reflexively in the public sphere.

As Habermas (2006: 1–4) explained, in the complex world of *multiple [ultra] modernities* there is no longer any place for exclusive truth claims or politically imposed religious doctrines. As the secular state guarantees that no one religion can dominate over others and encourages religious pluralism, it therefore enables religions to self-reflexively 'see [themselves] through the eyes of others' and therefore to renounce violence and exclusive truth claims (Habermas 2007: 10–11). In this way, ultramodern secular societies demand respect for all, providing a space for multiple, including religious, voices in the public sphere. Exclusive truth claims, both religious and non-religious, are replaced with rights-based frameworks that ensure freedom of religion yet guarantee that religious freedom does not impinge on the rights of others. Therefore, cosmopolitan secular and multifaith societies encourage peacebuilding principles by enabling a critical, self-reflexive, deliberative public sphere in which there is no place for religious violence, whether direct or structural, but in which faith-based wisdom can influence policies toward the common good.

The Multifaith Movement's Critical Mass

The clash between cosmopolitans and anti-cosmopolitans, between exclusivists and pluralists, be they religious or market fundamentalists, is one of the most pressing issues affecting the survival of our entire planet. As Gibbs <2007, USA> remarked, '[w]e're seeing a drama for the future of humanity being played out', '[w]ill we go the way of fear and hatred and division, violence and destruction, or will we find a different way?' Gibbs <2007, USA>, posited that 'the best of the interfaith movement is shining a light on a different way, a way [in which] we can invest in cultivating the technologies of peace and mutual understanding and respect', drawing on spiritual and religious traditions as resources. According to Gibbs <2007, USA>, while humanity has expended an enormous amount of effort on perfecting the ability to be violent, we have invested comparatively little in perfecting the ability to be peaceful. Despite the fact that the negative aspects of religion have dominated the media since September 11, the multifaith movement has continued to grow and to seek collaborative solutions to global crises, thus leading the way forward in the creation of new mazeways of global responsible living:

> … [the multifaith movement] is also growing in strength. It's growing in tiny ways … as John Paul Lederach says in *The Moral Imagination*, if you look at mass when you're baking bread it's the flour and you can put a little bit of yeast into a lot of flour and it has the potential to transform it … [W]e are creating, to use his term, "critical yeast" now and I'm really hopeful … our earth is letting us know that we can't continue being as foolish as we've been and survive, so we have to find a new way. We have to stop wasting our resources in division and domination, oppression, and dedicate them to creating a new tomorrow and from my perspective it's critically important in that regard that we claim … a consciousness that we are from the same source and we're citizens of this planet and we darn well better understand that first, and then say how can I and we, whoever the we is … identify with, contribute to that whole … <Gibbs 2007, US>

Similarly, Shaw <2007, AUS> compared the steady growth of peacebuilding movements, including the multifaith movement, and the emerging cosmopolitan condition to 'an underground river':

> When you go to Central Australia, you'll see the white ghost gums, and they're growing, they're quite flourishing, but it's completely dry on the surface. So underneath, the roots are down there, they're tapping into the water that's allowing the growth of the desert to bloom. But occasionally, when it rains, there's an inundation and overflow, and that allows the

> Berlin Wall to fall down, or Apartheid [to end]… or a big demonstration to happen, and then it goes back and continues to bubble on … the underground movement that's there, that bubbles up every now and again in Seattle or Genoa, in multifaith and interfaith. It's not on the surface, but it's such an important development, and there are so many people involved, that it can shift, and so the interfaith can meet with the environment [movement] can meet with the social justice [movement] and we can turn things around … <Shaw 2007, AUS>

Finally, Trebilcock <2008, AUS> suggested that it is the diversity of interconnected actors within the peacebuilding movement—including multifaith actors—that provides its momentum and strength:

> … the truth that you share between different religions is a transcendental one, but at the same time I also read this really cool book … on the scheme of bio-diversity … and it was basically this idea that there's … this movement at the moment … 250,000 different groups of people around the world, who are all doing different things … there'll be an environmental group over here or there'll be a different group over there doing something else. But just the sheer number of them, and the fact that they are diverse, and there is … that scheme of diversity, means that they … are almost indestructible in a way because they're all different people acting independently, yet they're unconscious of the fact that they're all interconnected because they're so … disparate, there's so many of them but they're so small, so unconnected. So that really got me thinking, this diversity that you have between faiths or between movements is really, really important, because it's strengthening … <Trebilcock 2008, AUS>

These actor perspectives demonstrate that the multifaith movement, alongside other ultramodern social movements, has maintained a commitment to forging new peacebuilding collaborative frameworks to advance common human and environmental security, despite vehement opposition from anti-cosmopolitan actors. While the multifaith movement has been largely ignored by the media and by sociologists of religion, these actor perspectives provide much-needed evidence of the steady growth of this movement in ultramodernity and of its role not only in promoting peacebuilding principles between faith-based communities but also between other sectors including government and UN agencies. It is precisely multifaith actors' capacity for collaboration with one another, and their ability to form multi-actor peacebuilding networks, that is modelling a new form of cosmopolitan governance founded on a public language of mutual understanding and respect. Genuine peacebuilding demands a multi-dimensional approach, where diversity is seen as an asset, yet where commitment to the common good is the central principle. Therefore, the multifaith movement and multi-actor peacebuilding networks are aligned with ultramodern cosmopolitan principles, as they strive to improve society through non-violent, deliberative, democratic processes.

Conclusions

These actor perspectives demonstrate that the multifaith movement seeks to affirm common values, and to strengthen the role that religions can play in encouraging their adherents to develop positive qualities such as compassion and altruism.

Based on cosmopolitan peacebuilding principles they encourage respect for diversity within a framework of commitment to equal rights for all. As a result, they have encountered much opposition, especially from anti-cosmopolitan, conservative religious and state actors. However, in ultramodern times, liberal and conservative faith communities have increasingly been uniting in response to common issues, such as terrorism and climate change. Through increased contact and communication this has in some cases enabled conservative actors to become more open to respecting diverse religious traditions. In these ways, religious peacebuilders have fostered processes of cosmopolitanisation in ultramodern societies. Indeed, a new emphasis on practical action rather than dialogue has enhanced the scope and efficacy of the multifaith movement. However, the increased participation of conservative actors in multifaith networks raises some concerns that the multifaith movement is in danger of compromising its peacebuilding potential, particularly in relation to structural violence and the rights of women, children and animals, by giving a platform for conservative voices within a movement that has traditionally been progressive. These are issues that require further investigation.

These actor accounts also lend further evidence to the claim that one of the most critical problems of the ultramodern era is not a clash *between* civilisations but a clash between exclusivists and pluralists *within* civilisations. The ambivalent nature of religion creates both closed, exclusivist mindsets and open, pluralist ones. However, the particular strength of multifaith initiatives, due to the emphasis they place on valuing diversity, is their ability to transform narrow, exclusive viewpoints into broad, open visions, thereby altering 'cognitive frames' from ignorance to mutual understanding. Perhaps, the greatest challenge currently facing humanity, as we confront a number of global risks including poverty, terrorism and climate change, is whether we will work together to solve these problems, recognising our interdependence, or whether we will continue to compete against one another so that only some will thrive while others' lives are devalued, exploited and ultimately destroyed. The multifaith movement has been gradually building, alongside other social movements in the twentieth century, modelling new cosmopolitan mazeways and thereby demonstrating that collaborative peacebuilding frameworks are effective strategies for countering global risks and advancing common security.

Finally, for multifaith engagement to be truly effective many participants agreed that it must be embodied—in role models, in personal stories and real relationships. It is these interactions that lead to the expansion of cognitive frames first at the individual and eventually at the collective level. In the words of the Australian songwriters Paul Kelly and Kev Carmody (1991), 'from little things big things grow'. While the multifaith movement, alongside other cosmopolitan social movements, has operated largely on the fringes of society, in the twenty-first century, in the face the global risks of terrorism and climate change, multifaith and environmental movements are becoming more mainstreamed. However, as in previous times in history, these cosmopolitan collaborative mazeways are constantly under attack from anti-cosmopolitan forces within societies whose interests are threatened by the changes that these new mazeways entail.

References

Abdo, Geneive. 2008. False prophets. *Foreign Policy*, July/August, 51–53.

Abu-Nimer, Mohammed. 2001. Conflict resolution, culture, and religion: Toward a training model of interreligious peacebuilding. *Journal of Peace Research* 38(6): 685–703.

Appleby, R.Scott. 2003. Retrieving the missing dimension of statecraft: Religious faith in the service of peacebuilding. In *Faith-based diplomacy: Trumping realpolitik*, ed. Douglas Johnston, 231–258. Oxford: Oxford University Press.

Benhabib, Seyla. 1992. *Situating the self gender, community and postmodernism in contemporary ethics*. New York/London: Routledge/Kegan and Paul.

Benhabib, Seyla. 2004. *The rights of others: Aliens, citizens and residents*, The John Robert Seeley memorial lectures. Cambridge: Cambridge University Press.

Benhabib, Seyla. 2007. Democratic exclusions and democratic iterations: Dilemmas of "just membership" and prospects of cosmopolitan federalism. *European Journal of Political Theory* 6(4): 445–462.

Bharat, Sandy, and Jael Bharat. 2007. *A global guide to interfaith: Reflections from around the world*. Winchester: O Books.

Braybrooke, Marcus. 2007. *Interfaith witness in a changing world: The world congress of faiths, 1996–2006*. Abingdon: Braybrooke Press.

Brodeur, Patrice. 2005. From the margins to the centers of power: The increasing relevance of the global interfaith movement. *Cross Currents* 55(1): 42–53.

Cox, Harvey. 1988. Many mansions or one way? The crisis in interfaith dialogue. *The Christian Century* 105(24): 731–735.

Habermas, Jürgen. 1984. *The theory of communicative action: Vol. 1. Reason and the rationalization of society*. Cambridge: Polity Press.

Habermas, Jürgen. 1987. *The theory of communicative action: Vol. 2. Lifeworld and system: A critique of functionalist reason*. Cambridge: Polity Press.

Habermas, Jürgen. 2005. Equal treatment of cultures and the limits of postmodern liberalism. *The Journal of Political Philosophy* 13(1): 1–28.

Habermas, Jürgen. 2006. Religion in the public sphere. *European Journal of Philosophy* 14(1): 1–25.

Habermas, Jürgen. 2007. *The divided west*, ed. and trans. Cronin, Ciaran (2007). Cambridge: Polity Press.

Halafoff, Anna, and Conley Tyler Melissa. 2005. Rethinking religion: Transforming cultures of violence to cultures of peace. In *UNESCO Paris and International Outlook Conference, Religion in Peace and Conflict: Responding to Militancy and Fundamentalism*. UNESCO, Paris, 12–14 April 2005, pp 365–371.

Hick, John. 1985. *Problems of religious pluralism*. Basingstoke/London: Macmillan.

Hick, John. 2001. *Dialogues in the philosophy of religion*. Basingstoke/New York: Palgrave.

Hollinsworth, David. 2006. *Race and racism in Australia*. Melbourne: Thomson Learning/Social Science Press.

Huff, Peter A. 2000. The challenge of fundamentalism for interreligious dialogue. *Cross Currents Spring* 50(1/2): 94–102.

Johnston, Douglas. 1994. Looking ahead: Toward a new paradigm. In *Religion, the missing dimension of statecraft*, ed. Douglas Johnston and Cynthia Sampson, 316–338. Oxford: Oxford University Press.

Kelly, Paul, and Carmody, Kev. 1991. From little things big things grow [song]. Comedy [Album]. Paul Kelly & the Messengers. Melbourne: Mushroom Records.

Kirkwood, Peter. 2007. *The quiet revolution: The emergence of interfaith consciousness*. Sydney: ABC Books.

Knitter, Paul F. 1995. *One earth many religions: Multifaith dialogue and global responsibility*. Maryknoll: Orbis Books.

Little, David, and Scott Appleby. 2004. A moment of opportunity? The promise of religious peacebuilding in an era of religious and ethnic conflict. In *Religion and peacebuilding*, ed. Harold Coward and Gordon S. Smith, 1–26. Albany: State University of New York Press.

Niebuhr, Gustav. 2008. *Beyond tolerance: Searching for interfaith understanding in America*. New York: Viking.

Sampson, Cynthia. 1997. Religion and peacebuilding. In *Peacemaking in international conflict: Methods and techniques*, ed. I. William Zartman and J. Lewis Rasmussen, 273–318. Washington, DC: United States Institute of Peace Press.

Vendley, William, and David Little. 1994. Implications for religious communities: Buddhism, Islam, Hinduism, and Christianity. In *Religion, the missing dimension of statecraft*, ed. Douglas Johnston and Cynthia Sampson, 306–315. Oxford: Oxford University Press.

Wuthnow, Robert. 2005. *America and the challenges of religious diversity*. Princeton/Oxford: Princeton University Press.

Chapter 8
Multiculturalism, Multifaith Initiatives and Countering Violent Extremism in Victoria

Following a cosmopolitan methodology, having established an overview of the multifaith movement in Chaps. 3, 4, 5, 6 and 7, this chapter presents a local case study of multifaith initiatives in the Australian State of Victoria. In particular, it examines how multifaith initiatives were successfully implemented as strategies to counter violent extremism in response to the events of September 11. At the same time, several problematic elements regarding multifaith engagement in Victoria emerged from viewing the local context from a global perspective, particularly those arising from the growing proximity between state and religious actors in Victoria and also the lack of inclusive religions and ethics education in Victoria's Government schools. This chapter therefore cites the Victorian approach to multifaith engagement as a best practice model, yet also seeks to aid the refinement of Victorian multifaith practices and policies based on insights gained from international contexts, particularly the UK and the USA.

Cosmopolitanism and Anti-cosmopolitanism in Australia

In order to understand Victorian multifaith initiatives, they need to first be examined within a broader context of multiculturalism and multifaith engagement in Australia, and in particular the clash between cosmopolitans and anti-cosmopolitans that has pervaded Australian history. As described in the introduction and previous chapters, in the wake of crisis events—including September 11, and the Bali and London bombings—religious communities in Australia have been pro-active in initiating multifaith activities to dispel negative stereotypes and to promote understanding between people of diverse faith traditions. In the State of Victoria, culturally, religiously and linguistically diverse (CRALD) communities have collaborated with state actors, including police, with the aim of building positive community relations that are informed by the principles of multiculturalism. These initiatives have been successful in advancing social inclusion and common security in Victoria (Cahill et al. 2004: 84–85; Halafoff 2006: 3, 9–12; Bouma et al. 2007: 5–6, 22–26, 43–60, 65–68).

A. Halafoff, *The Multifaith Movement: Global Risks and Cosmopolitan Solutions*,

DOI 10.1007/978-94-007-5210-8_8,

Conversely, Victorian CRALD communities have reported that rising narrow nationalism and a return to assimilationist immigration strategies, as promoted by the former Australian Federal Government under the leadership of John Howard, have legitimised prejudices in Australian society and exacerbated feelings of exclusion among minority groups, thereby potentially increasing security risks (Bouma et al. 2007: 5–6, 52–53, 65–68; Halafoff 2006, 2007). It follows that a narrow nationalism, which propagates either an anti-religious secularity or a particular faith tradition over and above others, is likely to lead to conflict in an ever more globalised world in which societies are becoming increasingly religiously diverse and faith traditions continue to play a central role in the majority of people's lives.

When people are denied access to opportunities and excluded from political processes, grievances abound and local and global risks are thus escalated. It follows that inclusive participatory processes provide a much-needed antidote to counter crisis events. In societies in which people feel a sense of belonging and where participation in the political process is encouraged the conditions for peace are enabled. In Australia in recent years, the Howard Government's exclusivist anti-cosmopolitanism approach to countering terrorism and to advancing social cohesion can be contrasted with the Victorian leaders' inclusive cosmopolitan approach to governance. With regard to the latter, the Victorian State Government has worked cooperatively with faith communities, successfully placing multiculturalism as a central pillar of its counter-terrorism and community-building strategy (State Government of Victoria 2005: 3). Therefore, it can be argued that cosmopolitan principles and policies of multiculturalism—provided they affirm a commitment to upholding the law and to human rights alongside respect for diversity—constitute the best foundation for building genuinely secure multifaith societies at the local and global level.

An Ambivalent History of Exclusion and Multiculturalism

Australia has an ambivalent history of exclusion and multiculturalism. British occupants committed gross injustices against Indigenous Australians, who were politically excluded until 1967. In the mid-nineteenth century, the Gold Rush brought waves of Chinese immigrants to Australia, who experienced discrimination and were victims of violent attacks. The Immigration Restriction Act, popularly known as the White Australia Policy, was implemented in 1901, restricting migration to European communities (Jayaraman 2000: 137–142). Subsequently, Australian immigration policy focused on assimilation to an 'Anglo-Saxon and Celtic ideal' until 1973 when Al Grassby, the Labor Government's Immigration Minister, delivered a speech titled *A Multi-Cultural Society for the Future*, emphasising the need to affirm cultural diversity with reference to the UN International Covenant on Civil and Political Rights (Theophanous 1995: 4–9; Hollinsworth 2006). In 1978 the Liberal Government, under the leadership of Malcolm Fraser, replaced assimilationist policies with policies of multiculturalism at the national level, establishing the Australian Institute of Multicultural Affairs (AIMA) in 1979 (DIAC 2007). *The Australian Institute of Multicultural Affairs Act 1979* outlined the following objectives:

> (a) To develop among the members of the Australian community: (i) an awareness of the diverse cultures within the community that arose as a result of migration; (ii) an appreciation of the contributions of those cultures to the enrichment of the broader community; (b) To promote tolerance, understanding, harmonious relations and mutual esteem among the different cultural groups and ethnic communities in Australia; (c) To promote a cohesive Australian society, and to assist in promoting an environment that affords the members of the different cultural groups and ethnic communities the opportunities to participate more fully in Australian society and achieve their own potential. (Parliament of the Commonwealth of Australia 1979 cited in Theophanous 1995: 17)

Multiculturalism enjoyed growing support and in 1982 was put 'at the heart of Australia's developing nationhood and national identity' (Galligan and Roberts 2003: 7). Former Labor Prime Minister Bob Hawke entered office in 1983, and in 1987 AIMA was replaced by the Office of Multicultural Affairs (OMA) in the Department of the Prime Minister and Cabinet. In 1989, the *National Agenda for a Multicultural Australia* received bipartisan support (DIAC 1989a) and multiculturalism was defined as not only affirming a commitment to respecting diverse cultures but also as having limits, particularly concerning the need to respect the rights of others, limits that were summarised as follows:

- multicultural policies are based upon the premises that all Australians should have an overriding and unifying commitment to Australia, to its interests and future first and foremost;
- multicultural policies require all Australians to accept the basic structures and principles of Australian society—the Constitution and the rule of law, tolerance and equality, Parliamentary democracy, freedom of speech and religion, English as the national language and equality of the sexes; and
- multicultural policies impose obligations as well as conferring rights: the right to express one's own culture and beliefs involves a reciprocal responsibility to accept the right of others to express their views and values (DIAC 1989b).

However, during the 1980s there were emerging challenges to policies of multiculturalism. Conservative historian Geoffrey Blainey was among their harshest critics (Theophanous 1995: 33–39) and *The Fitzgerald Report* of 1988 made 'strongly nationalistic' recommendations that emphasised the need to promote 'Australian identity' as preferable to multiculturalism (Committee to Advise cited in Galligan and Roberts 2003: 9). Former Prime Minister John Howard, then the leader of the opposition, echoed these views, calling multiculturalism an 'aimless, divisive policy', asserting the need to affirm a 'common Australian identity' in its place (Galligan and Roberts 2003: 1). The Liberal–National Coalition lost the 1990 and 1993 elections and Labor Prime Minister Paul Keating continued to be promote multiculturalism, with a new emphasis as an economic asset aimed at facilitating global trade (Lopez 2005: 39).

However, former leader of the One Nation party Pauline Hanson's rise to power in the mid-1990s provides further evidence of growing anti-multicultural sentiments in Australia. Hanson attacked Aboriginal communities for receiving so-called special treatment and also Asian Australians as presenting threats to the Australian way of life. Howard was elected as Prime Minister in 1996, and refused to condemn Hanson's views, instead voicing support approval for her right to air them (Jayaraman 2000: 151). Howard's 1996 election campaign was titled 'For All of Us', where the implied '(but not them)' (Pearson quoted in Clark 2006: 109) represented the special interest groups who under Keating had apparently 'made the majority feel left out' (Williams 1997: 59 cited in Maddox 2005: 77). In 1996 the OMA became absorbed into the Department of Immigration and Multicultural Affairs and in 1997 a new National Multicultural Advisory Council (NMAC) was formed, which was dissolved by the Howard Government in 1999 (DIAC 2007).

Moreover, Howard's 2001 election campaign was 'dominated by the dehumanisation of asylum seekers, by fear and xenophobia—the fear of strangers and a rejection of "the other"', implying that the route of asylum seekers arriving by boat was 'potentially a pipeline for terrorists' and describing the increase in numbers of asylum seekers as an 'urgent threat to Australia's very integrity' (Lawrence 2006: 39–41). Following the events of September 11, 2001, the former Howard Government 'linked anxiety about terrorism with anxiety about ethnic and religious difference' (Connell 2006: 35), and the London bombings in July 2005 reignited the multiculturalism debate, with many arguing that multiculturalism was a contributing factor in producing 'homegrown' terrorists (Lopez 2005: 33). According to Petro Georgiou (2005):

> The analysis generally runs along the following lines: multiculturalism has encouraged Muslims to maintain their identity without becoming part of the community at large; this has led to separatism, the free propagation of extremist views and contempt for the Australian nation and its core values.

While multiculturalism was mischaracterised as promoting difference and 'offering no central core of values to provide a shared identity', since the 1980s, as evidenced in the excerpts drawn from policies cited above, multiculturalism in Australia has always affirmed commitment to the law, to the rights of others and to common values alongside respect for diversity and equity of opportunity (Georgiou 2005). Despite this fact, after the London bombings, the former Howard Government frequently made numerous attacks on multiculturalism and employed divisive rhetoric against migrant and Muslim communities, fuelling fears and prejudice in broader Australian society. Some notable examples of this discourse emanating from members of Howard's Government in what became popularly known as the 'Australian Values Debate' included former Education Minister Brendan Nelson's (quoted in Grattan 2005) statement in July 2005 that, 'if people don't want to be Australians and they don't want to accept Australian values and understand them, well basically they can clear off', and former Treasurer Peter Costello's (quoted in Lewis 2006) speech at the Sydney Institute in February 2006, in the wake of the Cronulla riots, against 'mushy misguided multiculturalism', in which he stated that Muslims who do not abide by Australian values should be stripped of citizenship, calling for a 'more muscular nationalism'. Comments such as these, which attacked multiculturalism and targeted the Muslim community, were widely criticised by politicians, journalists, academics and Muslim leaders for: fuelling division in the community (Coorey 2006); feeding 'Muslim-bashing' (Ray quoted in Coorey 2006); increasing alienation that could 'lead to violence'; and antagonising youth (Aly quoted in Packham 2006). These divisive comments were consequently described as demonstrating an alarming lack of responsibility on the part of the nation's leaders (Halafoff 2006: 3).

Several Australian scholars have linked Howard's anti-cosmopolitanism with the anti-cosmopolitanism of the Bush Administration and the American Christian Right. According to Raewyn Connell (2006: 37), the Howard Government, following the Bush Government's lead, 'reproduced America's lies … created a local climate of fear about terror, and sparked massive prejudice against Muslims'. Marion Maddox (2005: 81, 294, 198–199) described Howard's ascent to power in 1995 as largely driven by his family values crusade, imported directly from the US Christian Right, and his marriage of economic neoliberalism and social conservatism as paralleling the 'American theology of Christian supremacy' known as Dominionism. After the events of September 11, Bush (quoted in PBS 2004 cited in Maddox 2005: 270) pledged to 'rid the world of evil', and stated that 'the liberty we prize is not America's gift to the world, it is God's gift to humanity' (Bush 2005 quoted in Maddox 2005: 174), revealing his Dominionist strategy which defined the War on Terror as a holy war and saw America's mission as the world's saviour. Howard (quoted in Hage 2001: 28) also expressed the notion of a grand plan, in which Western society is on a civilising mission, declaring, 'We are, as all of you know, a projection of Western Civilisation in this part of the world. We have inherited the great European values of liberal democracy'. Ghassan Hage (2001: 29, 31) exposed Howard's 'fundamentalism' in his vision of universal values such as commitment to tolerance and democracy as inherently Australian and Western, thus implying that certain 'other' nationalities and civilisations do not uphold such values. Howard's fundamentalism, like all fundamentalisms, also discouraged critical reflexivity, as 'anyone who trie[d] to emphasise a different reality [wa]s clearly on the side of the Bad other'. Those who promoted multiculturalism and Aboriginal land rights; 'black-armband' history; left-wing intellectuals; Christians who work for social justice; gay couples; single mothers; Muslim and migrant communities; in short, all the so-called 'out groups' who had played a critical role in the public sphere, were thereby demonised. In their place, under the former Howard Government—as was the case during the Bush era in the US—Australia witnessed a rise in the influence of right-wing think-tanks, conservative press and talkback radio, which propagated neoliberal family values and Dominionist agendas (Maddox 2005: 210–221).

The so-called Australian Values Debate of 2005 had disastrous consequences. Carmen Lawrence (2006: 35) described how since the 2005 London bombings 'many ethnic groups in Australia, especially those who are identified as Arab or Muslim have reported a climate of fear', that 'racism has hit peaks not seen since One Nation was in full flight', and that a doubling of complaints of religious discrimination have been reported by the Victorian Equal Opportunity Commission since 1999. Several recent Australian studies similarly documented a rise of Islamophobia, and of discrimination against Arab and Muslim Australians, following September 11, the Bali and London bombings (HREOC 2004: 43–62; Cahill et al. 2004: 84–85; Bouma et al. 2007: 5, 43–48). In addition, many communities who were incorrectly perceived as Muslim, including 'non-Muslim Arab, Lebanese, Indian, Sikh, Pacific Islander, and African communities', were also been targets of *misplaced Islamophobia*. CRALD communities in Victoria and Queensland also reported a rise in migrantophobia, xenophobia, racism and religious vilification during this period (Bouma et al. 2007: 5, 48–52).

Governments and media have played a significant role in determining the extent of the impact of these crisis events. Negative impacts have been attributed to the mainstream media's 'misrepresentation of culture and religion' and fear mongering; 'lack of support for multiculturalism at the Commonwealth Government level'; and 'an emerging narrow nationalism in Australia, evident in the "Values Debate"'. Most disturbingly, this collective rise in inflammatory and divisive rhetoric led to violent acts against CRALD communities, as evidenced in the Cronulla beach riots in Sydney in 2005 (Bouma et al. 2007: 5–6, 52–53, 65–68). The Cronulla riots were a hideous display of nationalism and racism, fuelled by 'shock jocks' and also in part by the Values Debate. Youths on a mission to protect 'our' beaches and 'our' women, draped in Australian flags singing *Waltzing Matilda*, chanting 'Aussie! Aussie! Aussie!', 'Fuck off Lebs! Fuck off wogs! Let's keep our country clean!' and 'Go home!', brutally attacked two men of so-called of Middle Eastern appearance (Lawrence 2006: 32–34). The Cronulla riots took most Australians by surprise. However, when you consider Australia's history of exclusion, especially our recent history including the ill treatment of asylum seekers and demonisation of Muslim communities, it was hardly surprising at all.

In the wake of the Cronulla riots in Sydney in 2005, 44% of Australians thought that Australian society was racist (Newspoll cited in Shannahan 2005) and 75% believed 'there is an underlying racism in Australia' (ACNielson cited in Shannahan 2005). Concurrently, 70%, according to Newspoll (cited in Shannahan 2005), and 81%, according to ACNielson (cited in Shannahan 2005), of Australians said they supported multiculturalism. However, in 2007 the Howard Government, in its final blow to multiculturalism, replaced the Department of Immigration and Multicultural Affairs with the Department of Immigration and Citizenship (DIAC) and implemented a citizenship test for new immigrants that included a section on Australian Values. Despite the Howard Government's demise in late 2007, the title of DIAC remains unchanged to this day.

Multiculturalism and Multifaith Initiatives in Victoria

Despite the constant attacks by the right-wing press, academics and the former Howard Government, multiculturalism was defended and promoted as a strategy for building social inclusion and common security in the State of Victoria during the Howard years.

As a primary site for the discovery of gold in the late 1800s, Victoria has a long history of cultural and religious diversity as a result of immigration. While religious diversity in Victoria declined following the introduction of the 1901 White Australia Policy, following its demise in the late 1960s diverse CRALD communities immigrated to Victoria in large numbers. Growing numbers of religious persons in Victoria can be attributed to two factors: firstly migration particularly of Jews, Buddhists, Hindus, Sikhs and Muslims from Europe, Asia and the Middle East, and to a lesser degree conversion in relatively large numbers to Buddhism and Islam. Victoria's city and regional areas now include many temples, shrines, domes, minarets and mosques alongside churches (Bouma 2006: 52, 56). Consequently, Victoria has been at the forefront of multicultural policy development in Australia since the 1970s (Clyne and Markus 2001: 84). The Ethnic Communities' Council of Victoria (ECCV) was established in 1974 to represent Victoria's diverse immigrant communities. The Victorian Ethnic Affairs Commission, which was to later become the Victorian Multicultural Commission, was established in 1983. The *Ethnic Affairs Commission Act (1983)* was passed in that same year and the terms 'race', 'religion' and 'culture' were included in the Victorian *Equal Opportunity Act (1984)*. The *Victorian Multicultural Commission Act (1993)* superseded the *Ethnic Affairs Commission Act (1983)* and in the early 2000s the *Racial and Religious Tolerance Act (2001)* was passed followed by the *Multicultural Victoria Act (MVA) (2004)*, and the *Charter for Human Rights and Responsibilities Act (2006)* (Lentini et al. 2009: 14–15).

The principles of multiculturalism, as outlined in the *Multicultural Victoria Act (*2004*)*, are to recognise and promote cultural diversity in Victoria within the framework of a common law:

(a) Mutual respect and understanding for all Victorians regardless of their cultural, racial and linguistic backgrounds;
(b) The promotion and preservation of this diversity and cultural heritage by individuals and institutions;
(c) The encouragement of co-operation between people of different backgrounds so as to continue to build a positive and progressive future;
(d) Equal opportunities and access to participate in and contribute to social, cultural, economic and political life of the State; and
(e) The responsibility of all Victorians to abide by the State's laws and respect the democratic processes under which those laws are made. (*Multicultural Victoria Act* 2004: 3–4)

Indeed, despite national and international debates and critiques concerning multiculturalism, CRALD communities and so-called 'host' (Anglo-Celtic and European) communities throughout Victoria reported widespread support for multiculturalism in the late 2000s (Bouma et al. 2007: 6, 55; Lentini et al. 2009: 4, 21, 26–27). CRALD communities also described how they implemented a multitude of peacebuilding strategies to stem the negative impact of crisis events and attacks on multiculturalism at the Federal Government level. A significant rise in educational activities promoting awareness and understanding of Muslim culture and of multifaith engagement occurred in Victoria after September 11, and the Bali and London bombings (Bouma et al. 2007: 6, 55, 57–59). Muslim communities in particular have also been active in addressing the negative effects of divisive and ill-informed media reporting through positive engagement with the media (Bouma et al. 2007: 59–60), and Muslim public intellectuals have countered negative stereotypes and sought to promote understanding of their communities through commercial and independent media (Lentini 2007: 56).

In Victoria, these community-led initiatives, such as Mosque open days, multi-faith educational programs, symposia and festivals, have received State Government support in the form of funding. The Victorian Government, Victoria Police and several local councils have also initiated a plethora of multifaith activities in partnership with faith communities, including the Victorian Government's *Community Accord, Celebrate our Cultural Diversity Week*, the *Premier's Multifaith Leaders Forum, Multifaith, Multicultural Youth Forums,* the Australasian Police Multicultural Advisory Bureau (APMAB) and Victoria Police's *Multicultural Advisory Unit* and *Multifaith Council* (Bouma et al. 2007: 22–26). These initiatives have been aimed at fostering an inclusive Victorian community in which: religious diversity is welcome; religious traditions and practices are respected as long as they are consistent with the law and human rights; and good relations are developed and maintained between diverse communities and state actors that assist new communities with settlement and in managing tensions, whether old or new, should they occur. These initiatives have contributed to building genuinely secure communities and have also formed a significant part of preventive countering violent extremism strategies. The Victorian Government and former Premier Steve Bracks have been praised for their commitment to multiculturalism as a strategy to promote social inclusion (Bouma et al. 2007: 25). CRALD Victorians have also expressed an overwhelmingly positive view of Victoria Police, notably for their high level of community engagement and willingness to work in partnership with communities to address critical issues (Bouma et al. 2007: 71–72, 111; Pickering et al. 2007: 107, 109). Moreover, Victoria Police's community policing approach has been cited as an effective counter-terrorism strategy (Pickering et al. 2007: 115–116).

Indeed, the State Government of Victoria's counter-terrorism policy declares that a long-term view to attacking the causes of terrorism must include 're-affirming Australia's commitment to multiculturalism' (State Government of Victoria 2005: 3). The former Premier stated that:

> Governments must take a long-term view to address the causes of terrorism. The Victorian community gains great strength from its long history of democracy, diversity and harmony. The Government believes that an effective approach to terrorism must include measures to prevent, at its roots, the rise of radicalism that advocates terrorism. This can only be achieved through cooperation and partnership with faith and community leaders together with their communities. (State Government of Victoria 2005: 3)

These cosmopolitan strategies act primarily as preventive counter-terrorism measures by including religious leaders and communities in counter-terrorism networks, thereby establishing trust and understanding between communities and state actors such as police. These networks have provided additional benefits; for example, the arrests of suspected terrorists in Melbourne and in Sydney as part of Operation Pendennis on 8 November 2005 allegedly took place as a result of a 'tip-off from an Australian Muslim' in addition to the usual surveillance and intelligence operations of state and federal law enforcement actors (Lentini 2008: 186).

As described above, the Victorian Government approach of building networks with multiple faith communities in order to enhance preparedness for future crises and to promote multifaith engagement as part of a broader peacebuilding strategy has been largely acknowledged as beneficial to building positive community relations. In addition, these CRALD community perspectives demonstrate that multifaith and multi-actor peacebuilding initiatives in Victoria have played a positive role in formulating strategies to counter extremism and promote common security, particularly by normalising cultures of religious pluralism, thereby lessening the potential for alienation and radicalisation in multifaith societies. They have also encouraged deliberative processes between religions and states, thus assisting religious actors to play a non-violent role in effecting social change by influencing policy. State support of these initiatives has therefore been welcomed, especially in Victoria.

Thus, promoting multiculturalism not only enables multifaith engagement, it also provides the foundation for genuinely peaceful societies. Indeed, Victorian policies of multiculturalism have encouraged an equitable participation of diverse cultural and religious communities in processes of governance and have enshrined respect for diversity and rights into law. Both the Victorian Government and Victoria Police have moderated religious practices by affirming a commitment to common law and rights according to a cosmopolitan framework. Deliberative forms of democracy that encourage multifaith voices to have input into devising and revising these policies thus enable both the state and religious organisations to work collaboratively on developing and refining policies according to cosmopolitan principles. As a result, CRALD communities feel included in society and also in governance in the Victorian context, thereby lessening the risk of alienation and increasing feelings of empowerment to effect non-violent social change toward the common good.[1]

Critical Issues Facing Multifaith Initiatives in Victorian

Victorian actor perspectives gathered in the course of this study largely affirm the positive views previously expressed by Victorian CRALD communities regarding post–September 11 multifaith initiatives, yet new concerns have arisen particularly

[1] This study was undertaken well before the spate of attacks against Indian students occurred in Victoria. In recent years there has been a dramatic rise in the number of Indian international students enrolled in Victorian universities. Victoria is not immune to difficulties, yet in the past, as racism has shifted from community to community, Victorian's CRALD communities and state actors have effectively addressed tensions quickly and cooperatively. However the persistence of racism in Australian society is yet to be sufficiently acknowledged or remedied by state actors. In a city such as Melbourne, that prides itself on intercultural and interreligious harmony, perhaps it is our pride that has gotten in the way of an honest appraisal of these issues.

regarding the growing proximity between multifaith and state actors in Victoria. These concerns were raised by Victorian participants themselves, and also emerged by viewing the Victorian context in light of UK and USA experiences.

When situated within a global context, it is possible to see that many of the developments in multifaith relations in Victoria reflect global trends. Conversely, the extent of collaboration between state and religious actors in Victoria is closer than in the UK or the USA, a fact that has raised some new issues which have not been examined in previous Australian studies. Overall, the picture remains largely positive, and the Victorian model can be described as a best practice example of how inclusive cosmopolitan strategies can assist in ameliorating community tensions and preventing negative impacts of crisis events on communities. In addition, according to cosmopolitan principles, these models need to be constantly reviewed, and this study provides insights into aspects of multifaith engagement in Victoria that may well need to be refined and revised in the future.

Australia, like other Western multifaith societies such as the USA and the UK, has a long history of multifaith engagement. The first formal attempts at multifaith dialogue occurred in Melbourne, Victoria in the 1960s, predating the introduction of multicultural policies. Anglican Archbishop Frank Woods began inviting diverse faith leaders to meet for a meal and discussion at Bishopscourt, which enabled a greater level of understanding to be developed between faith traditions and for religious leaders of these traditions to start forming friendships. In the 1980s, the Council of Christians and Jews was established in Australia, notably later than in other Western societies (Baldock 1997: 193–196). The multifaith movement in Victoria was described as having been influenced by the Second Vatican Council, with its initial emphasis on Jewish–Christian relations in the 1960s, which then shifted to an interest in East–West dialogue in the 1970s <Dupuche 2008, AUS>. Multifaith engagement in Victoria arose in a period when there was greater contact among diverse religious traditions due to a rise in immigration and improved access to international travel. During the 1970s and certainly by the 1980s a new focus on multifaith peacebuilding initiatives emerged in Australia, especially during the Cold War period with the looming threat of nuclear war <Jones 2008, AUS>.

Gradually a wider interest in multifaith engagement occurred, particularly in Victoria where the Office of Multicultural Affairs assisted in the establishment of a Multi-faith Resource Centre, which functioned as an unofficial interreligious council. However, only a few years later the Centre dissolved as a result of division and conflict. In 1987, the decision was made to hold the 1989 fifth World Conference of Religions for Peace (WCRP) World Assembly in Melbourne at Monash University. From 1987 onward, the WCRP began to play an influential role in Australia. The event was a great success, with 700 delegates, half of who were international, and the Australian WCRP national office was moved to Melbourne where it has remained active to this day (Baldock 1997: 193–196).

The 1990s was a time of increased multifaith engagement in Australia at the federal, state and local council levels. The Uniting Church set up working groups with both Jewish and Muslim communities, the Council of Christians and Jews expanded throughout Australia, the Australian Council of Churches established a

Commission for Dialogue with Living Faith and Community Relations and also a Working Group on Religious Liberty. Multifaith organisations were also formed in Adelaide, Perth, Brisbane and New South Wales during this period. In Melbourne, Victoria, Monash University conducted several research and community engagement projects and the Springvale City Council formed a multifaith network (now the Interfaith Network of the Greater City of Dandenong) that still organises tours to the variety of places of worship in the area. Faith leaders also joined together in 1993 to support Aboriginal land rights and to raise concerns over the decrease of social services in Victoria. Christian and Jewish groups also reached out to assist Muslim communities during and after the Gulf War (Baldock 1997: 197–199).

Victorian participants described how following the end of the Cold War in the early 1990s, the multifaith movement in Australia focused on addressing rising economic inequities, on human rights and on environmental issues alongside other social movements of that period <Toh 2008, AUS>. There was also a particular focus on Indigenous issues <Shaw 2007, AUS; Jones 2008, AUS> and on New Age and Eastern spirituality <Shaw 2007, AUS; Dupuche, 2008, AUS>. A notable shift occurred in Australian multifaith engagement away from an emphasis on dialogue towards the application of wisdom from diverse traditions to the most pressing global risks of our times <Camilleri 2008, AUS>. Muslim communities in Australia also began to be active in multifaith initiatives in response to growing international tensions in the late 1990s <Hassan 2008, AUS; Ozalp 2008, AUS>, resulting in a rise of bilateral interfaith dialogues between Jews and Muslims or Muslims and Christians <Dupuche 2008, AUS; Jones 2008, AUS> and in Victoria specifically between the Victorian Council of Churches (VCC) and the Islamic Council of Victoria <Postma 2008, AUS>. The Leaders of Faith Communities Forum, a peak multifaith grass-roots council, was also established in Victoria in 1995 (FCCV 2010) under the auspices of the VCC.

The Catholic Interfaith Committee was established in 2000 in Melbourne as a subcommittee of the Ecumenical and Interfaith Commission <Dupuche 2008, AUS>, and the Jubilee 2000 celebrations in Melbourne included a major multifaith event entitled a 'Collaboration for Peace' <Dupuche 2008, AUS>. The Victorian Government was also described as beginning to develop collaborative relationships with faith communities in the 1990s as a flow-on effect of their commitment to multiculturalism <Postma 2008, AUS>. These local developments reflect global trends in the multifaith movement, as described by Braybrooke (1992) and by participants in the global overview of this study. Moreover, they affirm that the two key principles of multifaith engagement are: firstly, a genuine interest in developing greater understanding of diverse faith traditions, as evidenced by the increased interest in Hindu and Buddhist religions from the 1970s onwards in Australia; and, secondly, that multifaith initiatives have a long history of being implemented as peacebuilding strategies in response to global risks. The focus of multifaith initiatives in Victoria has shifted from one faith community to another over time, in response to international crisis events, a pattern that has also occurred globally.

Following September 11, the focus of multifaith engagement, as in other Western societies, shifted towards dialogue among the monotheistic faiths of Judaism,

Christianity and Islam. Muslim communities and academic and state actors began to initiate multifaith activities, increasingly incorporating social cohesion and counter-terrorism agendas (Halafoff 2006: 11–12, 2007: 3–5). Indeed, since September 11, issues of national security have been imposed on multicultural, multifaith organisations and Muslim communities, which are well positioned to promote harmony through commitment to social cohesion (Lopez 2005: 35) by challenging cultures of violence and promoting cultures of peace in their stead.

Subsequent to the events of September 11, an increase in multifaith activities also occurred in Victoria at the local council level in Dandenong, Moreland, Geelong, Hume and Kingston. The Turkish-based Fethullah Gülen Movement's Australian Intercultural Society in Melbourne and Affinity in Sydney have also been active in organising multifaith events and initiatives, often in partnership with academic institutions. The Australian National Dialogue of Christians, Jews and Muslims, including the Australian Federation of Islamic Councils, the Executive Council of Australian Jewry and the National Council of Churches of Australia also became increasingly active following September 11, and at a national level, the Federation of Ethnic Communities' Councils of Australia (FECCA) established a special multifaith committee, the Australian Partnership of Religious Organisations (APRO), in April 2003 (Cahill et al. 2004: 86–88). While the former Howard Government frowned upon multiculturalism, multifaith initiatives continued to enjoy growing government support throughout the nation throughout the 2000s.

As a result of the events of September 11, Victorian participants described how the visibility of the multifaith movement in Victoria increased as religious leaders joined together to condemn the terrorist attacks <Postma 2008, AUS>. By building on networks previously established among faith communities and also between non-religious and religious actors, multifaith initiatives provided a forum in which to dispel negative stereotypes <Aly 2008, AUS; Hassan 2008, AUS; Woodlock 2008, AUS>, and to affirm commitment to peace and the common good <Woodlock 2008, AUS>. Victorian faith communities reached out to Muslim communities, offering support and thereby awakening a new level of interest among Muslim communities in multifaith engagement <Woodlock 2008, AUS>. Consequently, Muslim communities, and the Islamic Council of Victoria in particular, became more active in initiating multifaith activities with an educational and peacebuilding focus <Dellal 2008, AUS; Hassan 2008, AUS; Postma 2008, AUS; Woodlock 2008, AUS>. Multifaith initiatives continued to be implemented as peacebuilding tools after the 2002 Bali and 2005 London bombings <Hassan 2008, AUS>. The success of these initiatives <Hassan 2008, AUS; Woodlock 2008, AUS> and multifaith engagement more generally as a means of developing greater understanding across faith communities has been widely recognised across CRALD communities <Aly 2008, AUS; Dellal 2007, AUS; Pascoe 2008, AUS>.

Victorian multifaith initiatives were also cited as providing opportunities for people from diverse communities to voice grievances in a non-violent way <Hassan 2008, AUS>, thereby contributing to countering processes of alienation <Woodlock 2008, AUS>. In addition, the London bombings placed a new emphasis on multifaith youth initiatives <Dellal 2008, AUS>. A new focus on the global risk of climate change also began to emerge in Victorian multifaith initiatives and organisations <Summers 2008, AUS> following the release of Al Gore's *An Inconvenient Truth*, reawakening a sense of global interdependence and the need for collaborative responses to environmental crises that had previously emerged in the multifaith movement in the 1990s <Landau 2008, AUS>.

Media interest in religion also increased in Australia as a result of September 11 and was described as being largely negative, spreading fear and prejudice in the broader community <Shaw 2007, AUS>. This was seen by some as occurring largely as a result of the irreligious orientation of journalists, and consequently had a negative effect on multifaith relations <Aly 2008, AUS>. Conversely, Victorian Muslim communities experienced some benefits by working with the media, including having access to a greater platform from which to counter fears and ignorance in the broader community. *Salam Café*, a Muslim current affairs and comedy program produced in Victoria, was viewed as a positive means of challenging negative stereotypes and of 'normalis[ing] Muslims' on Australian television <Aly 2008, AUS; Hassan 2008, AUS>. An increase in academic research and study programs for university students on religion also occurred in Victoria after September 11 and the London bombings <Dellal 2008, AUS>, as evidenced by the establishment of the UNESCO Chair in Interreligious and Intercultural Relations, Asia-Pacific at Monash University in 2004, the Australian Catholic University's Asia-Pacific Centre for Inter-religious Dialogue and the La Trobe University Centre for Dialogue in 2006 <Dupuche 2008, AUS>.

A growth in multifaith engagement, particularly a rise of participation of Muslim communities in Victorian multifaith initiatives following September 11, was consistent with global trends. Furthermore, the participants' perspectives indicate that Muslim communities in Victoria have been proactive in working with the media to counter negative stereotypes and that these efforts, despite the negative impacts of mainstream media reporting, have been effective in promoting positive community relations. An increase in academic interest in religion and multifaith engagement in Victoria during this period was also mirrored by similar trends in the USA and UK.

The main difficulty Victorian religious actors involved in multifaith activities, and Victorian Muslim communities in particular, experienced was a lack of resources and personnel to carry out their educational work as they were largely dependent on volunteers <Hassan 2008, US>. While Victorian participants viewed increased engagement of Muslim communities in multifaith initiatives alongside Christian and Jewish traditions as a positive development, they stated that there is also a need to broaden this engagement to include Hindu, Buddhist and Sikh religions, Indigenous spiritualities and New Religious Movements <Woodlock 2008, AUS>, as well as non-religious persons <Shaw 2007, AUS>. Religions were described by participants as offering the moral imperative and the inspiration for action to counter global risks and to work collaboratively for social change <Landau 2008, AUS; Pascoe 2008, AUS; Young 2008, AUS>; however, it was also observed that there is a need for religious leaders and communities in Victoria to do more on environmental issues <Landau 2008, AUS>. Victorian respondents also raised concerns that multifaith initiatives are viewed with scepticism <Woodlock 2008, AUS> for 'preaching to the converted' <Hassan 2008, AUS> and 'singing to the choir' <Aly 2008, AUS>, rather than reaching more isolated individuals and communities at greater risk of being radicalised <Aly 2008, AUS>. In addition, Victorian respondents cited more conservative elements of religious communities as opposing multifaith engagement <Pascoe 2008, AUS; Summers 2008, AUS> and calls were made for more intrafaith peacebuilding initiatives <Postma 2008, AUS; Summers 2007, AUS>. There was also a sense among participants that while affirming the benefits of common action and values, multifaith activities too frequently avoided dealing with 'tough issues' <Hassan 2008, AUS>.

Many of these issues, faced by Victorian communities, were identical to issues facing the multifaith movement in the UK and USA, particularly the need to: obtain more resources; extend beyond preaching to the converted; overcome resistance from conservative religious actors toward multifaith initiatives; be more inclusive, beyond Jewish, Christian and Muslim communities; and engage in more 'difficult conversations'. Whereas in the USA a rise of multifaith environmental initiatives was reported, in the UK multifaith engagement on environmental issues was hardly mentioned, and in Victoria it is clearly still an emerging area that requires more attention.

In addition, many participants described how, in response to the events of September 11, the Victorian Government increased its interest in religion, and in multifaith activities in particular, due to their capacity to promote community harmony <Aly 2008, AUS; Camilleri 2008, AUS; Dellal 2008, AUS; Dupuche 2008, AUS; Hirst 2008, AUS; Pascoe 2008, AUS; Postma 2008, AUS>. Victoria was cited as a leader among other Australian states for initiating an immediate multifaith response to the events of September 11 in consultation with the Victorian Council of Churches, and for promoting multifaith relations as part of a broader social inclusion strategy <Pascoe 2008, AUS>, initiatives made possible because of the existence of previously established grass-roots multifaith networks. The Victorian Multicultural Commission (VMC) provided financial support for multifaith initiatives <Hirst 2008, AUS> throughout the State of Victoria during this time, and local councils were praised for establishing multifaith networks <Aly 2008, AUS> to deal 'not with abstract dialogue but with concrete issues to do with local community needs' <Camilleri 2008, AUS>. Victoria Police was also commended for prioritising engagement and cooperation with Muslim <Hassan 2008, AUS> and Jewish communities <Hirst 2008, AUS>. As described above, despite the divisive rhetoric emanating from the former Howard Federal Government, the Victorian Government maintained its commitment to multiculturalism and was praised for being more supportive of multifaith initiatives, more inclusive of diverse faith communities and more consistent in matters of faith than the former Howard Government <Postma 2008, AUS>. Whereas the Howard Government attempted to silence religious communities in the public sphere when they criticised government policies <Pascoe 2008, AUS>, religious communities in Victoria were encouraged through these multi-actor partnerships to voice their concerns and to participate in deliberative processes of governance, countering processes of marginalisation and thereby reducing vulnerability to radicalisation <Woodlock 2008, AUS>.

Following the London bombings and the Cronulla riots, the VMC formed a Multifaith Multicultural Youth Network (MMYN) in response to concerns that young people, especially from CRALD communities, were experiencing discrimination and were consequently feeling excluded from mainstream Australian culture <Young 2008, AUS>. While this support of young people from CRALD communities was appreciated, concerns were raised that the MMYN, as a government initiative, was more focused on building relationships between the state and community groups than among community groups themselves. Consequently, while increased state interest in multifaith relations was viewed as positive, it was seen to be less effective than community-led multifaith initiatives. Moreover, young people felt that they needed to be able to implement their own initiatives and not have these initiatives imposed upon them by state actors <Young 2008, US>.

Multifaith initiatives that were focused on common action, for example, around environmental issues, were described as effective strategies for developing relationships among young people of diverse faith communities <Woodlock 2008, AUS>. Young people were also said to be playing an important role in multifaith initiatives as they had been raised with an understanding of global interdependence and responsibility <Young 2008, US>. As a result, young people can play a significant role in normalising religious pluralism and affirming the peacebuilding aspects of religious traditions that stress the interconnected nature of life <Trebilcock 2008, AUS>.

One Victorian participant raised the issue of unequal power relations among faith communities in dealing with Victorian state actors. Communities with weaker leadership structures, newly arrived communities, and economically poorer communities were described as lacking in the requisite skills and resources when dealing with state actors compared to better-organised and more established faith traditions. This participant was also concerned that state involvement in multifaith initiatives led to competition for funding between communities, thus creating tensions between communities, especially around the need for equitable assistance—highlighting the need to ensure that more powerful groups do not come to dominate the conversation <Aly 2008, AUS>. Similar issues were raised in the USA.

Indeed, Victorian participants felt that the primary role of partnerships between religious and state actors was for religious representatives to act as advisors on issues that were of concern to their communities, according to principles of deliberative democracy. Concerns were raised over whether governments were actually willing to listen to challenging opinions <Dupuche 2008, AUS>, while some participants noted the need to include more people with experience at the grassroots level in innovative multifaith activities rather than heads of faith in multi-actor peacebuilding networks <Camilleri 2008, AUS>.

Again, these concerns were consistent with issues raised at the global level, specifically calls to include religious voices in deliberative processes, and for states to moderate exclusivist religious discourses and ensure equitable participation of multiple faith traditions in these conversations <Landau 2008, AUS>. Following this argument, Victorian participants' views were congruent with USA participants that a secular pluralism involving the separation of religion and state was necessary to ensure that one religion did not dominate the political process. They also believed that policies of multiculturalism in Australia, and pluralism in the USA, whereby all religions should be treated equally, needed to be affirmed as the best way forward to build genuinely peaceful and deliberative societies according to cosmopolitan principles. Participants stated that in multifaith societies such as Victoria, as microcosms of a multifaith world, immigrant communities and multifaith peacebuilders have an important role to play in advancing these principles. A deliberative public sphere, where diverse religious actors are included, enabled them to effect social change and to build more equitable and inclusive forms of governance that emphasise collaboration between state actors and multiple faith communities at the local and global level <Ozalp 2007, AUS; Woodlock 2007, AUS>.

These actor perspectives demonstrate that the Victorian Government approach of building networks with multiple faith communities in order to enhance their preparedness for future crises and to promote multifaith engagement as part of a broader peacebuilding strategy was largely acknowledged as beneficial in building positive community relations. Victorian Government support of these initiatives has therefore been welcomed among faith communities.

In addition, these participant observations demonstrate that the greatest differences between multifaith engagement in Victoria, the UK and USA occur at the level of government participation in multifaith relations, which has been far closer in Victoria than in the USA and even in the UK. Both Victorian and UK Governments have prioritised working collaboratively with CRALD communities to prevent extremism and to promote social cohesion in response to September 11 and the London bombings. However, in the UK, state bodies did not establish multifaith networks, which instead remained autonomously run by community organisations that received increased state support. Conversely, in Victoria, local councils and the Victorian Government created networks, in collaboration with faith communities, within local and State Government structures. Due to the prominent role that communities have played within these networks and the success of these initiatives, especially as they have enabled deliberative processes between religious communities and state actors, these multifaith and multi-actor networks have been widely praised in previous studies. Actor perspectives gathered in the course of this study have also been largely positive regarding this increased collaboration between religious and state actors, thereby contributing to evidence documenting the success of these initiatives. However, both locally and globally some concerns have been raised regarding the growing proximity between governments and religious actors and the problems that this could create for CRALD communities.

The Religion in Schools Debate

Despite the many peacebuilding initiatives described above, and the Victorian Government's impressive overall record of promoting multifaith engagement, the way in which religion is currently being taught in Victoria's government schools has recently generated considerable controversy as it potentially undermines the success of Victoria's social inclusion strategies (Bachelard 2011a, b, c, d; Bouma 2011; Bouma and Halafoff 2011; Halafoff 2011; Topsfield 2011a, b, c; Zwartz 2011a, b, c). Christian volunteers currently teach 96% of children attending Special Religious Instruction (SRI) classes in Victoria's Government schools. Faith communities, including Buddhists, Jews, Hindus, Baha'is and Greek Orthodox, also provide SRI taught by accredited volunteers. Concerns have been raised that the exclusive nature of these programs, coupled with an emphasis on instruction *into a* particular religious tradition, is problematic in an increasingly multifaith society such as Victoria (Bachelard 2011a; Bouma et al. 2007: 78–79; Bouma and Halafoff 2009: 20–21). While the 2006 Victorian Education and Training Reform Act finally allowed the teaching of General Religious Education (GRE) in Government schools, GRE programs are yet to be developed and implemented. The current public debate regarding the teaching of religion in Government schools in Victoria, can be viewed as a clash between cosmopolitan actors, who are campaigning for more equitable SRI programs coupled with General Religions and Ethics Education (GREE), and their anti-cosmopolitan opponents who wish to preserve the Christian bias inherent in the current system.

The positive role that interreligious education can play in building a socially inclusive society has been widely acknowledged in a number of recent Australian studies (Cahill et al. 2004: 126; Erebus International 2006: 109; Bouma et al. 2007: 85–86, 2011: 80: Bouma and Halafoff 2009; Engebretson 2009; Lentini et al. 2009: 7) and educators shaping Australia's new National Curriculum, which will begin to be introduced in 2013, have stressed the 'need to nurture an appreciation of and respect for social, cultural and religious diversity' among Australia's youth (*Melbourne Declaration* 2008: 4). However, religious education in Australia's Government schools has been described as 'lagging behind other nations' (Byrne 2007: 45 citing Rossiter 2001). Catherine Byrne (2007: 32–34, 15) has expressed grave concerns about what she calls 'Australia's Christian privilege' in Special Religious Education (SRE), as it is known in NSW, and states that the need for a 'broad based comparative religious education is yet to be widely accepted' in Australia. Culturally, linguistically and religiously diverse communities and scholars have also made numerous requests for education *about* diverse religions to be included in the curriculum from the first years of schooling (Bouma et al. 2007: 78–79, 2011: 58–59, 80; Lentini et al. 2009: 7). By contrast, the United Kingdom is widely recognised as the leader in the field of interreligious education where World Religions Education (WRE) replaced Christian religious education in the state education system in the mid-1970s (Rossiter 2001; Lovat 2002). More recently, the Government of Québec has also introduced a more inclusive common Ethics and Religious Culture program in its primary and secondary schools (Ministère de l'Éducation, du Loisir et du Sport 2005).

Up until recently, public education has been the responsibility of State Governments in Australia. Consequently, each Australian State has its own unique history, laws and policies concerning SRI/SRE. The 1872 and the 1928, Victorian Education Acts stated that '[i]n every State school only secular instruction shall be given' during the 'school day', which was specified as 2 h before and 2 h after lunch. The Acts also stated that there was nothing to 'prevent the State school buildings from being used for any purpose on days and at hours other than those used for secular instruction'. Consequently, the 1872 and 1928 Acts forbid religious education to be included in Victorian Government school curricula yet allowed for religious instruction (RI) to be delivered by 'outsiders', namely Christian volunteers, in schools before or after the prescribed four school hours (The Victorian Statutes 1929: 248 quoted in Newell 1968: 1–2, 275).

The 1950 amendment to the Education Act, maintained the 4 h of secular instruction provided by teachers, and continued to forbid the teaching of religion in the core curriculum. RI was now permitted to be taught during school hours by 'accredited representatives of religious bodies… approved by the Minister' of Education. However, RI wasn't made compulsory as students could be 'excused from attending' at their parents' request (The Education (Religious Instruction) Act 1950 quoted in Newell 1968: 83, 274). By according a place for RI within school hours, the 1950 Act established RI as a norm for most students, given that parents had to seek an exemption for their children not to attend RI classes. The 1950 Act also made provision for Roman Catholic and Jewish RI in Victorian Government schools (Russell 1974: 12) and parents had to opt their children into these alternative programs.

While the multifaith movement, and the World Congress of Faiths in particular, played a prominent role in introducing WRE in England in the 1970s (Braybrooke 1992: 85–86) it is important to note that there wasn't a multifaith movement in Victoria at that time.

Rather than campaign for a shift from RI to WRE, Religions for Peace Australia (RfPA) lobbied instead for so-called minority faiths to deliver RI programs alongside Christian and Jewish providers in the late 1990s. These providers now include Baha'i, Buddhist, Hindu, Muslim and Sikh groups. Another notable change, which occurred in the 1990s, was that The Council for Christian Education in Schools (CCES), which had previously coordinated the Christian SRI classes, began trading as ACCESS Ministries. Many concerns have been raised about the Evangelical nature of ACCESS Ministries, and its CEO Evonne Paddison and Chairman Anglican Bishop Steven Hale's links with 'Arrow Leadership, which subscribes to the "Lausanne Convention", the evangelical manifesto which believes in making "[Christian] disciples of every nation"' (Bachelard 2011d). Both ACCESS and RfPA receive financial assistance from the Department of Education to administer their RI programs, yet RfPA receives a pittance, compared to ACCESS Ministries. Moreover, only ACCESS receives government funds to publish, provide and evaluate its curriculum materials, that aren't granted to any other faith community (DEECD 2009, 2010).

The 2006 Education and Training Reform Act, finally included the provision for teaching GRE within the core curriculum by qualified teachers, however, to this date there have been no allocation of financial resources by the Education Department to provide GRE curricula or to train teachers to deliver GRE programs other than in the final 2 years of secondary schooling. The 2006 Act distinguishes 'special religious instruction' (SRI) from 'general religious education' (GRE).

It defines SRI as '[i]nstruction provided by churches and other religious groups and based on distinctive religious tenets and beliefs' and GRE as '[e]ducation about major forms of religious thought and expression characteristic of Australian society and other societies in the world'.

Indeed, mounting concerns regarding SRI/SRE in Australia have prompted scholars, religious educators, religious community leaders and parents to convene roundtables and form networks, including the Religions, Ethics and Education Network of Australia (REENA 2011) and Fairness in Religion in Schools (FIRIS 2011), to call for a review of the way SRI/SRE is taught in Australian Government schools (REENA 2011; Zwartz 2011b) and to investigate best practice international examples of religious education (REENA 2011).

In March 2011, a group of concerned parents lodged a complaint against the Department of Education, Early Childhood Development (DEECD) in Victoria with the Victorian Equal Opportunity and Human Rights Commission, regarding the discrimination that their children were facing having been opted-out of SRI (Zwartz 2011b; Bachelard 2011d). Since then a public debate has been raging in Victoria, including state actors, ACCESS Ministries, REENA representatives, parent groups, religious community leaders and peak multifaith bodies such as the Multifaith Advisory Group (MAG), the Faith Communities' Council of Victoria (FCCV), The Multicultural Multifaith Youth Network (MMYN) and InterAction. Newspaper articles featured in *The Age* and the *ABC religion and Ethics* website on this topic have generated hundreds of letters and Tweets (Bachelard 2011a, b, c, d; Bouma 2011; Bouma and Halafoff 2011; Halafoff 2011; Topsfield 2011a, b, c; Zwartz 2011a, b, c). The prominence of this debate in Victorian newspapers, and on social media, indicates that the current model of SRI is untenable and that significant changes are afoot. Broad based support, among diverse religious and non-religious actors, is growing for a more inclusive model of GREE, taught by qualified educators, within the core curriculum, as opposed to the current divisive system.

Cosmopolitan Alliances and General Religious and Ethics Education

As described above, Australia witnessed a rise of political influence from the Christian Right under the former Howard Government. However, the current Federal and State Governments are failing to recognise that the world and their political constituencies are changing. There has been a widespread backlash against conservative religions in recent years, as witnessed by the rise of interest in atheism in both militant and moderate forms. Australians treasure their freedom, and the more progressive groups, be they religious or not religious, and are stepping forward to fight for their rights and for the rights of others. This has created new holy-unholy cosmopolitan alliances, among progressive actors, to call for changes on a wide array of issues such as marriage laws, religious education and climate change. It's therefore incorrect to frame the current SRI debate as one of the religious vs.

the anti-religious–it is rather a clash between cosmopolitan and anti-cosmopolitan actors–between those who seek equal rights for all and those who seek to preserve their positions of power, at the expense of others (Halafoff 2011).

Within a cosmopolitan framework, given religions' ambivalent roles in creating and ameliorating social problems, it is the responsibility of the state to guard against exclusive religious narratives that are capable of perpetuating prejudices and inspiring conflicts. It is also vital that no one religion should dominate within a genuinely secular system of state education. Therefore instead of instruction *into* a particular faith, providing a critical education *about* diverse religions and ethical traditions is a central tenant of cosmopolitan education strategies.

Currently, the State Government of Victoria's SRI model is contravening cosmopolitan principles, such as advancing equal rights and respect for diversity, crucial to socially inclusive societies. Providing a space within a secular education system to propagate exclusive religious views, and by allocating vast amounts of funding to Christian groups–to promote their values and to develop their curriculum–and not to other religious groups, risks undermining the positive outcomes of the Victorian Governments' vast investment in promoting multiculturalism and multifaith initiatives as foundations of its community building and resilience strategies.

A review of SRI needs to be conducted by the Victorian Government, in consultation with religious and non-religious groups, with teachers, parents, scholars and young people, in order to arrive at a solution that is beneficial for the whole community, and not simply for the most vocal anti-cosmopolitan actors, in this case the Christian evangelicals who run and support ACCESS Ministries.

A genuine commitment to the development of GREE programs and teacher training is also needed from the Victorian Government. In addition, as the State Government of Victoria currently supports many multifaith activities targeted mainly at immigrant communities, educational programs also need to be developed and delivered to all young people in Victorian, including 'host' communities, to promote religious literacy and to counter prejudices against religions and religious people.

Conclusions

In summary, Victorian experiences demonstrate the efficacy of multi-actor peacebuilding networks in countering risks, in this case terrorism, and in advancing common security. Including religious actors in multi-actor peacebuilding networks alongside state actors—such as police, education and media actors—which are informed by the principles of multiculturalism, has been a highly effective strategy for promoting social inclusion and thereby genuine security in Victoria.

Exclusion is a major contributing factor to global risk. While concerns have been raised that multiculturalism 'undermines solidarity and trust' because 'people are more likely to afford equal treatment to others with whom they share a common identity and common values', lessening marginalisation of minority groups through inclusive policies such as multiculturalism, can actually encourage their participation in society and therefore increase feelings of solidarity (Miller 1998: 48 cited in Eisenberg 2006: 19, 21). Moreover, promoting a multicultural view of Victorian identity also ensures that a common unity can be found beyond the oppositional 'Us and Them' of monoculturalism and policies of assimilation.

That is not to say that acts of racial or religious vilification do not occur in Victoria, or that multiculturalism in Victoria does not have its critics. However, in the face of such obstacles, the State Government of Victoria maintained its commitment to promoting an inclusive multicultural and multifaith community as a peace-building strategy, against global trends and against the divisive policies of the former Howard Government. The decision arguably protected the Victorian community from terrorism at a time when terrorism, homegrown terrorism in particular, posed a significant threat to Western societies. However, the future of multiculturalism, globally and locally, remains uncertain. Currently it remains cloaked in fears and misconceptions that it promotes disloyalty to the state and increases the risks of radicalisation. Victorian experiences indicate that it is perhaps premature to give up on multiculturalism, and that in a globalised world in which cultural and religious diversity will only increase perhaps the backlash against multiculturalism will in time be recorded as a temporary impulse born of a fear of change.

In terms of multifaith engagement specifically, employing a cosmopolitan methodology in this study has demonstrated that multifaith initiatives in Victoria have developed largely in line with global trends affecting the growth of multifaith engagement in Western societies. For the most part, the main aims, characteristics and trends of ultramodern multifaith initiatives have been very similar in Western, increasingly multifaith societies of Australia, the UK and the USA. A summary of these 'global' developments is presented in the concluding chapter. However, multifaith initiatives, despite global similarities have certain characteristics particular to each locality or region. This Victorian case study demonstrates that in our increasingly globalised age, viewing local situations through a global lens can shed new light on local issues and that, in turn, insights produced at the local level can inform global perspectives. In particular, the challenge of a growing proximity in religious-state relations, as they seek to collaboratively counter risks—be they of terrorism, environmental or economic security—emerges as one of the most significant issues of this study.

State-implemented multifaith initiatives in Victoria were criticised for being more focused on building positive relations between communities and states than among communities themselves, and for being led by state actors, thereby allocating a more passive role to communities. Young people especially viewed this as problematic. In so far as communities lack resources to initiative their own multifaith activities, and despite the good intentions of the Victorian Government, these actor perspectives indicate that perhaps assistance would be better provided in the form of funding to existing or new community-led multifaith initiatives, rather than for the creation of local and State Government multifaith bodies. It follows, according to the USA model, that ideally religious and multifaith organisations should be self-funded or at least funded by non-state actors, such as philanthropic organisations, in order to best maintain their autonomy and critical voice.[2] Indeed, following the Melbourne 2009 Parliament of Religions, the VMC provided funding to the Leaders of Faith Communities Forum, the multifaith grass-roots body established in 1995, to establish the Faith Communities Council of Victoria (FCCV) as Victoria's umbrella multifaith body. While still dependent largely on State Government funding, it sits outside of government institutions, which is a positive and significant development (FCCV 2010).

As there is definitely a need for state actors to develop a better understanding of religion, increased opportunities for contact, conversations and developing mutual understanding between state and religious actors should be encouraged, as has been the case in Victoria. CRALD communities have highly appreciated state support for Muslim organisations and multifaith initiatives following the events of September 11. Therefore, in countries such as Australia and the UK, where there is a tradition of state support for CRALD communities, especially in times of crisis, it is vital to ensure that resources be distributed equitably and not necessarily equally among diverse faith communities, cognisant of disparities among them, and also of the fact that certain communities are impacted more than others by crisis events at different times. These actor perspectives also suggest that states are wise to be as inclusive as possible in their support of religious organisations and multifaith initiatives, and that the Victorian model of multifaith engagement provides a best practice model as it concurrently offers more assistance to those communities who are experiencing trauma, while also including a diverse range of communities in broader consultations to minimise exclusion. It also demonstrates that multifaith practices and policies in Victoria need to be refined in order to ensure that communities are leading these activities, and not states, and that a culture of depending upon state funding for multifaith initiatives be gradually replaced with a more self-sufficient and thereby self-determined model of multifaith engagement, by drawing more on financial support from philanthropic organisations and benefactors within and beyond faith communities.

It also demonstrates that while significant progress has been made in recent years, Victoria is yet to develop a comprehensive program of General Religions and Ethics Education. As religions are playing an increasingly prominent role in the public sphere, there is a growing need for a critical education about diverse religions and ethics for all Australian school children in order to counter ignorance and advance a greater level of interreligious awareness, respect and understanding. In short ignorance about religions leads to the kinds of disrespect that greatly undermines social inclusion strategies and places our common security at risk. As described above, allowing a potentially narrow religious message to be

[2] It is of particular interest to note that following his election in 2008, President Obama's administration established the Centre for Faith-Based and Community Initiatives, which brings diverse religious groups in much closer proximity with state actors than previously in the USA. While a detailed discussion of this new development is beyond the scope of this book, the findings of this study could serve to inform the Obama administration, and faith-based and community groups, of the potential benefits and challenges that may arise from deepening religious-state collaboration.

taught to young Australians could sustain interreligious ignorance and heighten social tensions among Australian communities. Consequently, it is crucial that a greater understanding about current levels of religious and interreligious literacy among Australian children and youth is developed in order to identify potential areas of risk and also best-practice models of religions and ethics education to promote social inclusion and advance common security. As stated in previous chapters, if ignorance is the root cause of many interreligious tensions it follows that educational programs, which focus on generating a greater understanding of diverse worldviews, can provide the foundation for socially inclusive and peaceful societies. Moreover, for such GREE programs to be effective they need to be developed by collaborative networks comprised of religious and non-religious, state and community actors.

References

Bachelard, Michael. 2010. Thou shalt not teach humanism: ALP. *The Age*, November 7.

Bachelard, Michael. 2011a. Backlash as god forced into schools. *The Age*, March 27.

Bachelard, Michael. 2011b. Priest slams religion curriculum as "appalling". *The Age*, April 3.

Bachelard, Michael. 2011c. Anger at schools Christian bias. *The Age*, April 10.

Bachelard, Michael. 2011d. The god complexity. *The Age*, July 24.

Baldock, John. 1997. Responses to religious plurality in Australia. In *Many religions, all Australian: Religious settlement, identity and cultural diversity*, ed. Gary D. Bouma, 193–204. Melbourne: The Christian Research Association.

Bouma, Gary D. 2006. *Australian soul: Religion and spirituality in the twenty-first century*. Cambridge: Cambridge University Press.

Bouma, Gary D. 2011. Getting facts straight about religious education in schools. *ABC religion and ethicswebsite*.[Online]Availableat:http://www.abc.net.au/religion/articles/2011/05/23/3224745.htm. Accessed 29 Aug 2011.

Bouma, Gary D., and A. Halafoff. 2009. Multifaith education and social inclusion in Australia. *Journal of Religious Education* 57(3): 17–25.

Bouma, Gary D., and A. Halafoff. 2011. 'Time to review religious instruction in schools. *ABC Religion and Ethics Website*. [Online] Available at: http://www.abc.net.au/religion/articles/2011/04/08/3185955.htm. Accessed 29 Aug 2011.

Bouma, Gary D., Sharon Pickering, Anna Halafoff, and Hass Dellal. 2007. *Managing the impact of global crisis events on community relations in multicultural Australia*. Brisbane: Multicultural Affairs Queensland.

Bouma, Gary D., Desmond Cahill, Hass Dellal, and Athalia Zwartz. 2011b. *Freedom of religion and belief in 21st century Australia*. Canberra: Australian Human Rights Commission.

Braybrooke, Marcus. 1992. *Pilgrimage of hope: One hundred years of global interfaith dialogue*. London: SCM Press Ltd.

Bush, George W. 2005. *State of the Union Address*, January 28.

Byrne, Catherine. 2007. *Spirit in the 'expanding circle' why learn about religion in Australia in the 21st century? Can comparative religion knowledge enable cultural diversity capacity?* Master of Arts thesis, University of Queensland, Brisbane.

Cahill, Desmond, Gary D. Bouma, Dellal Hass, and Michael Leahy. 2004. *Religion, cultural diversity and safeguarding Australia*. Canberra: Department of Immigration, Multicultural and Indigenous Affairs.

Clark, Anna. 2006. Flying the flag for mainstream Australia. *Getting smart: The battle for ideas in education, Griffith review* 11: 107–112.

Clyne, Michael, and Andrew Markus. 2001. Attitudes towards immigration and multiculturalism. In *Building a new community: Immigration and the Victorian economy*, ed. Andrew Markus. Crows Nest: Allen & Unwin.

Connell, Raewyn. 2006. Chicago values: The Neoliberal Dream and Howard Government Politics. *Overland* 183(Winter): 32–38.

Coorey, Philip. 2006. Labor MPs divided on values pledge. *The Sydney Morning Herald*, September 13: 2.

Department of Education and Early Childhood Development (DEECD). 2009. Agreement between the State of Victoria and ACCESS Ministries for Chaplaincy and Religious Instruction Project.

Department of Education and Early Childhood Development (DEECD). 2010. Agreement between the State of Victoria and World Conference of Religions for Peace.

Department of Immigration and Citizenship (DIAC). 1989a. *National agenda for a multicultural Australia: Index*. [Online] Available at: http://www.immi.gov.au/media/publications/multicultural/agenda/agenda89/toc.htm. Accessed 19 Mar 2008.

Department of Immigration and Citizenship (DIAC). 1989b. *National agenda for a multicultural Australia: What is multiculturalism?* [Online] Available at: www.immi.gov.au/media/publications/multicultural/agenda/agenda89/whatismu.htm. Accessed 19 Mar 2008.

Department of Immigration and Citizenship (DIAC). 2007. *Fact sheet 6 – The evolution of Australia's multicultural policy*. [Online] Available at: www.immi.gov.au/media/fact-sheets/06evolution.htm#history. Accessed 19 Mar 2008.

Education and Training Reform Act 2006 (Victoria).

Eisenberg, Avigail. 2006. Education and the politics of difference: Iris Young and the politics of education. *Education Philosophy and Theory* 38(1): 7–23.

Engebretson, Kath. 2009. *In your shoes: Inter-faith education for Australian schools and universities*. Ballan: Connor Court Publications.

Erebus International. 2006. *Encouraging tolerance and social cohesion through school education*. Canberra: Department of Education, Science and Training.

Fairness in Religion in Schools (FIRIS). 2011. *Fairness in religion in schools*. [Online] Available at: http://religionsinschool.com/. Accessed 10 Apr 2011.

Faith Community Council of Victoria (FCCV). 2010. Available at: http://www.faithvictoria.org.au/about-fccv. Accessed 29 July 2011.

Galligan, Brian, and Winsome Roberts. 2003. *Australian multiculturalism: Its rise and demise*. Refereed paper for Australasian Political Studies Association Conference. [Online] University of Tasmania, Hobart. Available at: http://www.utas.edu.au/government/APSA/GalliganRoberts.pdf. Accessed 1 Sept 2006.

Georgiou, Petro. 2005. Multiculturalism and the war on terror. [Online] *AustralianPolicyOnline*. Available at: http://www.apo.org.ay/webboard/results.chtml?filename_num=41084. Accessed 1 Sept 2006.

Grattan, Michelle. 2005. Accept Australian values or get out, Nelson declares. *The Age*, August 25, p 1.

Hage, Ghassan. 2001. The politics of Australian fundamentalism: Reflections on the rule of Ayatollah Johnny. *Arena* 51(February–March): 27–31.

Halafoff, Anna. 2006. UnAustralian values. In *Cultural Studies Association of Australasia annual conference, UNAustralia*. University of Canberra, Canberra, 6–8 December 2006 (electronic resource).

Halafoff, Anna. 2007. Advancing Australian "shared security": Secular-religious peacebuilding networks. In *Australian Sociological Association (TASA) and the Sociological Association of Aotearoa New Zealand (SAANZ) joint conference, public sociologies: Lessons and trans-tasman comparisons*. University of Auckland, Auckland, 4–7 December 2007 (CD-Rom).

Halafoff, Anna. 2011. The SRI status quo is simply not tenable. *ABC Religion and Ethics Website*. [Online] Available at: http://www.abc.net.au/religion/articles/2011/05/28/3229553.htm. Accessed 29 Aug 2011.

Hollinsworth, David. 2006. *Race and racism in Australia*. Melbourne: Thomson Learning/Social Science Press.

Human Rights and Equal Opportunity Commission (HREOC). 2004. *Isma` – Listen: National consultations on eliminating prejudice against Arab and Muslim Australians*. Sydney: Human Rights and Equal Opportunity Commission.

Jayaraman, Raja. 2000. Inclusion and exclusion: An analysis of the Australian immigration history and ethnic relations. *Journal of Popular Culture* 34(Summer): 135–155.

Lawrence, Carmen. 2006. *Fear and politics*. Melbourne: Scribe.

Lentini, Pete. 2007. Countering terrorism as if Muslims matter: Cultural citizenship and civic pre-emption in anti-terrorism. In *Terrorism, organised crime and corruption: Networks and linkages*, ed. Leslie Holmes, 42–59. Cheltenham: Edward Elgar.

Lentini, Pete. 2008. Antipodal terrorists? Accounting for differences in Australian and "global" neojihadists. In *The globalization of political violence: Globalization's shadow*, ed. Richard Devetak and Christopher W. Hughes, 181–202. London: Routledge.

Lentini, Pete, Anna Halafoff, and Ela Ogru. 2009. *Perceptions of multiculturalism and security in Victoria: Report to the Department of Premier and Cabinet, State Government of Victoria.* Melbourne: Global Terrorism Research Centre, Monash University

Lewis, Steve. 2006. Costello urges migrant loyalty. *The Australian*, February 24, p 2.

Lopez, Mark. 2005. Reflections on the state of Australian multiculturalism and the emerging multicultural debate in Australia. *People and Place* 13(3): 33–41.

Lovat, Terence. 2002. *What is this thing called RE: A decade on?* 2nd ed. Katoomba: Social Science Press.

Maddox, Marion. 2005. *God under Howard: The rise of the religious right in Australian politics*. Sydney: Allen & Unwin.

Maddox, Marion. 2011. Welcome address. *Religion and Education Roundtable II*. Sydney: Macquarie University

Melbourne Declaration on Educational Goals for Young Australians. 2008. Melbourne: Ministerial Council on Education, Employment, Training and Youth Affairs.

Miller, David. 1998. The left, the nation-state, and European citizenship. *Dissent* 48: 47–51.

Ministère de l'Éducation, du Loisir et du Sport. 2005. *Establishment of an ethics and religious culture program: Providing future direction for all Québec youth. Québec City: Government of Québec*. [Online] Available at: http://www.mels.gouv.qc.ca/lancement/Prog_ethique_cult_reli/prog_ethique_cult_reli_a.pdf. Accessed 7 May 2011.

Multicultural Victoria Act. 2004 (Act No. 100/2004 Version No. 003). Melbourne.

Newell, Phillip K. 1968. *The enactment and operation of the 1950 amendment to the Victorian Education Act*. Master of Education thesis. University of Melbourne, Melbourne.

Packham, Ben. 2006. PM firm on Muslim line. *Herald Sun*, September 2: 2.

Parliament of the Commonwealth of Australia. 1979 (Act No. 154, Section 5). Canberra.

PBS. 2004. *The Jesus Factor*, [TV programme] screened in the US on May 2004.

Pickering, Sharon, David Wright-Neville, Jude McCulloch, and Pete Lentini. 2007. *Counter-terrorism policing and culturally diverse communities*. Melbourne: Monash University.

Religions, Ethics and Education Network Australia (REENA). 2011. *Statement of principles and actions*. [Online] Available at: http://reena.net.au/. Accessed 10 Apr 2011.

Rossiter, Graham. 2001. *Finding the balance: Religious education in Australia*. International Association for Religious Freedom in consultation with the Economic and Social Council of the United Nations. [Online] Available at: http://www.iarf.net/REBooklet/Australia.htm. Accessed Jan 2007.

Russell, H.B. 1974. Religious education in schools. Report to the Committee on Religious Education. Victoria.

State Government of Victoria. 2005. *Protecting our community: Attacking the causes of terrorism*. Melbourne: State Government of Victoria.

The Education (Religious Instruction) Act 1950 (Victoria).

The Education Act 1928 (Victoria).

The Victorian Statutes. 1929. *The general public acts of Victoria* (in five volumes), Act 3671 Vol. II.
Theophanous, Andrew C. 1995. *Understanding multiculturalism and Australian identity*. Melbourne: Elika Books.
Topsfield, Jewel. 2011a. Let us get god out of the classroom. *The Age*, April 4.
Topsfield, Jewel. 2011b. Call to teach students the ethos of all religions. *The Age*, April 18.
Topsfield, Jewel. 2011c. Students who pass on religion win fight. *The Age*, August 26.
Williams, Pamela. 1997. *The victory: The inside story of the takeover of Australia*. Sydney: Allen & Unwin.
Zwartz, B. 2011a. Religious study contested. *The Age*, March 24.
Zwartz, B. 2011b. Academics call for review of school religious teaching. *The Age*, April 7.
Zwartz, B. 2011c. Why Christianity should be taught properly in our schools. *The Age*, April 11.

Chapter 9
Conclusion: *Netpeace*

This chapter summarises the main findings of this study and describes how multifaith initiatives have been implemented as cosmopolitan strategies to address the risk of radicalisation at the turn of the twenty-first century. It examines the issue of state–religious relations and proposes a new *netpeace* framework, arguing that a cosmopolitan approach to governance constitutes the most effective method for advancing common security in a globalised world. Finally, it argues that the anti-cosmopolitan *politics of fear* can best be countered not by hope alone but by a cosmopolitan *politics of understanding*.

Aims, Benefits and Challenges of Multifaith Engagement

This study has investigated how multifaith initiatives have been implemented as cosmopolitan strategies to counter global risks—such as terrorism and climate change—and to advance common security in ultramodern Western societies.

As described in Chap. 3, the global multifaith movement, comprising numerous local and global multifaith networks, arose largely through interaction between Hindu, Buddhist, Christian and Jewish religious actors at the turn of the twentieth century. The multifaith movement has four principal aims of:

1. *developing understanding of diverse faiths and of the nature of reality;*
2. *challenging exclusivity and normalising pluralism;*
3. *addressing global risks and injustices; and*
4. *creating multi-actor peacebuilding networks for common security.*

The first three aims have been present since the 1893 Parliament of the World's Religions (PWR). Following WWII the third aim, of addressing global risks and injustices, became more prominent within the multifaith movement in response to crisis events such as the Holocaust and the nuclear bombing of Hiroshima and Nagasaki. This change in focus also shifted the emphasis within the multifaith movement from dialogue to action. The second aim, of challenging exclusivity and

A. Halafoff, *The Multifaith Movement: Global Risks and Cosmopolitan Solutions*,

DOI 10.1007/978-94-007-5210-8_9,

normalising pluralism, was highlighted by the multifaith movement during the 1960s, 1970s and 1980s in response to processes of globalisation and rising immigration to Western societies. The fourth aim, of creating multi-actor peacebuilding networks that included religious actors, IGO, NGO and state actors, emerged in the latter half of the twentieth century, and focused on issues of common human and environmental security such as poverty alleviation and global warming.

From the 1960s onward, the multifaith movement, alongside other ultramodern social movements including the peace, women's and environmental movements, non-violently addressed injustices committed by global capitalism and led the way forward by creating new collaborative cosmopolitan mazeways of responsible global living. Multifaith actors also challenged cultures of violence, both direct and structural, within their own religious traditions, such as terrorism, exclusivity and gender inequality. A dramatic rise in multifaith engagement occurred in the early 1990s, accompanied by an increased interest in religious peacebuilding initiatives after the end of the Cold War, a period that can be described as a cosmopolitan moment in history. However, these processes of cosmopolitanisation met with much resistance, as witnessed by the rise of anti-cosmopolitan movements, including religious extremist movements in the mid to late 1990s. Thus, a clash occurred *within* civilisations, between cosmopolitan and anti-cosmopolitan actors, at the turn of the twenty-first century.

During the 1990s, as Muslim communities increasingly found themselves at the centre of crisis events and of discrimination in Western societies, Muslim peacebuilders began to take a more proactive role in multifaith initiatives. By the end of the 1990s the multifaith movement was well poised to counter the negative effects of September 11. Religion assumed a prominent place in the public mind during the 2000s, largely as a result of the events of September 11 and the subsequent 2005 London bombings. Multifaith initiatives suddenly became more visible as they were implemented as counter-terrorism strategies in Western multifaith societies and to remedy the negative impact of these crisis events on community relations.

The tragedy of September 11, similar to previous crisis events such as the Holocaust and the bombings of Hiroshima and Nagasaki, served as a stimulus for multifaith engagement at local, national and global levels. Therefore the multifaith movement has always been highly responsive to global risks and the focus of peacebuilding initiatives has shifted over time. As the process of 'othering' shifted from community to community immediately following a crisis, so too did the need to provide support to communities at risk or under pressure. Multifaith organisations reached out to Muslim communities, and Muslim communities themselves became more active in initiating multifaith and educational events to dispel negative stereotypes that were being perpetuated by the media following the events of September 11. Due to the homegrown nature of the London bombings youth also began playing a more prominent role in multifaith initiatives, alongside a rise in women's multifaith networks. In the USA, foundations provided a significant amount of funding to support religious and multifaith programs in the early to mid-2000s. Multifaith initiatives in Australia and the UK also received increased state funding support as they began to be implemented as part of social cohesion and counter-extremism strategies, particularly after the London bombings. As a result, the multifaith movement continued to grow during this period when other social movements, such as the environmental and women's movements, were marginalised by conservative governments, especially in the USA and Australia.

In addition, academics and universities played an important role as facilitators of multifaith initiatives and in conducting research on religion's role in the ultra-modern public sphere. The UN took a stronger interest and role in multifaith initiatives during the 2000s. In more recent years, a focus on environmental issues has re-emerged within the multifaith movement, after the release of Al Gore's *An Inconvenient Truth* in 2006. Consequently, the impetus to address global risks and injustices, to counter extremism and normalise pluralism and to develop understanding of diverse faiths has strengthened following the events of September 11. However, the increased focus on human security lessened the focus on developing understanding of the nature of reality within the multifaith movement at the turn of the twenty-first century.

However in more recent years, and particularly in response to the re-emerging global risk of climate change, the multifaith movement can still be described as having a 'mutual mission' (Hick 1985: 44) of: developing understanding of diverse faiths and the nature of reality; and addressing global risks and injustices through collaborative action. These two interweaving aims continually inform one another as theological and philosophical perspectives inspire multifaith practices—transforming self-centred individualism to a more altruistic and interdependent worldview—thereby countering risks and advancing common security.

In addition, the main benefits of multifaith initiatives are that they:

- provide opportunities to develop mutual understanding among communities of diverse faiths;
- offer opportunities for contact between people of diverse faiths, thus dispelling common misperceptions and fears and countering ignorance through educative and communicative processes;
- address the root causes of problems and effectively enact social change;
- affirm common values, and strengthen the peacebuilding role of religion; and
- encourage respect for diversity within a framework of commitment to equal rights for all.

The main challenges for multifaith initiatives include:

- that they are perceived a 'soft' and therefore ineffective strategies to counter radicalisation;
- a lack of resources;
- the need to be more inclusive of all faith and no-faith communities;
- the need for more cooperation and less competition between multifaith organisations; and
- the need for further research into their efficacy, particularly through longitudinal evaluative studies.

Moreover, two key issues have emerged in this study that raise some concerns about the multifaith movement's future directions. Firstly, the growing proximity between religious and state actors, as they partner on issues of common security, raises questions regarding whether increased state support of multifaith initiatives might impede the critical voice of religious actors in the ultramodern public sphere. Secondly, in recent times, more conservative faith communities have joined the multifaith movement as a new emphasis on practical action in place of dialogue has increased the scope of the movement's activities. On the positive side, this has led conservative actors in some cases to become more respectful of, and open-minded about, religious diversity. Conversely, the multifaith movement may be in danger of compromising its peacebuilding potential—especially in relation to protecting the rights of women, children and animals—by giving conservative voices a platform within a movement that has been traditionally liberal. Both of these issues require further investigation.

One of the central arguments of this study is that the most critical problems of the ultramodern era is not a clash *between* civilisations but a clash between exclusivists and pluralists *within* civilisations. The ambivalent nature of religion creates both closed, exclusivist mindsets and open, pluralist ones. However, multifaith initiatives, due to their emphasis on valuing diversity, are capable of expanding 'cognitive frames' from ignorance to mutual understanding. As several participants noted, for multifaith engagement to be truly effective it must be embodied—in role models, in personal stories and real relationships—as it is these interactions that expand cognitive frames at the individual and eventually at the collective level.

The multifaith movement and multi-actor peacebuilding networks develop understanding of diverse faiths and the nature of reality through communicative and dialogical processes. Both the multifaith movement and ultramodern cosmopolitan theories stress the importance of developing mutual understanding, particularly of the underlying causes of conflicts in order to address them effectively and to prevent conflicts from reoccurring in the future. In addition, both the multifaith movement and cosmopolitan theories emphasise the need for collaboration across diverse sectors in order to address the most pressing risks confronting the entire lifeworld. Consequently, the multifaith movement and multi-actor peacebuilding networks can be described as pioneers of cosmopolitan mazeways, founded on a new public language of mutual respect.

The findings of this study therefore make the following contributions to knowledge in the field of sociology of religion. This is the first systematic sociological study to investigate the rise of the multifaith movement in ultramodernity. It is among the first studies to employ Beck's (2006) cosmopolitan methodology, by investigating the grand theory of cosmopolitanism by focusing on the rise of the multifaith movement in Western societies. By drawing on 56 interviews with leaders in the field of multifaith relations, it has presented empirical evidence to explain how multifaith initiatives have been implemented as cosmopolitan strategies aimed at countering global risks and advancing common security in ultramodern Western societies. In so doing, it has provided a missing narrative within the sociological literature, which is comprised of cosmopolitan peacebuilding religious responses aimed at collaboratively countering global risks. In addition, by documenting these peacebuilding aspects of the ultramodern resurgence of religion, it has contributed new evidence to further challenge the secularisation thesis. Finally, it has demonstrated that diverse religious groups have a critical role to play in cosmopolitan governance, alongside other actors, and that it is preferable to view the role of religions in the public sphere as part of a cosmopolitan framework rather than view religious diversity as needing to be managed or governed 'from above' by state actors and institutions.

Multifaith Initiatives and Countering Radicalisation

Despite the many benefits of multifaith engagement documented within this study, scepticism abounds regarding the effectiveness of multifaith initiatives in countering global risks such as terrorism. In particular, the multifaith movement has been frequently criticised for preaching to the converted and thereby not reaching those most at risk of radicalisation. Drawing on the findings of the previous chapters, the following discussion briefly outlines the precise role that multifaith initiatives and multi-actor peacebuilding networks—which include religious actors—can play in countering processes of radicalisation to dispel the misconception that multifaith initiatives are 'soft' and thereby ineffective strategies for countering violent extremism. It also explains how multifaith initiatives form part of broader counter-alienation strategies, and how many of the additional measures required to counter terrorism have also benefitted from increased collaboration between state and religious actors. Therefore, religious actors need to be included in counter-terrorism networks at multiple stages in order to enhance understanding of religious extremism and of how best to prevent it from leading to catastrophic consequences.

Firstly, promoting a multicultural and multifaith society, which affirms the value of diversity alongside an overriding commitment to abide by the law through policy and multifaith initiatives, can assist in encouraging social inclusion and thereby stem processes of alienation. By normalising cultures of religious pluralism people feel welcome and experience a sense of belonging in society, thereby fostering networks and relationships of trust across diverse communities and sectors. Simultaneously, by emphasising the importance of abiding by the law and of respecting rights, religious practices that propagate cultures of violence, be they direct or structural, are forbidden, thus minimising the risks posed to religious adherents themselves and to the broader community. In addition, responsible statements by political leaders, public intellectuals and the press that encourage inclusive, diverse, respectful and law-abiding participation in society can contribute to creating genuinely secure communities. Conversely, divisive rhetoric, such as Islamophobic and migrantophobic statements by leaders and journalists, can exacerbate feelings of alienation and exclusion, and thereby heighten security risks (Halafoff 2006: 3, 13).

Free press, free speech, and the right to voice concerns publicly and to air a diverse range of opinions need not be threatened by such statements; the emphasis here is on *responsible speech*, not on the regulation of speech. Indeed, the right to voice concerns, to critique the state and to engage in non-violent protest and dissent must be encouraged in order to provide outlets for grievances and to encourage a participatory and deliberative form of governance, thereby assisting religious actors to play a non-violent role in effecting social change by influencing policy. Consequently, multifaith initiatives, Mosque open days, op-ed pieces, TV shows such as *Salam Café*, multifaith leaders and youth forums all form part of inclusive peacebuilding and thereby counter-terrorism strategies. Such initiatives are largely preventive measures; once a person has already become alienated from society other initiatives are required, which are based on similar principles of collaboration between state and religious actors.

Policy-makers and the general public often do not see the benefits of multifaith engagement or educational activities because they are perceived as 'soft' options. However, placing them in this context they are not 'soft' at all, but rather are among the most effective methods of stemming processes of alienation in multifaith societies and in the global arena. When viewed in this way, 'hard' options such as promoting a narrow nationalism, citizenship testing or proposing a return to Judeo–Christian values can be seen as exclusive and thereby dangerous as they can alienate minority groups and aggravate grievances instead of alleviating them.

Community-policing initiatives can also be effective preventive strategies that play a crucial part in curbing processes of violent radicalisation in situations where individuals and communities have already become alienated from mainstream society. Police, by encouraging positive community relations, such as playing soccer with youth, attending community events and offering assistance to newly arriving communities, can foster a culture of inclusion, thereby lessening the risk of alienation. When states and police allow non-violent processes of dissent and provide avenues for grievances to be safely aired, religious communities can continue to play their traditional role in critiquing states and markets through non-violent means. By consulting with multifaith and youth councils established by communities, governments encourage deliberative forms of governance and communities genuinely feel heard and respected, thereby decreasing the risks of alienation.

Once members of faith communities have become deeply alienated from society, religious communities are the best actors to intervene as they can provide guidance and counselling to those at risk. In addition, when religious actors can no longer help those in need, or when they are alerted to a breach of law or possible danger, they can assist authorities if networks of trust are already well established between state agencies, such as police, and religious communities. Religious leaders are also in the best position to challenge extremist leaders within their own communities and to destabilise their power bases with the assistance of state authorities.[1] These initiatives are best undertaken by religious leaders who are active within their own communities but not necessarily within multifaith networks as it is imperative that

[1] See Lambert Robert (2008a, b) 'Empowering Salafis and Islamists against Al-Qaeda: A London Counterterrorism Case Study', *PS* January 2008: 31–35 and Lambert, Robert (2008b) 'Salafi and Islamist Londoners: Stigmatised Minority Faith Communities Countering Al-Qaida', *Crime Law Social Change* 50: 73–89.

at this stage of the process they are directly connected to individuals and communities in need, and not brought in from outside.

As mentioned above, multifaith networks can be most effective in preventing processes of alienation. However, in the case of youth, it is possible that encounters with multifaith networks could assist in stemming processes of more advanced radicalisation as multifaith youth networks can provide communities of support and methods of non-violent social change that could be appealing to alienated individuals, offering them an alternative to the methods employed by violent radical movements. Finally, involving religious actors in de-radicalisation strategies in prisons can also be highly effective, by providing theological imperatives for non-violent social change instead of violent ideologies.

Arriving at *Netpeace* and the *Politics of Understanding*

As described above, not only do multifaith initiatives have an important role to play in counter-radicalisation strategies, but they also provide much-needed evidence of the efficacy of cosmopolitan approaches to countering risks and advancing common security more generally. While John Arquilla's and David Ronfeldt's (2001: 15) observation that 'it takes networks to fight networks' achieved almost axiomatic status in much contemporary scholarship on counter-terrorism that emerged during the Bush and Howard eras, this book argues that *netpeace* is a preferable option to netwar for countering global risks such as terrorism and climate change.

The concept of *netpeace* acknowledges the interconnectedness of global problems and solutions, and particularly the capacity of critical and collaborative networks, including state, non-state and religious actors co-committed towards common good, to solve the world's most pressing problems. That is not to deny the potential for power imbalances within these networks or that they could be used to form alliances aimed at violent means or ends. Those possibilities are ever present. However, the development of multifaith and multi-actor peacebuilding networks according to cosmopolitan principles lends itself to *netpeace*—to an optimistic and practical vision—whereby seeking mutual understanding and enabling non-violent critique will increase equitable participation in responsible local and global governance.

As global risks and concerns shift away from terrorism towards global warming, new more collaborative frameworks for dealing with global risks are emerging. However, anti-cosmopolitan elements within religious traditions and broader society remain prevalent. Indeed, the rise of climate change sceptics and the Tea Party in the USA demonstrate that conservative forces are gathering new momentum in Western societies.

Perhaps the issue of climate change, more than any other issue, demonstrates that 'we are all in this together', and that the future of humanity and all forms of life will benefit from a more collaborative and cosmopolitan vision, which sees beyond us/them divisions. As many participants in this study have described, it is the acknowledgement of our interdependence and the ability to act altruistically, for the collective good, which holds the key to our survival. Faith traditions offer this much-needed wisdom, understanding that ultimately, despite our differences, we are dependent on one another.

From its inception the multifaith movement—through dialogue between diverse religious actors—envisaged a new way forward founded on an awareness of our interdependence, respect for diversity and a commitment to collaboratively countering risks and advancing common security. The social movements of the 1970s and 1980s, and the peace, women's and environmental movements, all awakened to this reality and created new collaborative cosmopolitan mazeways in the face of global crises. Despite the regressive decade at the turn of the twenty-first century—from the mid-1990s to the mid-2000s—we find ourselves in a new era in which cosmopolitan visions are becoming more mainstreamed. Will we go the way of fear and hatred, of ignorant self-centredness and mass destruction? Or will we find new altruistic mazeways to benefit the entire lifeworld? The multifaith movement is modelling a new way forward in which the wisdom of theological and philosophical traditions can play a role in cosmopolitan governance, informing policies on which the survival of humanity and the planet depend.

The multifaith movement has created a new language of mutual respect, which enables mutual understanding to develop among diverse religious and non-religious actors. As our societies become increasingly culturally and religiously diverse, and as global communication systems bring us all closer together, this new language is becoming increasingly useful to multiple sectors. Politicians, academics, teachers, doctors, scientists, teachers, artists and entrepreneurs, among others, would all benefit from acquiring the skill set of developing multifaith understanding. If we are to build a genuinely peaceful and secure lifeworld, hope alone is insufficient to counter the politics of fear. We need a new cosmopolitan *politics of understanding*, as described and practised by participants in this study, not only of one another but also particularly of the interdependent nature of reality. For fear is derived from ignorance, primarily the ignorance that makes us think that we are somehow separate from one another.

References

Arquilla, John, and David Ronfeldt. 2001. The advent of netwar (revisited). In *Networks and netwars: The future of terror, crime, and militancy*, ed. John Arquilla and David Ronfeld, 1–25. Santa Monica: RAND.

Beck, Ulrich. 2006. *The cosmopolitan vision*. Cambridge: Polity Press.

Halafoff, Anna. 2006. UnAustralian values. In *Cultural Studies Association of Australasia Annual Conference, UNAustralia*. University of Canberra, Canberra, 6–8 December 2006 (electronic resource).

Hick, John. 1985. *Problems of religious pluralism*. Basingstoke/London: Macmillan.

Lambert, Robert. 2008a. Empowering Salafis and Islamists against al-Qaeda: A London counterterrorism case study. *Political Science and Politics* January 2008: 31–35.

Lambert, Robert. 2008b. Salafi and Islamist Londoners: Stigmatised minority faith communities countering al-Qaida. *Crime Law Social Change* 50: 73–89.

Appendix 1

The following expert professionals participated in this study[1] and are listed alphabetically. Their affiliation, at the time of the interview, is also provided below:

Dr. Umar Faruq Abd-Allah*, Chairman of the Board and Scholar-in-Residence, Nawawi Foundation, Chicago, USA.*

Prof. Mohammed Abu-Nimer*, Director, Peacebuilding and Development Institute, International Peace and Conflict Resolution Program, School of International Service, American University, Washington, USA.*

Waleed Aly*, Lecturer, Global Terrorism Research Centre, School of Social and Political Inquiry, Monash University, Melbourne, Australia.*

Nurah Amatullah*, Executive Director of the Muslim Women's Institute for Research and Development, New York, USA.*

Dr. Patricia Blundell*, Coordinator Chaplaincy, Griffith University, Brisbane, Australia.*

Rev. Professor Marcus Braybrooke*, President, World Congress of Faiths, Oxford, UK.*

Rev. Dr. Chloe Breyer*, Executive Director, The Interfaith Centre of New York, New York, USA.*

Prof. Joseph Camilleri*, Director, Centre for Dialogue, La Trobe University, Melbourne, Australia.*

Josh Cass*, Youth Worker, Encounter, London, UK.*

Dr. Bulent (Hass) Dellal*, Executive Director, Australian Multicultural Foundation, Melbourne, Australia.*

Joyce S. Dubensky*, Executive Vice-President and CEO, Tanenbaum Centre for Interreligious Understanding, New York, USA.*

[1] Unfortunately, two of the interviews, one with Prof. Perry Schmidt-Leukel in Glasgow and one with Dr. Lucinda Mosher in New York, weren't able to be included in this study due to technical difficulties.

A. Halafoff, *The Multifaith Movement: Global Risks and Cosmopolitan Solutions*,
DOI 10.1007/978-94-007-5210-8, © Springer Science+Business Media Dordrecht 2013

Fr. Dr. John Dupuche*, Chair, Catholic Interfaith Committee of the Catholic Archdiocese of Melbourne, Melbourne, Australia.*

Greg M. Epstein*, Humanist Chaplain at Harvard University, Cambridge (interviewed in Chicago, USA at the Interfaith Youth Core Conference), USA.*

Rev. Dirk Ficca*, Executive Director, Council for a Parliament of the World's Religions, Chicago (interviewed in Melbourne, Australia), USA.*

Rev. Charles Gibbs*, Executive Director, United Religions Initiative, San Francisco, USA.*

Dr. Maurice Glasman*, Director, Faith and Citizenship Program, London Metropolitan University, London, UK.*

Rev. Fletcher Harper*, Executive Director, GreenFaith, New Brunswick, USA.*

Sherene Hassan*, Interfaith Officer, Islamic Council of Victoria, Melbourne, Australia.*

Dr. Karin von Hippel*, Director, Post-conflict Reconstruction Project, Centre for Strategic and International Studies, Washington, USA.*

Di Hirsh*, Interfaith and Intercultural Chair, National Council of Jewish Women of Australia, Melbourne, Australia.*

Sheherazade Jafari, *Assistant Program Director, Religion and Conflict Resolution, Tanenbaum Centre for Interreligious Understanding, New York, USA.*

Jeremy Jones*, Co-Chair of the Australian National Dialogue of Christians, Muslims and Jews, Sydney, Australia.*

Assoc. Prof. Laurel Kearns*, Associate Professor, Sociology of Religion and Environmental Studies, Drew Theological School and Graduate Division of Religion, Drew University, Madison, USA.*

Simon Keyes*, Director, St. Ethelburga's Centre for Reconciliation and Peace, London, UK.*

Shah Nazar Seyyed Dr. Ali Kianfar*, Co-founder and Co-director of the International Association of Sufism, Novato, California.*

Sr. Joan Kirby*, United Nations Representative, The Temple of Understanding, New York, USA.*

Prof. Paul F. Knitter*, Paul Tillich Professor of Theology, World Religions and Culture, Union Theological Seminary, New York, USA.*

Josie Lacey*, Convener, Women's Interfaith Network, Sydney, Australia.*

Catriona Laing*, Project Manager of The Cambridge Inter-faith Programme, Faculty of Divinity, University of Cambridge (interviewed in London, UK), UK.*

Melanie Landau*, Lecturer in Jewish Studies, Australian Centre for Jewish Civilisation, School of Historical Studies, Monash University, Melbourne, Australia.*

Anushavan Margaryan*, Program Associate, The Interfaith Centre of New York, New York, USA.*

Katherine Marshall*, Senior Fellow, Berkley Center for Religion, Peace and World Affairs, Georgetown University, Washington, USA.*

Shaykh Ibrahim Mogra*, Chair, Interfaith Relations Committee, Muslim Council of Britain, London, UK.*

***Alison Murdoch**, Director, Foundation for Developing Compassion and Wisdom, London, UK.*
***Mehmet Ozalp**, Chief Executive Officer, Affinity Intercultural Foundation, Sydney, Australia.*
***Dr. Susan Pascoe**, Chair, Australian National Commission for UNESCO, Canberra (interview conducted in Melbourne), Australia.*
***Dr. Eboo Patel**, Executive Director, Interfaith Youth Core, Chicago, USA.*
***Brian Pearce**, Director, The Inter Faith Network for the UK, London, UK.*
***Janet Penn,** Executive Director, Interfaith Action Inc., Massachusetts, (interviewed in Chicago, USA at the Interfaith Youth Core Conference) USA.*
***Maureen Postma**, General Secretary, Victorian Council of Churches, Melbourne, Australia.*
***Ibrahim Abdil-Mu'id Ramey**, Director, Human and Civil Rights Division, Muslim American Society Freedom (MAS Freedom), Washington, USA.*
***Amal Saffour**, Muslim Youth Worker, King's College London, UK.*
***Dr. Chris Seiple**, President, The Institute for Global Engagement, Washington, USA.*
***Stephen Shashoua**, Director, The Three Faiths Forum, London, UK.*
***Dr. Sylvie Shaw**, Lecturer in Religion and Spirituality Studies, The School of History, Philosophy, Religion and Classics, University of Queensland, Brisbane, Australia.*
***Dr. David R. Smock**, Vice-President, Centre for Mediation and Conflict Resolution, Religion and Peacebuilding Center of Innovation, United States Institute of Peace, Washington, USA.*
***Rev. Helen Summers**, Director, The Interfaith Centre of Melbourne, Melbourne, Australia.*
***Prof. Toh Swee-Hin**, Director, Multi-Faith Centre, Griffith University, Brisbane.*
***Krista Tippett**, Broadcaster and Author, Speaking of Faith, American Public Media, (interviewed in Chicago, USA at the Interfaith Youth Core Conference), USA.*
***Freeman Trebilcock,** Secretary, Loving Kindness, Peaceful Youth (LKPY), Melbourne, Australia.*
***Dr. William F. Vendley**, Secretary General, Religions for Peace, New York, USA.*
***Prof. John O. Voll,** Associate Director, Prince Alwaleed Bin Talal Center for Muslim-Christian Understanding, Georgetown University, Washington, USA.*
***Rachel Woodlock**, Researcher, Centre for Islam and the Modern World, School of Social and Political Inquiry, Monash University, Melbourne, Australia.*
***Elizabeth Young,** Student and Multifaith Youth Worker, Flinders University, Adelaide (interviewed in Melbourne), Australia.*

About the Author

Dr. Anna Halafoff is a Research Fellow at the Centre for Citizenship and Globalisation (CCG) at Deakin University. Previously, Anna was a lecturer in Sociology and in Politics at the School of Political and Social Inquiry, Monash University. She was also a researcher for the Global Terrorism Research Centre (GTReC) and the UNESCO Chair in Interreligious and Intercultural Relations – Asia Pacific, Monash University. She continues to collaborate with the UNESCO Chair and GTReC on interreligious relations and countering violent extremism research in and beyond Australia.

Anna holds degrees from Monash University (Ph.D. 2010), the University of New England (Master of Letters in Peace Studies 2000 and Grad. Dip. Ed. 2005) and the University of Melbourne (B.A. 1991). In 2011, Anna was named a United Nations Alliance of Civilizations Global Expert in the fields of religion, terrorism, war and conflict and became an Associate of the UNESCO Chair in Interreligious and Intercultural Relations – Asia Pacific in 2012. She is currently the Co-coordinator of The Australian Sociological Association's (TASA) Sociology of Religion Thematic Group, and the Secretary for the Australian Association for the Study of Religion (AASR).

Anna's current and recent research interests include: intercultural and interreligious relations; cosmopolitan governance; multiculturalism; community engagement and countering violent extremism; religions and beliefs education; and Buddhism in Australia. She is the co-editor of *Terrorism and Social Exclusion* (Edward Elgar, 2010) and her work has been published in the following books and journals: *Australian Soul*: *Religion and Spirituality in the 21st Century* (Cambridge University Press, 2006); *International Handbook of Inter-religious Education* (Springer, 2010); *Buddhism in Australia: Traditions in Change* (Routledge, 2011); the *Journal of Research in International Education* (2008); *Studies of Conflict and Terrorism* (2009); the *Journal of Religious Education* (2009); *Political Theology* (2010); the *Australian Religious Studies Review* (2011), *Islam and Christian-Muslim Relations* (2011), and the *Journal of Global Buddhism* (2012).

A. Halafoff, *The Multifaith Movement: Global Risks and Cosmopolitan Solutions*,

DOI 10.1007/978-94-007-5210-8,

Index

A. Halafoff, *The Multifaith Movement: Global Risks and Cosmopolitan Solutions*,
DOI 10.1007/978-94-007-5210-8, © Springer Science+Business Media Dordrecht 2013